Stuart was a great fitter and my was a true professional and he took the strenuous day very seriously *which has left a lasting impression with me. He cared…and I always appreciated that about Stu.*

—Ryan Hall/Head Golf Pro Golf Club of Avon (CT) 2005-2014

Stuart went well beyond being a golf rep. He became much more, a loyal friend to my family.

—Fred Lux, Jr. Head Golf Pro Duchess Golf & Country Club
Poughkeepsie, NY 1982-2005

My times spent with Stuart Miller, the BEST golf salesman I encountered during my career as a PGA member.

—Mike Rosenquist/Head Golf Pro Potsdam Town & CC
Potsdam NY 1980-2005

For over 20 years Stuart has been helping me grow business in my pro shops. He has been nothing but helpful and professional. Any company, including PING, are lucky to have him representing their lines.

—Roger King/Director of Golf Sugarbush Resort 2015 to present

Superlatives to describe Stu Miller: hardworking, honest, knows his products through and through, pride in his approach, respectful, considerate, and detail driven. If a problem needs solved, he thinks solution.

—Bob Burg, President CMC Golf Design

Stuart was and will always be a true to the bone, aggressive yet flexible, forthright, and competent sales and marketing genius. Above all else, Stuart has perfected the lost art of listening. Perhaps we could all take a page from this book and learn to listen. You may be surprised by how much you learn.

—James Jeffers, Director of Golf Hiland Par CC
Queensbury, NY 2009 to present

A
WONDERFUL JOURNEY
IN THE
GAME OF GOLF

STUART MILLER

Legacy Book Press LLC
Camanche, Iowa

Dedication:

Dedicated to all the golf professionals and buyers (at golf specialty shops) for the business they have gave to me during my 40 year-plus career as a golf sales representative. It has been a pleasure and honor working with all of you both during my 28-year run with PING and my 14 years and counting as an independent rep. Without all of my dealings with you all, I would not have had the career that I have accomplished so far. I hope to see many of you soon.

Acknowledgement

I wrote this book during the COVID pandemic break out in the summer of 2020. It is a simple snapshot of the past 40 years of my life working in the golf industry as a sales representative.

One of the major factors for me to compose this book was the fact that I started this "wonderful journey in the game of golf" by working during the summer break from college for the PING Golf Company which at the time (1978) was still a very young company. I feel like I was part of something special working for a family-owned company that was still in its infancy stage. I wanted to express my gratitude once again to the Solheim family for hiring me all those years ago and allowing me to represent the PING brand in my area for 28 years (ending in July 2009).

One of the highlights of the book for me are the many testimonials that were given by former PING accounts and some active accounts commenting on my new role as an independent rep.

At this time, I also want to express my gratitude to several individuals for their help with this project. First and foremost is Rick Wright, the former head pro at The Edison Club in Rexford, NY (very close to my home town of Clifton Park). Throughout my writing of this project Rick would give me his honest opinion coming from the lens of a true PGA club professional. Rick was instrumental in helping me along the way, complimenting me quite often, which only gave me the confidence that what I was doing was profound and worthwhile.

I also want to thank Bob Smith of Beverly, MA, who ran the blanket company I repped for when I first began my new career as an independent rep. Through his reading of my manuscript,

Bob could see the dedication I gave to my former company, and he also knew that PING was lucky to have me as their rep. Bob recently passed away at the end of 2021, but I want to express to his family how influential he was for me while I was writing this book.

I want to thank my editor Alex McMillin for all of his fine work in getting my manuscript done so professionally so we could present to publishers to finally get it turned into a book. I also want to thank my mother, Elayne, for her constant encouragement in getting me to finally write the book that I had been thinking of doing for the past five years.

I want to send out a big shout out to all my companies that hired me to be their rep as my independent career started in the fall of 2009. And lastly, I wanted to send a big thank you to all of my accounts both present and past for giving me the opportunity to service their accounts.

In closing, if you are a golfer with as much enthusiasm about the game of golf as I have and would like to follow my path in this industry as a golf representative, then I have only one thing to say to you: If you have the drive then please go for it as I did and maybe with a little luck, good timing, and hard work, you too can find the success and joy that I have had. ENJOY MY BOOK!

Stuart Miller
MON 7/4/22

1.
THE BEGINNING

I really can't explain the why I called up professional golfer Bill Garrett of Phoenix, Arizona, one day way back in the spring of 1978. Nevertheless, this phone call pretty much set in motion the beginning of my professional business career in the great game of golf. I didn't know it then, but this day was surely the genesis of my life as I know it today. This spring (of 2020) marks my 40th year as a sales representative in the golf industry and my 43rd year overall in the business.

Maybe my decision to call Bill Garrett was simply due to the boredom of being a then-19-year-old who'd just finished his first year of school at Glendale Community College and was now looking for something new to do. However, I had heard through the grapevine of other avid golfers that there was a major golf event in the area soon, and golf pros were looking for caddies to carry their heavy "staff" golf bags during the competition. I reached out to Bill not knowing who he was, nor did he know me from Adam.

I could tell from speaking with him on the phone that he had an accent I had never heard before. Bill spoke in very slow words and was somewhat difficult to understand, but after only a five-minute conversation, he'd hired me. He told me to meet him at Pinnacle Peak Country Club in Scottsdale in a few days to caddy for him in the Arizona Open, which was considered one of the major tournaments on the calendar for club professionals and amateurs sporting a handicap of two or less.

This was not going to be the first time I had caddied for a pro golfer. In the spring of 1974, my dad (stepfather) was still a Chief Petty Officer in the U.S. Navy, and we were living in the Pensacola, Florida, area. Many of the golfers on my high school golf team were trying to find a job as a caddy for the Monday qualifier of the then-Monsanto Open on the PGA Tour. I drove out to the host club, Perdido Bay Country Club, with my friend of mine who was going to be a senior at Tate High School. I was 15 years old and didn't even have a driver's license yet.

We both found tour players to caddy for in the qualifying tournament. I approached several pros in the parking lot at Perdido Bay. After three of them declined, saying they already had a regular tour caddie, I was fortunate to meet up with Jim Ahern. He was a rookie on the tour out of South Dakota. He gave me the job and man, was I excited... I gave it the sort of fist pump you make when you've just drained a tough 30-footer for birdie. My pal also got a loop with a pro competing in the event.

The first day of the qualifier was canceled late in the afternoon due to heavy rain. Jim had shot an even-par 72 to make it through to the Monsanto Open itself, but now we had to come back the next day and do it all over again. Jim recorded another 72 and qualified easily.

Jim was the epitome of the word, "rabbit," as that is what he and many other rookie tour players who had to qualify each week to get into events were called. Back then, only the top 60 money winners were totally exempt for the season. The rest of the players had to Monday-qualify. For example, at this tour stop, there were over 120 players vying for 30 spots to get into the tournament's final field of 156 players. If you did make the 36-hole cut in the event, you were exempted into next week's event. If you were fortunate enough to finish in the top 25 of that event, you were automatically exempt to play in that tournament the following year.

Anyway, I was very pleased with Jim's successful qualification and was very much looking forward to going to the Pensacola Country Club, where the Monsanto Open would be contested. However, Jim decided to go with the full-time tour caddie for Mark Hayes (a pro who failed to qualify). Hayes went on to win the first-ever Tournament Players Championship two years later at Sawgrass Country Club in Ponte Vedra, Florida.

I was devastated not to have the opportunity of going to the "Big Show," but Jim offered me $20 and a dozen used Titleist balata golf balls, and I was happy again. My friend's man did make it, and since he was older, his player did bring him to the event as his caddy, although they didn't make the cut.

Even though I didn't get to work the Tour event, the new experience of being behind the ropes as a professional golfer's caddy was an invaluable lesson that would pay dividends for me in the future.

As an interesting sidenote, during our time living in the Panhandle area of northwest Florida, I was on the golf team at Tate High, which was also the high school of Major League Baseball pitching great and future Hall of Famer Don Sutton (of Los Angeles Dodger fame).

I was playing in a practice round with our number one player. I noticed he was playing with different-looking equipment, and I asked him about his clubs.

"These are PINGs," he said with pride. I'd never heard of this brand before. My friend from the Monsanto Open also had a putter from PING (It was the ANSER model). When I looked at it, I noticed that it was stamped Phoenix, AZ, U.S.A.

"Wow, that's where my family is moving to in the summer after school gets out in a few months!" I said.

• • •

At the 1978 Arizona Open golf event, I met up with Bill Garrett on Wednesday near Pinnacle Peak C.C.'s practice putting green. Bill was a massive man, coming in at about 6' 6". Despite his size, he seemed like a pretty normal guy with short wavy brown hair and a friendly demeanor. His Texas upbringing had given an interesting slow drawl accent to his voice.

After he warmed up on the driving range for 30 minutes or so, we were ready to tee off. I can't remember exactly who we played with in that first round. All I can say is that Bill played very well, and it was a pleasure to caddy for him.

I remember Bill had a very nice all-white golf bag that was stamped "PING." The bag also had his name in red script letters, with "KARSTEN MANUFACTURING" in block letters just below his name. I had an odd feeling when I saw the PING name, as it reminded me of when I saw my first PING putter four years earlier in Florida.

The event spanned three rounds and 54 holes. I believe we finished in the top ten when it was all said and done. Well, Bill finished in the top ten. It's common practice for a caddy to always say "we" when describing how his player fared in competition. Anyway, Bill was very pleased with my performance.

"Stuart, you are an excellent caddy, and if you're interested, I would like for you to work for me again this summer."

"Absolutely!" I replied. "May I ask what your position is with PING?"

"I am their PGA Tour representative for Tour events and all the major competitions in the local area."

"Do you know if they're hiring extra workers for the upcoming summer months?"

I was on college break and looking for steady work.

"As far as I know, summertime is the busiest the factory gets."

"May I use your name as a reference?"

"Of course, Stuart," he replied.

That was the end of our first collaboration on the golf course. In the next two years, we would partner up in over a dozen events. We truly had a great relationship on the golf course.

I drove my 1976 Green Gremlin (a "classic" by the now-defunct American Motors Company, better known as AMC) straight to 2201 W. Desert Cove Drive, which was the address for Karsten (PING) Mfg. Corp. It turned out that this facility was only a 15-minute drive from where my family and I lived in Phoenix.

I went into the lobby, where a very large image of Karsten Solheim—the creator and owner of the company—was on display. The plush carpet had a unique design featuring what they now call the "PING man." After filling out an application, I was greeted by two gentlemen: Alan Solheim, who was a plant employee and one of Karsten's three sons, and Doug Hawken, the foreman for the woods department.

Doug took me into one of the factories and had me do a few basic tasks to see if I was coordinated enough to work in that department. As it turned out, I was. He was very pleased with me and told me I was hired, asking if I could start to work on Monday.

The day I was hired was Friday, May 23rd, 1978. I will never forget that day…That was the day I began my career in the golf industry with PING.

2.

THAT FIRST SUMMER
AT PING

It was the last Monday in May 1978, and I was on my way to PING to start my first day of work in the wood roughing department. I checked in at the employee timecard machine area and was greeted by Doug Hawken, who was the foreman of this department and the person who had hired me 48 hours earlier. Several years later, this same individual would become the President of PING.

I would describe Doug as a man of average height and build with a nice head of slicked-back hair. He walked me over to a very large white building, the same one where I had interviewed with him. This building was just one of many that dotted the sprawling campus of the Karsten Manufacturing Corporation, or KMC PING for short. It was also very early in the morning—6 a.m. to be exact. That day, and for the first full week, I was taught by several veteran workers who patiently and methodically showed me the ropes in that short period of time.

My work regime, which was basically the same every day, ran from 6 a.m. to 5 p.m. on weekdays and from 7 a.m. to 12 p.m. on Saturday, totaling 55 hours in a week. Here is a rundown of a typical day's work:

First, we would work on iron grinding. Then, we would come back to the woods department and do a different task for a few hours. By the time we were finished, it was time for lunch. After lunch, we would do a job called "The Bucket." This was the worst job you could do, but it was also very rewarding.

Imagine a wheel with holes on it that would spin around in a timely motion. From what I could recall, this was one of the first steps of making the woods after they had been roughed out, which is what I did. The ladies would put the black paint on them. The paint was a special solution that would fill all the pores on the wooden head (that is how it was explained to me). The clubhead would go around on the wheel for a few minutes before coming to me and one other worker, also a newbie or rookie as only rookies got this poor assignment. We would use a special burlap cloth to take all this solution off of the wood heads. Again, from what I recall there would be at least 50 wood heads on a tray, and we would do at least ten trays a day. This process would always take 90 minutes. Once that was over, the rest of the day was gravy.

From 3 p.m. to 5 p.m., we would be back in the woods roughing department doing another task. This would go on day after day for the entire summer. What I can tell you about all this work was that I was making some real money for the first time in my life. I was working 55 hours a week at I believe only $3.00 an hour, but I did get overtime pay on Saturday only. I believe I was bringing home $180 a week (before taxes) or $720 a month. This allowed me to buy a lot of neat things and pay for my car, which my dad had bought with me. I was paying him back.

The thing I remember most about that first summer at **PING** was the many different machines I was working on in the woods roughing department. My mentor, who taught me the tools of the craft. At the time of our introduction, he had been with the company for several years and was a seasoned veteran of this department. From what I could see, he was one of Doug's best employees and a great teacher.

I learned fairly soon in my employment that only a few years earlier, when he had been running for the Arizona State University track team, Doug had set a either a U.S.A. or world record in the 100-meter dash.

The very first machine that Joe had me work on was called the "neck cutter." I would take a raw wood head and simply clamp it into the machine, and it would cut off the neck of the item. Just imagine a round barrel about five-feet tall that held close to 1,000 wood heads. We did all the #1 woods at the same time, all the #3 woods at the same time, and so on. I would work on a barrel that only had driver heads in it. We also had #3, #4, #5, and #7 wood heads…in other words we had a lot of woods. All these were called laminated maple woods and were produced by a company called Birchwood Manufacturing out of Rice Lake, Wisconsin. After looking on a map, I saw that this was in a very remote northwestern part of the state about an hour away from Madison.

From hearing conversations from other higher up company employees, I learned it took approximately 25 days for a club head in our department to be ready to move onto the next big building. This was the woods finishing building (where The Bucket was located).

When you started a barrel of woods in the neck cutting machine, you would finish that barrel before you took on the next task. The neck operation, which was fairly easy to do, might take only an hour or so.

To summarize this methodical routine, here is what we did:

1. Cut the necks off the wood heads.
2. Create the hole for the hosel of the club.
3. Use a special routing machine to create the bottom of the club, where the sole plate would go.
4. Use a special routing machine to create a cavity, where the face epoxy would go.

This pretty much sums up the machine tooling aspect of the daily routine. When the majority of the machine work was completed, we would then put weights in the heads to create the proper weighting options. Then the final job, "the pour," had to be completed.

This was done every week. We would carefully place the heads near each other on very large tables, then pour special red epoxy into them.

After the heads were dried overnight, we would then take off all the extra tape and place them on tables that were carried over to the woods finishing building. Here, they were prepped for final paint jobs before assembly. This took another five days or so. In all, it was a good 30 days to make a wood golf club at PING.

Every one of these special machines was designed by Karsten himself. They all served one purpose. When they were working in concert with each other, they performed like an orchestra and produced (at the time) the best wooden product on the market.

The company sold a ton of these woods. Most orders were 1-3-5 combinations but the 7-wood (with a loft of around 21 degrees) was very popular. It replaced the #3 iron, which most golfers could not hit anyway. This was a time when hybrid woods were not even made, and the beginning of the metal wood revolution was still several years away.

One final note on the woods—and I heard this again through company channels—there was a three-month backlog of orders, which meant the production line just kept on going day after day (and this was just the woods department).

The biggest sellers at that time for KMC/PING were putters and irons. Again, there was always a two- to three-month demand for both items, which meant the factory floors were always busy, which was a great thing for the company.

A few interesting things happened to me during this first summer. Working on these machines made me focus as much as I ever had in my life. They could be dangerous if you were not careful due to the sharpness of the saw and the way they operated. Only one time did I have an issue that I can vividly remember.

I lost my concentration for just a second when I was working on the hosel machine. This machine enabled you to lock the wood head into the device, lining it up with a sharp thin pole that would make the hole where the shaft would enter the clubhead.

I lost control of my hand on the clubhead, and I could sense it immediately moving awkwardly and spinning rapidly. At that moment, I had no option but to let go, and the clubhead flipped through the air several feet from where I was standing. No one was in danger as no one was near me. That was the last time that happened.

I also remember that after I'd worked only a few weeks, John A. Solheim (one of Karsten's three sons and a high ranking official of the firm) walked into the building when I was working on the first machine in the process (the neck cutting machine). John suddenly reached into the barrel I was working on and grabbed one of the heads, taking it with him when he walked out without saying a word or addressing me. Being a new employee, I really didn't worry about it as I'm sure he had a purpose for doing that.

Another interesting thing happened to me that first summer at PING: There was a golf league for the employees, and each week we would play a match at Bel Aire Golf Course—a public par

60 executive course. As I was a pretty good player, I was put into the A flight with the better players. We would play a match each week to win points.

In the very first week, I was pitted up against the company's credit manager and a scratch golfer who also won the Arizona Amateur Championship multiple times. He had to give me one stroke in the match. As it turned out, I didn't need it. I edged this gentleman (who was at least ten years my senior) on the front nine by shooting a natural 30—even par—to nip him by one stroke. It was, for sure, considered an upset. Everyone at the main plant was pleased with my achievement.

My boss Doug was so thrilled for me that he did me a favor. It is customary that after a new employee finishes one month of work at the company, they are gifted a PING putter, usually the Anser model, which has a manganese bronze putter head. I wanted to get the same putter that my player Bill Garrett was using, which was the ZERO 2 model. It was stainless steel, which costs more, but Doug let me have it for my accomplishment. They etched my name on the sole of the putter in white script, which I found to be extremely neat.

Throughout the entire summer, Karsten himself would come into our building with several people. He was giving them a tour of the facility, and he took a lot of pride in doing that. He was especially proud when showing them all the machines that he designed. I just know that whenever Karsten came into sight it got all the employees' attention in a good way (especially me).

My first-ever Karsten story is from the fall of 1976 when I was at Moon Valley Country Club practicing on the putting green as a member of the Thunderbird High School golf team. I was there for a few minutes, and I spotted three golfers on the driving range. One was a very tall man, while the other two were on the shorter side. Within five minutes, they all started to walk directly toward me. I could then see that one of the gentlemen was older, with all-white hair and a little white patch of hair on his chin. I thought it might be Karsten himself, as I knew PING was located in Phoenix, but I had no idea it was him. He never really identified himself to me, but the tall golfer who was with him was George Archer, who had won the 1969 Masters title. He had a white PING bag with his name on it in red letters. I assume he was just testing out some equipment for Karsten.

As it turns out, it was indeed Karsten Solheim, and this would be my first real in person encounter with him (and fortunately for me there would be several more in the years to come). I really don't recall what was said but I do know that Karsten asked me, "Can you please take a picture of the three of us?"

"Gladly," I said eagerly, thinking I was the luckiest guy on the planet. All I know is after I took the picture, I heard Karsten tell me that my technique needed a little adjustment to secure a better outcome, so I did what he instructed and took another shot.

I did just that and it was over in a flash. I had my first Karsten moment. I would then continue to practice my putting before heading back home. Working at PING was not even on my radar at that time.

3.

THOSE EARLY DAYS

When our family lived in Rhode Island from late 1971 to spring 1973 (when Dad was stationed at Quonset Point Naval Air Station on Narragansett Bay), we lived in a very nice home just a short pitching wedge from Lake Tiogue, a major lake in the town of Coventry, where we called home for a short time.

The Picketts, whose patriarch was a retired oil executive (from Shell if I remember correctly), lived in a neighboring house. Mr. Pickettt needed a lot of help with his yard and his property. I worked for Mr. Pickett whenever I could, and he paid me very handsomely because I was a good worker.

In the meantime, my family constructed a fence in our front yard to keep our property from sloping too much. We used large rocks, which were plentiful in the heavily forested lot just next to us. For that entire summer, I helped Dad build the rock fence, which seemed to go on forever in our front yard.

Dad did leave us for one year as his squad was deployed to Asia to serve the Vietnam War effort, which was beginning to come to an end. I was the man of the house while he was away. The time went by very fast, and he was safely home before I knew it.

The extra money I received around this time from helping Mr. Pickett allowed me to buy whatever items I desired. As I grew older, I always had a desire for nicer things. I knew I could obtain them due to my work ethic.

My golfing career kind of took a break when we were living in the northeast, as summers were very short, and the winters were very long. I did play POP Warner football in the fall both years and was our leading running back on our team. I was about to be offered a football scholarship to attend a private prep school in nearby North Kingston, but Dad was transferred back to Florida as President Nixon decided to close several military installations in the United States. My father's base was one of them. I was very relieved, as this allowed us to return to the Pensacola area where we had lived from 1968 to 1972.

Living in Florida for just a short time was a great time for the growth of my golf game. From 1973 to 1975, I really started to figure things out, and my game was getting better. I still remember sitting in a school bus at the age of 12 and watching one specific hole from a local course pass by.

The hole was always active with a group assembled on the tee ready to strike their shots. I vividly remember the green being mowed in such a way that it looked like cut ribbons of paper with the afternoon sun bouncing off multiple shades of green. Back in those days, they used to double-cut the greens, which gave them a cool look not often seen today. The course was only open for play to golfers over the age of 12 so I had to wait for a spell. This only made my level of anticipation that much higher. In the meantime, I continued to play at Saufley Field Golf Course—the par three course where I began my golfing career.

When that time finally came in the spring of 1972, I went to play the big course. It was called Osceola Golf Course, named after both the county and the great Indian warrior who roamed these lands a few hundred years ago. It was a municipal golf course, and it was the best golf course I had ever played in my young life.

It was a par-72 with each nine a par-36. It measured out at 6,800 yards from the back tees, but my age group played the middle tees. It was a true test, for sure.

The three years in Pensacola went by very quickly as I played a lot of golf and competed in my fair share of junior events during the summer. I also had my first real-life experience of being in the company of greatness when I played in the 1974 Southern Juniors Championship at Perdido Bay.

The great Jack Nicklaus came out to play the day before the main event in the father-son tournament with his son Jackie Jr. Mr. Nicklaus gave a short speech afterward and signed several autographs. I was one of many players who stood in line to finally meet Mr. Nicklaus and get his autograph as well as a picture of that moment. Please see the images of this moment on next page along with his autograph.

ELEVENTH ANNUAL SOUTHERN JUNIORS

GOLF CHAMPIONSHIP

August 19, 20, 21, 22, 1974

Sponsored by

the Pensacola Sports Association

at Perdido Bay Inn & Golf Club

Pensacola, Florida

We all remember watching the 1986 Masters championship on CBS some 14 years later as "The Golden Bear came out of hibernation" (a quote by then-rookie broadcaster named Jim Nantz that I believe fast-tracked his career). That same young man, Jackie II, was now 26 years old and the winning caddy for what was his father's sixth and final Masters win.

My brother Marcus was born in 1974 when I was a freshman at J.M. Tate High School in Gonzales, Florida (just outside Pensacola). Since my mother Elayne had married my stepfather, Paul Myers, Marcus was my half-brother and had a different last name, but I considered him my whole brother. Marcus, who later changed his name to Marc, came into this Earth in July 1974, right in the middle of summer break from school. I also had a sister, Rheta, who was two years older than I and at that age where she did her thing and I did my thing, as teenage siblings do. She was due to graduate from high school in 1975.

The whole family agreed that when Dad was ready to retire from the Navy after 21 years, we were all going to move to Phoenix—where my Mother's mother, my Yaya, was living with my Uncle Ted and his family. This is exactly what we did. My days of living in Florida were over.

4.

THE 2ND SUMMER AT PING

The fall 1978 saw me start my second school year at Glendale Community College and my second year on their golf team. The squad was loaded with talent during my first year, making it impossible for me to qualify to play in any team matches. However, a terrific round of golf I shot at the end of the first season cemented my status on the team for the 1978 to 1979 campaign.

We played on our home course at The Wigwam Resort in Litchfield Park, primarily playing the Gold Course. On this particular day, we were teeing it up on the Blue Course, which is the shortest and easiest of the three courses on the property. It was late May, school was almost over, and this was our last day of practice sessions for the year. Coincidentally, my game had started to bloom, just like many of the local plants.

I shot a one-over-par 36 on the front nine. After getting it up and down from the greenside bunker on my final hole by canning a four-footer on the par three, I posted a three-under-par 32—firing a 68 (two under par and the best round from the two groups that were competing that day). My coach, Ken Weis, was ecstatic with my performance and gave me a scholarship for the following year to pay for my books (which I graciously accepted).

I ended up playing in only four of the team's matches that school year, as we still had an outstanding team. Just getting in those matches was a significant accomplishment for me because it made me feel part of the team, which was something I had long strived for. My best performance came in our final outing of the season at Randolph Park Golf Course in Tucson, where I finished the 36-hole event with an even-par 72 that was the best score of the day on our team and even got me in the top ten for the competition. That accomplishment alone pretty much wrapped up my college golfing career as a successful one and one I was proud of. I knew I was never going to be a great player or play on the PGA Tour. That was never my intent; just playing to my ability was always my goal. I got there with these two years at Glendale Community College.

I ended up getting my Associate of Arts degree from G.C.C. I was able to take the 64 hours of credits I'd earned and transfer them to Arizona State University, where I was signed up to enroll in the fall.

First, I had my second year of work all lined up at KMC/PING. Since I was already trained, I was welcomed back to start another season in the Woods Roughing Department under the guidance of Doug Hawken.

When I started back at PING in late May, I got right back into doing the prep work: getting all those barrels of wood heads on those many machines and readying the heads to go next door to be painted. From there, the heads went to the shipping department to be boxed and shipped out to various golf courses in America. The PING wood's popularity (with its distinct look of a black head with a red insert marking the hitting zone) was still the craze of the industry. Sure, there was competition out there, but the PING woods, at only $300 retail for a set of three woods, were still in high demand. I was glad to do my part to pump them out by the hundreds every day.

I would put in regular 55-hour workweeks, which did not leave much time to play competitive golf. Every once in a while, I would get some time off to play in some bigger events. However, my focus was on work and saving as much money as possible. My car was now all paid off, and I was able to start putting more money into my savings account.

My younger brother, Marcus, was five years old by then. Our dad was going back to college on the GI Bill (from the Navy) to get his teacher's degree. In fact, at one time that past semester, he was on campus with me along with my future brother-in-law Bill Van Cott—all at the same time. I don't believe it gets any stranger than that, but also very neat at the same time. I would also play every month at the company's monthly golf event. We would inevitably travel north to Prescott or Sedona, as it was always 15 to 20 degrees cooler than those hot Phoenix days where temps were always hovering around the century mark.

When Doug Hawken agreed to welcome me back to work for him, I had asked nicely if I could be exempt (we golfers love this word) from having to do "The Bucket," and he said this wasn't a problem. This, by itself, made the summer that much more fun. Before I knew it, the summer was over, and the time to leave PING for school was there again—but I wouldn't be leaving PING entirely.

From what I recall, PING worked out a deal with the city of Phoenix involving property on a former landfill. They built a state-of-the-art driving range, and Bill Garrett was going to run it along with Pam Barnett, a former LPGA player from the '70s. When I began attending ASU in the fall of 1979, Bill asked me to work at the range part-time (or just weekends to get started). Of course, I said yes. This was my opportunity to stay connected year-round to the company that would ultimately become the centerpiece of my life.

5.
"Best Time of my Life" as a Golfer

I started my two-year stint at Arizona State University in 1979 as a business major specializing in marketing. I commuted from our home in Phoenix, taking three classes on Monday, Wednesday, Friday, and two on the other days. It was a good 45-minute drive each way to get to campus, but it was not a problem at the time. Looking back on that period, I don't remember the first three weeks of classes as I was entrenched in what would turn out to be the busiest and most rewarding stretch of competitive golf that I've experienced in my lifetime.

In August, one week before starting classes, I competed in the qualifying round for the United States Public Links Championship at Papago Park golf course. Since the temperatures were above 110 degrees each day, the USGA allowed our state two days to play instead of cramming all 36 holes into one day. My first day, I shot a ho-hum 77 or five over par and was positioned in the middle of over 120 golfers vying for only four coveted spots.

When I came out the next day, I noticed several golfers had already dropped out, so I was paired with different players. As it turned out, I was going to play with only one other golfer for the final round, and we were one of the last groups to tee it up. I was paired up with an older gentleman whose name escapes me all these years later. He was an excellent player and a pleasure to play with.

As it turned out, this gentleman held a high-ranking position with the Phoenix Suns in the NBA.

"Wow," I said, "That must be a cool thing to do."

"It has its moments. I've been doing this for over 15 years now."

"Good for you. I was always a big Suns fan, especially in 1974, when I was living in Rhode Island and watched them play the

Celtics in the NBA Finals. That was special." (Phoenix did not win the title; instead, the Celtics won under the leadership of John Havlicek and Coach Tom Heinson.)

"Those were good times for sure," he said, following up by asking, "What do you do, Stuart?"

"I am just about to start at ASU as a junior and just finished up working at PING for the summer."

"That sounds terrific. PING is a great company, good for you."

He and I played as a twosome that hot afternoon. In reflection of that day, all I can say is it was the best ball-striking day of my career, and that is past and present. I hit 17 greens and shot 71 or one-under-par, one of the best competitive rounds of my life. My two-day total of 148 (four-over-par) missed out on qualifying by only three strokes. It didn't dawn on me that I was still in the hunt for one of the spots until an official from the Arizona Golf Association, the late John Riggle, was following me around to see how I was doing those last few holes (which on the Papago course are very demanding). I was able to bring it home with all pars. My playing partner congratulated me on a great round and told me it was a pleasure to meet me and play with me. I drove home and shared the great news with Mom and Dad (and Marcus), and they were all so pleased with me.

There are so many times in all our younger days when parents, especially mothers, do a lot of driving around for their kids and don't get much thanks for it. However, I was always pleased to thank my parents for what they did for me when I was younger. It is incredible when you look back on how important parents are in helping to shape our ultimate characters.

The first few days of class were really neat, being at such a big school as ASU. I was taking basic business classes, including Finance and Business Statistics. Just as school was starting, the Phoenix City Championship was being conducted at historic Encanto Golf Course, one of the oldest public venues in the area. It was a short track of about 6,400 yards from the tips with a par of 70 (35 on both sides).

I ended up shooting 75-74 the first two days, and my 149 total score was good enough to make the 36-hole cut with over 120 players in the field. I shot another decent score of 74 in the third round to make the final cut, which allowed me to be among the final 36 players to play the final round. I then had my best round of the week, posting a 73, and my four-day total of 296 is still the best total I ever had over that many holes (which is like competing in a PGA Tour event). A few other players from PING were also playing in the event and my total was the best, which made me feel pretty good. It also helped my name become a little more known in company circles, which is never a bad thing.

You would think I was ready to hunker down with schoolwork and make that my priority, but you would be wrong. Even at such a big school as Arizona State, which historically has one of the best golf programs in the country (men's and women's), they have to have an open qualifier for any students wanting to make the ten-man roster. So, I went out for the team, knowing there wasn't a chance in high heaven I would grab one of the two spots. But hey, it was free golf, so why not go for it.

The first day was at Ahwatukee Golf Links not far from campus, and over 144 players were there. I shot a decent round of 78, and from what I could remember, anyone breaking 80 that day made it to the second round. At that time, then-men's golf coach, George Boutell, would put a list of players on his office door after each round. If your name was still on the list, you were in for the next round. I ended up making the list four times, which meant I made it to the final round of qualifying (the fifth round), which made me feel so good and gave me so much confidence with my game moving forward.

We ended up playing the final round at Dobson Ranch in Mesa, a very short and tight layout that meandered through a community of homes, so out of bounds was pretty much on both sides of the course on most holes. I played a very steady round, shooting a one-over-par 73, but two of the players in our foursome shot 65 and 67, with the last player posting an 80. Those two golfers ended up making the team with their final round performances, and I just felt great being able to see that happen. I knew these players had so much more skills than I did and deserved to be on the team, but they too would have to go out and qualify to gain entry into matches as the team already had a stable nucleus of players returning. For the record, this qualifying exercise took two and a half weeks, and a good three weeks of the 16-week semester had been completed.

My final event of this torrid golf run was the Arizona Amateur, held the following week at nearby Mesa Country Club, a course I had never played before. I had to alter my class schedule for this one as there was a two-day qualifier on Wednesday and Thursday; only 64 spots were available for the match-play portion of the tourney. The top 32 would be in the Championship Flight, and the next 32 made it into the President's Flight. Over 140 players were competing.

Again, I was playing my best golf ever, so I was able to shoot solid rounds of 77 and 75 for a two-day total of 152. This got me into match play in the President's Flight, which was fine by me as it meant I was one of the best 64 players at the time in the state of Arizona, and that was a pretty good feeling. In the previous two times I played in this event, I did not make the match play.

The first round of match play was held on Friday. I ended up winning my match one-up on the last hole. We all played two matches that day, so after a quick lunch break, I was on to my next match. I was paired up against an excellent established player from Tucson. I played a good match, but my competitor was too good for me and prevailed three and two. I gave it my all, and that was all I could do.

Officially, I had attended classes at my new college for four weeks, and I had not even read one page of any of my assignments. To put it mildly, I was behind and had a lot of catching up to do.

I remember those days so vividly now, as it was the best time of my life as a golfer. However, interesting things were about to happen off the golf course and out of the classroom that left an indelible mark on my career while at ASU.

6.

ENJOYING WRITING FOR THE SCHOOL PAPER

As the fall moved forward and I finally engaged myself with the whole college student atmosphere, I started to appreciate getting back to the basics again. Going to classes, doing the assignments, writing the term papers, and finally taking the exams. A lot harder than I imagined, but I was coping. A few things were also happening for me while going to ASU full time. I was working at PING's new driving range on the weekends, and I was also a contributing writer for the school's daily newspaper, the *State Press*.

When I was attempting to qualify for the golf team, I formed an interesting relationship with the coach, George Boutell. I informed him that I was in touch with the school's newspaper and had told them I would gladly submit weekly articles about both the men's and women's golf teams, and that they had granted me permission.

George was a unique individual. Standing at 5'11" tall, he was a little larger than average, and he was a charming man and very accessible. This was needed if I was going to be a reporter covering the golf team. In 1964, George, hailing from Minnesota, was ranked as one of the best amateur golfers in the entire country. He played golf for Arizona State and was an All-American selection two years running. He would compete on the PGA Tour for a few years with limited success. He was still a heck of a player just to go out there and give it a shot. The competition was so fierce that he ultimately found himself back at the Tempe campus, being named the men's golf coach in 1975.

When George was tearing up the college scene, so was another golfer named Allen Miller who hailed from Pensacola, Florida, where I had lived earlier in my life (also the hometown of Jerry Pate, who won the 1975 U.S. Open). Allen would go on to Georgia to become an All-American in the late '70s. I befriended his younger brother, John. We ended up playing some golf together when I was living in Pensacola. One time, he invited me to play his home course, Pensacola Country Club, possibly the most exclusive private club in the area. That was a treat for me. As it turned out, I would meet up with Allen shortly.

My job with the newspaper was to cover the team's main tournaments and do features on their many elite players. I remember the team playing events in Louisiana, Hawaii, California, Oregon, and locally. They were perennially ranked among the top 20 schools in the country, and always contended well in the NCAA Nationals, despite never winning the mythical title.

George always had time to meet up and give me his perspective on the players I was spotlighting. I did several player features, including one on Jim Carter, during that first fall semester and several more in the spring. Carter would win the NCAA individual title in 1983, finally bringing that coveted achievement to the Tempe campus. It was a lot of fun to interview these individuals. We usually did these interviews at the Hayden Library or at the Student Union, as there were plenty of places to conduct these conversations. All the guys were also excited to see their stories appear along with a picture of themselves in the paper the following week. The paper was readily available to all students on campus, which at that time had over 40,000 attendees. Looking back, it was an excellent experience for me too. I dreamed early in my life that I wanted to be a sportswriter, and this was pure food for that appetite.

In addition to the men, I also covered the women's team, reporting on their big tournaments and doing feature stories. My subjects included Pia Nilson from Sweden (who today is a nationally known golf instructor) and Lauri Merten (who would go on to win the 1993 U.S. Women's Open and was a personal friend of mine from playing junior golf together). Please see a poster of her victory on next page along with a personal note to me with her autograph.

The women's coach was Linda Vollstedt, who was just beginning her career at ASU and would guide the team to six national championships and coach countless All-Americans while at the school.

When I ponder this period in my life, I genuinely have no idea how I fit all those activities into one day. I guess I had the fountain

of youth working for me. Talk about being super busy. In addition to doing the *State Press* stories and going to class, I was putting in eight hours a day on both weekend days at the driving range, working under the tutelage of Bill Garrett and Pam Barnett. All I knew was that this weekend job kept me connected to PING, which at the time was very important to me—though I wasn't exactly sure why.

Soon the semester was over, Christmas came, and a new year also came along with a new decade. It was now 1980, and I was soon to be 21 years old. My second semester at ASU was pretty much the same, just a different medley of class subjects. All were focused on marketing. The best classes I had were Principles of Advertising, taught by Professor Vince Blasko, and Principles of Selling, taught by Professor Donald Jackson. For me to remember these gentlemen's names all these years later must have meant I enjoyed their classes and that their teaching left a pleasant impact on me. As I recall now, both were golfers, and since they knew of my connection to PING, I believe they paid a little more attention to me. This, in retrospect, meant a lot to me.

I got an A in both courses and ended up with a 3.0 GPA that second semester, which was excellent. My writing for the State Press continued under the sports editor, Pete Prisco. They never paid me for my services since I was not officially on the staff, but they always gave me a byline. Seeing "Contributing Writer" below my name satisfied my desires. I found out many years later that Pete had a successful career for CBSSports.com.

In summary, I would go on to do several more feature stories about golfing greats, including the late Heather Farr, whom I interviewed during the spring season. She was a stalwart on the golf team and a phenom in the junior ranks. After several seasons on the LPGA Tour, she was diagnosed with breast cancer and succumbed in 1993 at age 28. A statue was later erected in Heather's honor at the Karsten ASU Golf Course, which was built a few years after her passing and acted as the home course for both teams.

School was now over, and it was summertime.

7.

THE BREAK THAT I WAS LOOKING FOR

I am sure you all have heard that expression "timing is everything" or "being at the right place at the right time." I witnessed this firsthand on many occasions. What happened to me in the summer of 1980 delivered a new road map for me and my plans. It was a real game changer.

I did the math, and I had to take just one course in summer school to graduate on time from ASU by obtaining the 128 credit hours required for my degree. I enrolled in a class called Business Law. It was being held in the basement space of one of the most popular shopping malls in Phoenix, aptly called Metro Center. The mall was also conveniently located only 15 minutes from my home. From my best recollection, we would meet up every day from 8 to 11 a.m. for four consecutive weeks. I will never forget what happened on the very first day.

"Good morning, I see you are taking this class too," said a familiar voice. I looked up, and it was none other than John Solheim, a vice president of the company I had been working for the last few years. I wasn't quite sure how he knew me except for the fact that people in high places usually have a pretty good idea of who is working for them. Back then, the company was still rather small with fewer than 1,000 employees (figures that I had read about in industry magazines).

"Hi, John. Yes, I had to take a course in order to graduate on time this spring."

"Good morning class," said our professor for this course, Mrs. Marianne Jennings. She was a tallish, slender, attractive woman in her late 30s or early 40s with the brightest red lipstick you could imagine.

"Good morning," we all said back. The session began.

For the next four weeks, we would come into class and review many notable cases of the law related exclusively to business matters throughout the United States and some worldwide. It wasn't the most exciting class, but it was bearable. During this time frame, I worked full time at the 19th Green Driving Range, played a few tournaments, and just enjoyed life as a 20-year-old. My relationship with John also got better.

He even asked me on a few occasions to babysit for his family's two young boys, Andy and John K. Again, this all occurred a very long time ago, and from what I remember, Andy was five or six, and John was two years younger. Their home was just around the corner from the Moon Valley Country Club (where I had practiced and played while at Thunderbird High School), so it was close to our home.

The elder Solheim also knew I was a fine golfer and let me try out the company's new balata golf ball. I had read that Karsten Solheim created a series of golf balls sometime near the late '70s. I am not 100% sure, but I believe the Karsten III model was his most recent development. All I know is that the most recent golf ball rendering was a balata covered ball, so it had a superior feel to it and spun well. The newly created Golf Ball Factory was the building just next to the one that I worked in those first two summers making woods.

Speaking of the Karsten golf ball, there was a unique incident while I was caddying for Bill Garrett. It was in January of 1980, and we were trying to qualify for the PGA Tour's Phoenix Open. It was on Monday of event week, and we started on the back nine at the famed and posh Phoenix Country Club. Bill's first shot of the event flared off to the right on the dogleg left hole and finished farther from the hole than we'd liked. However, that was not our most serious problem. When we got to where we thought his golf ball should be, we noticed several other balls were lying around. It turned out to be a practice chipping area for the club members.

Bill did not bother to mark his golf ball with a sharpie as most pros would do, as he played with the company's new PING balata ball and assumed he was the only one in the field playing with it. The problem was that Phoenix C.C. was an excellent PING account (like so many in the state), and the club had bought this new ball as one of their range balls to use for the year. All the other golf balls lying around this practice area were the same PING model that Bill was using. Oh boy, we all thought we were in serious trouble and would have to deem this ball lost and head back to the tee to hit another ball.

I was about to do something I had never done before. You could say it was the beginning of a new hobby of mine: problem solver. I knew from playing golf all those years that golf balls all had numbers and letters stamped into the covers. Not sure why, but they were there. The codes were very small, but you could read them. As a caddy, I always took a sleeve (package of three) of balls out and kept two of them in my pocket just in case my player needed another quickly.

I looked at both golf balls to see what code number was stamped on them. They had the same combination of numbers and letters as the ball Bill was using. Plus, they had the same number as the other two in the sleeve. I started to look around where I thought Bill's ball had come to rest and check the code letters on them. They were all different except for just one ball, which had the same code as the golf balls we had from the original sleeve. We were able to identify Bill's ball, and we played on. That was a good story as no penalty stroke incurred, but Bill didn't play his best that day, and we did not make it to the "Big Show." However, Bill was very impressed with my detective skills.

Our next to last week of class was approaching, and I was so glad as my daily routine was starting to wear me out. Don't forget it was over 100 degrees every day, thanks to the Arizona weather that includes over 300 days of sunshine in any given year. Unfortunately, on this first Monday back to class, my seating partner was not there. I was concerned.

I later found out that the distributor for PING in West Germany (East Germany was still a communist country back then) had died of cancer, and John had to travel there to sort things out but was gone only for a short stay.

As it turned out, my final assignment for the class was to review an actual business contract. At the time, PING had a contract with its sales force, all whom were independent contractors who happened to represent the Karsten family but could also sell other brands. John was back in the country, and I consulted with him on this. He provided me with the contract, and I asked him if he didn't mind working on it with me. He had done so well during the course from what I could recollect, and I just thought it would make him feel better if he consulted with me on it. He made the time in his busy schedule to do this, and before you knew it, we were done. I received an A+ on the assignment. I cannot speak for John, but I know this grade made me feel very good, and I hope it made him feel the same.

My sense of appreciation and gratitude for the PING company had vastly improved with this experience. You could say this was a pivotal moment. It was the break that I needed to continue my life at PING and form my aspirations as part of the company.

8.
THE FINAL YEAR
OF COLLEGE

The time was rapidly approaching, and I could really start to feel the excitement. I was on the verge of starting my final year of college at ASU, and ultimately, my last days of any schooling at all.

It was finally all coming to an end. There was also a change in my living accommodations for that year; I was going to be living near campus. I had arranged to room with a golfing friend I'd met several years ago, Roy McMillin, and another of Roy's friends. We lived in Roy's parent's home as they'd recently relocated to Oceanside, California, to enjoy their golden years in better weather. The house was in a very nice, established neighborhood; it was only about a ten-minute drive to the main campus.

I had met Roy for the first time four years prior to us getting together again. We were paired together on the first day of the Arizona Junior Championship at historic Arizona Biltmore's Adobe Course. This was my final summer of junior golf, and we were competing in the 15- to 17-year-old division. I had heard Roy's name before as he was a prolific golfer and considered one of the top young players in Arizona. At that time in my golfing life, he was the best player I had ever witnessed. Man, was he good, and he was wielding a PING Anser putter to boot. Roy shot a 66 that day and then followed that up with a 64 the next day, a two-day aggregate of 130 (or 14 under par). Who does that? Great players do, and Roy was in that class. He won the event by a whopping 12 strokes.

We enjoyed our round together and agreed to stay in touch. In fact, shortly after this tourney, we played a practice round together at Phoenix Country Club for the local qualifying round of the prestigious U.S. Junior Championship. There were only two spots up for grabs in this one, and Roy seized one position.

Two years later (1978), we also traveled together to Albuquerque, New Mexico, to compete in another prestigious event, the Western Juniors Championship. It was considered a major event on the junior circuit for golfers 16 to19 years old. We drove together with another golfer, Dave Swartz, who'd played with me and was a star on my Glendale C.C. team. There were close to 300 solid players from all over the country trying to qualify for 64 spots to get into match play. We all played 36 holes over two courses, including the well-known University of New Mexico Golf Club, which would host the match play.

Roy was the only one to make it into match play and was knocked out in the first round. A golfing phenom at the time, Bobby Clampett, who played for Brigham Young University, was low medalist and the ultimate winner. I mentioned earlier that players from all over were competing in this one, including my childhood friend from Pensacola, John Miller (younger brother of then PGA Tour player Allen). We were able to find each other and converse some during the week.

Shortly after this event, Roy and I talked about the upcoming school year (we were both going to be seniors) and Roy suggested I stay at his place. After talking this over with my parents, they gladly allowed me to do this. I continued to work at PING's driving range on weekends, so I would go to class during the week and come home on Friday and work the range all weekend long, getting in full eight-hour shifts. Mom would help me out with my laundry as she was great about things like that. Everyone was doing great at that time, too.

Another neat thing about the campus was that since we were all seniors now, all the classrooms we were in were elegantly designed and decorated in the finest décor possible. The seats were all leather and very comfortable. Each room was named after a local business that'd donated the money to create this environment, and I noticed and appreciated it. This was also the time frame where all my courses were all very specific to my marketing major. We had only the best professors teaching these courses, and quite often the actual textbooks we were reading were written by the same people teaching the class. Pretty cool stuff.

I learned so much that last year, and I also worked extremely hard. I believe in the time I was at ASU, I wrote approximately 12 lengthy papers spanning various disciplines. As I recall, I received an "A" on every one of them. One that stands out is the paper I did in my Transportation class in my junior year about Federal Express, which was still a new entity (created by Fred Smith, who remains its chairman and CEO). I remember writing that they had lost a little over $600 million during their first few years of business. Fred was quoted as saying, "When you borrow money from the bank, make sure to borrow a lot as they very much would like for you to pay them back." I thought that was interesting.

I also continued to write golf stories for the *State Press*. My new roommate Roy was also on the golf team. In fact, he was a starter, so he played in every one of the events, which meant he was gone on the road for half the semester. In addition to being a great golfer, he was also excellent in the classroom (he was studying accounting), so being gone did not affect his grades.

I even wrote a feature story on him for the paper, which we thought was neat. Our other roommate, who I had never met before, was a member of the school's ROTC and occasionally had to go on patrol assignments for several days at a time.

Once school was close to ending, I found out that several companies would come to campus to conduct interviews with students who were in hopes of landing jobs after graduation. Since my connection at PING was on solid footing now, and I hoped to continue to work there after college, I asked John Solheim if I should even bother with the interviews. He commented to me that I should interview to see what might be out there. I found this to be a little odd, but since he gave me this advice, I took it.

I ended up interviewing with only two companies that I found interesting. Gallo Winery, out of Modesto, California, is the only company with which I can recall doing this process. This company had two representatives on hand that day. I did very well in the first interview with the gentleman, so they asked me to come back the second day. I did, and the female interviewer, after talking to me about my aspirations, could read me like a book. She knew that my future was already determined. She told me they would hire me, but that would be a mistake. She told me in so many words that my future was with PING. I found this interesting as these are professional recruiting specialists looking for good talent, but they also know how to read people. I must have been expressing so many good things about PING that I left an indelible mark on them.

I told John the good news that I had interviewed with two companies, including Gallo Wines, and that I was not offered a job (something I knew John would already sense, but it made him feel better knowing I tried). I asked him politely if he thought I had a future with the company, and he said something to this effect: "Of course you do, we just need to figure out what that is."

The graduation ceremonies took place at the legendary Grady Gammage Auditorium in late May 1981. They were attended by my entire family including my Yaya, my grandmother on my Mother's side, and my younger, six-year-old brother Marcus. My time as a student was over. My education in the golf business was just about to start, and I could hardly wait.

9.

THE FRONT OFFICE EXPERIENCE

The process of exiting my position at the driving range and transitioning into my new role in the front office was simple. I believe it took only a few weeks for me to finish up my obligations at the range and say my final goodbyes to the entire staff, including my mentor, golf instructor, and pro Bill Garrett who I would still caddy with in the future, Pam Barnett, and my fellow workers.

We had a heck of a ride at this state-of-the-art facility (it was the only range at the time with automatic tees, another product that Karsten had a hand in creating from what I had heard). However, it was time for me to move onto my next chapter with PING. It was mid-June when I started in the front office. I remember that first day very well. I had no title at that time as the management team decided to make up a position for me. I ended up being a sort of jack-of-all-trades. I was assigned to work directly for the plant manager, who was an elderly gentleman, and with his assistant. They were all so friendly to me when welcoming me to the team. They even admitted that what I was about to do had never been done before by just one person, but it only seemed fitting for me to give it a try. The first few weeks, the assistant was training me on the basics of what I was going to do. Then they totally unleashed the reigns, and it was go-time.

My main responsibility was to be the liaison between the plant and the customer service department, which was made up of an all-female staff of about six people. To give an example, the account holder would call into PING's 800 number, trying to find out the status of the order they'd placed for one of their members. The customer service rep would note all the requests or changes on a standard green slip and put the slips into a basket which I would come to grab every hour or so. Then, I would simply go to the assigned department, ask to see the manifest of the orders, and ask the foreman how much longer before the order went to production.

At this time (June 1981), the company was always running behind in production and deliveries. The demand for the product was substantially higher than the supply. Not exactly sure that our founder Karsten Solheim envisioned this or sought this condition, but it for sure helped cast the PING mystique (in my opinion).

As I said earlier, I was put into a position with a myriad of responsibilities. In addition to checking the status of orders for the customer service department, my big role was what we called "returns." Returns were orders sent out in good faith that would get refused for some reason. The UPS driver would return it to the shipper, marking it as an "RTS." My role was to find out what happened to this item, then to make sure it was put back into the system somehow. This job ended up being my most time-consuming duty, yet it was also the most rewarding. At that time, the product backlog was very long, and this task allowed me to redistribute brand-new products into one of the orders waiting to go out the door and make some golfer out there happy to finally get their "PINGs."

Each day I reassigned items, but man was it a lot of work. There were always items that found their way back to the company, and it was my job to sort them all out, which for the most part I admit I did a very good job.

From time to time, I would do a static fitting for a customer interested in our product. We had an area just off the main lobby to do this. It was all based on the company's measuring figures, and it was a pretty good first step for a golfer who wanted to be fitted for our products. PING was the first major golf company in the industry to make fitting a main priority. They were the leader in this area, but it temporarily caused them to get behind in fulfilling orders.

The company at that time could only produce so many sets of irons a day, as each factory worker assigned to do loft and lie on an iron set would take several minutes on each set. At that time, there were eight different lie angles on the patented PING fitting chart, as Karsten made it rule number one that all golfers who were buying his clubs would be fitted first. A custom set would then be made for them, thus the delay in the production line.

Since a large percentage of clubs that did make it back to the "returns department" were irons, I got to know the iron foreman pretty well. He would keep all his orders for iron sets on spindles, as each order was printed on what was called a "golden rod." This was simply a computer printed-out order that included three copies. Each spindle contained roughly 100 or more golden rods from what I can recall.

When I would go to see this person about an inquiry from the front office, I had to find that exact order. I would end up having to look through his desk for it. On many occasions, since there were several spindles to search, it could take several minutes to find the order; but that was my task, and I handled every assignment with pride.

It was just an awesome sight seeing all these orders. It is something that I will never forget. Talk about job security. At that time, (and again these figures were all common knowledge within the company as I had to give quote times to our accounts) an order for a custom set of PING irons took six to eight weeks. The woods had a somewhat longer wait time at roughly eight to 12 weeks.

In summary, several times a day, I would go to the iron foreman and find an order that matched up perfectly with one of the sets of irons that was recently returned. All I had to do was update the serial number from the set to match up with the new order. It was that simple, and I would do this constantly. This process would also apply to a set of woods. Everyone was happy with how smoothly the process ran.

The last thing that I would do in my new job was serve as the factory tour operator. I did this very little, but if some very important person came in when no one else was available I would take this VIP on a quick tour of the factory—maybe 30 minutes— while showing the things that we could show.

That pretty much sums my new role at PING. I was loving every minute of it, as each day I worked I knew that I was an integral part of a world class organization. Each year, the company was becoming widely more recognized and its market share in the golf industry was exploding (again this is how I saw things shaping up). Of course, this was only the beginning and more great times were just on the horizon.

10.
FINDING MY WAY WITH MORE PAY

Summertime was now upon us, and the PING factory was cranked up to its full operating capacity. Orders were coming in from all over the United States due to the company's elite sales force and the many distributors that had been assembled along the way. I was now in my fourth full week of work in my new title role, but it dawned on me that I was still making the same basic hourly wage of $3.00 that I was earning at my former job at the 19th Green Driving Range. I still remember making only $2.30/hour when working as a carryout associate at Smitty's of Arizona grocery store during my senior year in high school four years earlier.

I finally got a chance to bring this up with John Solheim, who technically was the boss of all us at the company. John was the one son who followed his dad's footsteps the most, as he was engaged heavily in the design work of future club models and in overseeing the sales force. We set up a meeting soon after. I was able to get Karsten's three sons in the same room to decide my future pay sum.

This particular event happened close to over 40 years ago. Still, for whatever reason, when you are in the company of individuals who are not only older than you but are also high-ranking company officials, you tend to remember moments like this.

"Just because Stuart now has a college degree, he thinks he should be paid more money," said Alan Solheim, who was in charge of all employee relations at the firm (and was principally the one who hired me back in '78).

"That is not fair, Alan," I responded. "I am no longer working at the driving range picking up golf balls. My role here is so much different now."

Louis Solheim, who was also there, was the one brother I seldom had interactions with during those early years at the company. From what I recalled, he was a former IBMer from upstate New York and was responsible for the PING computer and operating systems. I vividly remember that IBM made all the hardware equipment and that the computer department was one of the crown jewels of the operation at the factory as Louis did a great job. My response seemed to satisfy Alan and the others in the room.

"If I were to make $6.00 per hour coupled with some overtime pay, I believe I can make $18,000 this year, and that would be great for me."

As soon as I mentioned the number, all three of them brought out their pocket calculators and started punching the keyboards. It was a unique moment for sure, but it must have been a good thing for me. After expressing myself to them, the meeting was over, and I left that room with a good feeling.

We got paid every two weeks, and when the office business manager was personally handing out the checks, he patted me on my shoulder and said, "Nice going, they took care of you." I quickly opened the envelope, almost destroying it in my anticipation to see what he meant. When I looked at the rate per hour on the check stub and saw the $6.00, my request had become a reality. I learned right then and there that if you ask for something that is both fair and reasonable, there is a good chance it can happen. That was a big moment in my new office career, and it boded well for me with the company going forward.

One of the best moments of each day with my new job was the correspondence I would have with the creator and founder. With my desk being positioned right near the door that led back into production, Karsten himself would walk right by me every day at the same time.

"Good morning, Karsten," I would say to him.

Without really making eye contact, he would reply, "It is a good morning, isn't it?" He did this every time. It was great. What a way to get your day started—by talking to the man himself.

I was getting very good at my job and was learning new things all the time. Concerning the return department, there would be times when I would have to personally call the sales representative up to discuss why something was returned. All documents shipped out had a sales number column on it, indicating the sales rep responsible for that account. I figured I should get to know these numbers by memory to know who the rep was. I was able to master this assignment, and in less than one month, I knew all the 40 or so independent reps we had in the field.

Sometimes, I would even meet some of the reps when they were in town for business functions. Quite often the reps would gather in the back office walking around, and if I saw them, I would recognize their names and always introduce myself and tell them what I did. Once that was done, they always thanked me for the job I was doing for them.

I even had time to caddy for my dear friend Bill Garrett on occasion as the company always gave me the day off to do this for Bill. During this first summer of my new job, I recall caddying for him in the Smitty's Southwest PGA Championship at the Arizona Biltmore's Adobe Course. This was a major championship on the calendar for the section's club pros and was well-attended. Bill played great in the event and shot well under par to tie for first place. This got us into a sudden-death playoff with someone who I had crossed paths with six years ago.

It was Jim Ahern, the same pro I caddied for in a qualifier for the Pensacola Open on the PGA Tour. And he, sure enough, remembered me like the qualifier was yesterday. Jim ended up making a birdie on the first hole, grabbing the championship and the winner's check of $3,500. I believe Bill fetched $2,500 and gave me a very nice bonus for our success.

In the many times I caddied for Bill, from my best recollection we only won one event: the Mountain Shadows Pro Classic, and that was in January of 1981. As I mentioned, Bill was considered one of the best players in the section. He was also a former PGA Tour player and winner of the 1970 Cape Coral Open in Florida, which I believe is now the Honda Classic.

He was also a valued employee for PING and Karsten's friend. Bill would always be one of the first players to test a new product for the company. We gave it a good try at the event, but it was not meant to be. I returned to 2201 W. Desert Cove Drive to make more memories.

11.

APPLYING FOR THE CREDIT MANAGER'S JOB

We were now entering the end of the fall season, with wintertime just around the corner. The best weather of the year was now upon us, with daily temperatures consistently in the low 80s and high 70s. The factory was still busy but was slowing down just a little. The return merchandise was still coming in.

Sometimes there would be cases when lots of product would come back, and I would have to get the credit manager involved. During this time period, I worked closely with this gentleman (who was in his mid-30's from what I recall) and had been with the company for most of his adult life. He was excellent at what he did. His best feature was that he was a smooth talker on the phone and successfully got delinquent accounts to pay their past due invoices. This way, they could get off credit hold and thus get their clubs shipped to them. He had replaced the previous individual who left three years prior to become the new salesperson for the Bay area in Northern California.

A development occurred in the sales force towards the end of this year 1981 that would have a domino effect. To make things simple, one of the first reps hired by PING was giving up some of his territory, and one of the areas involved was Colorado. The credit manager was picked to go out and service this region, starting in the new year.

With this person leaving, this created an open position in the credit manager role. I thought I would throw my name in the mix for this role, as it might be the only ticket for me to become the sales representative that I always wanted to be at PING.

So, I formally applied for the job. Several candidates were vying for this position. John Solheim called me into his office to explain that they gave the job to another employee who was several years older than I and had some experience in the credit industry (so he was well suited).

John asked me why I wanted to do this job, and I just told him I thought it might help me become a sales rep in the future. He quickly defused the situation and simply said in so many words that not getting this job will not be a factor at all in determining my future with the company. That, for sure, gave me some comfort. I quickly congratulated the new credit manager, and for my remaining time at the front office, we worked exceptionally well together.

During this time, PING was enjoying enormous success in the industry. They had created an allotment system for their accounts so that product was equally distributed to all its authorized dealers throughout the country. Let's just say due to supply and demand factors, the company created the allotment based on iron sets, sets of woods, and putters. Each account with a good credit rating would qualify for their monthly allotment. There was a fair amount of accounts that were taking their full allotments, thus creating a demand that was unparalleled at the time, which helped PING's market share in all categories increase.

It had been exactly one year since I started working in the marketing department, and things were going very well for me. My parents also had a trip they had planned for a while, which would include me traveling back east to my mother's hometown of Salem, Massachusetts, to see family members. This was mid-August, which was a perfect time for me to take some vacation time. I figured that no one would miss me for a short time. It has been so long since this time in my life that I don't recall all that happened on the trip except we all had a nice, relaxing time with family members.

One day in early September, I remember getting several sets of PING irons that had been returned from a club in Indiana due to the customer not paying for them (they were a cash on delivery account). After I investigated all the details, it turned out that the salesman in the area did some things that went against company policy, and unfortunately it cost him his job. Within a few days, the company announced that a new field representative would be going to Indiana. That person turned out to be me.

12.
FINALLY BECOMING A PING REP

In the early days of September, I got a call from John Solheim asking for me to come to his office, which was an uncommon request. I had only been in the front office for about 15 months, and I got the news I had been waiting for.

"How do you feel about going to Indiana to be our new salesman?"

"Really, what happened?"

"As you know, through your findings in the returns department, things were happening there that were against company policy, and we had to make a change; therefore, we want you to go there."

I wasn't sure how I felt at that very moment as I had looked forward to spending some time in Arizona as a young college grad. However, I quickly decided that I was up for the new challenge.

I remember the first thing I did was call Mom and Dad to tell them of the exciting news and that I had a few weeks to get ready before heading out. They were extremely happy for me, but also nervous. I went to the local AAA office and picked up some maps of Indiana and travel guides to help me navigate this new land.

I also needed some things for the trip. I recall going to Metro Center. Just a month earlier, I had purchased my first ever "brand-new" automobile. It was a Datsun 200X, a sporty four-door car with nice lines on it and a soft light blue exterior. I believe it cost me just over $10,000 at the time, and I financed it. The interest rate was almost 20%. However, it was mine, and I was going to pay for it over the 60-month plan.

I parked my car reasonably close to one of the entry points to the mall and headed in to get some warm clothing items that I would certainly need as fall was rapidly approaching. For some reason, I went by an entertainment store in the mall and started to watch the U.S. Open men's tennis tournament, which at the beginning of the second week and only the best players were still in the mix. I distinctly remember watching the John McEnroe-Ivan Lendl match, and for whatever reason I was glued to the set. I was just a big sports fan at heart and really liked to watch all sports events. I ended up watching it to the conclusion, which took well over an hour. (Lendl did win but lost to Jimmy Connors in the final.) At that time, my shopping was done, and it was time for me to head back out to the parking lot and get on home.

Then something eerie happened to me. I could not find my car. Watching that tennis match had taken a toll on me, as I was mesmerized by the excitement. For an instant, I could not remember where I had parked or what entrance I had come into the mall. Plus, with all that was going on with the new job, my mind was racing. I guess I just didn't have a good sense of what it looked like, because it was so new. After well over half an hour, I finally found it, and it was not even close to where I thought I had parked it. I made sure that was never going to happen to me again.

I got into the car and said a quick prayer to our Maker, thanking him for allowing me to find my car so I could get home and start the new journey in my life.

I was starting to picture things in my head about my destination. As I was a huge sports fan my entire life, I first thought of Notre Dame football in South Bend and thought of Indiana men's basketball in Bloomington and, of course, the Indianapolis 500 car race in the capital. Since I had never been to Indiana, this was all virgin land to me.

Only three days had passed, and I was in the front office working with John's assistant who was also in charge of the marketing department when he said that John needed to talk to me and it was important. He was in West Germany at the time, getting things updated since the long-time director Burt Lancaster had succumbed to cancer over one year before.

John told me that he forgot that the current sales rep for the upstate New York area had asked if an area ever opened up to the west, he wanted first dibs at it. So, John told me he had no choice but to give this state to the current rep. I understood and had no issues whatsoever with his decision. He wanted me to go to service the New York region, which also included neighboring

Vermont and Western Massachusetts. As an added twist, he also wanted me to go to Virginia where the long-time salesman recently suffered a stroke and had to retire to make a sweep through the state and call on the top accounts. John said I could pick wherever I wanted to locate after I toured both sections.

So, it was settled. I was heading to the northeast to be a new PING sales rep.

My vision of doing this was finally here. I must admit I thought I would spend at least three to five years in the front office learning more of the PING way before heading out on the road to become what was the company's crown jewel job at the time: a PING sales representative. It was revered as one of the best jobs in the entire golf industry, and now I had it. I was only 23 years old, which from what I could recall may have made me one of the youngest reps hired in company history at that time.

A few days later, when John returned from Heidelberg, West Germany, he congratulated me in person on my new appointment. I will never forget to this day what he said to me on that late September evening:

"We like you a lot and what you do for us here at the factory… But your future is out there." Man, did that make me feel so good and filled me with so much pride in going out on the road and representing this great company to the best of my ability. I was ready. Soon, I would be on my way.

13.

MEETING THE GREAT BERT READ

As part of my final preparations before embarking on my new wonderful journey as a golf sales representative, John Solheim wanted me to fly to southern California to work with legendary PING salesman Bert Read on some sales training. From my brief time with the company, I had heard nothing but great things about Bert and how he was revered as one of the best PING sales reps ever and on all accounts was a living legend. For the past few years, every new rep would go to see Bert for some pointers and tips. It was a trip I was very much looking forward to.

When my plane landed at the John Wayne Airport in Orange County, I was looking for Bert in the terminal but then heard a familiar voice.

"Over here, Stuart." I looked up, and it was another company sales rep who offered to drive me to my hotel. He covered the area just east of Bert's and lived in Bakersfield.

"Where is Bert?" I said.

"He had a meeting he could not get out of and will meet us at the hotel."

This gentleman was a former standout golfer at ASU and just became a PING rep three years prior. He was a super nice person, and every time we spoke on the phone in my previous job, he was kind to me.

"Just wanted to say congratulations on your new rep assignment. Now, where are you going again?"

"I'm going to take over the upstate New York region."

"Good for you." With that, we were off to my hotel.

When Karsten himself had hired Bert to be one of his early salesmen on the road in the early 60's, he was responsible for the entire state of California. Now that is a lot of territory, with the state covering over 163,000 square miles, making it the third-largest state in the whole country just behind Alaska and Texas. From my calculations, Bert would be in his early 70s and would be entering his 20th year working for the company.

I got to the hotel in the tony city of Laguna Niguel, a very affluent community just on the coast north of Dana Point. The Pacific Ocean beckoned with its majestic blue waters a stone's throw from the place I was staying in.

Since cell phones were still not the norm back then, I got a call in my room from Bert telling me to meet him in the lobby. I wandered down there, and within seconds I could hear Bert's unique raspy voice.

"How are you doing, young man? Great to see you."

"Thanks, Bert. It's so great to be here with you, how're you doing?"

"Just fine. Now let's get some coffee."

Bert and I would have one cup of coffee together (Bert really loved his coffee as I would in the years to come) in the hotel lobby, then we went off to have a nice dinner at one of the many spectacular restaurants that dotted the immediate area. This was a very affluent part of the greater Los Angeles metro area but was well south of L.A and located just north of the La Jolla region. Over dinner, I asked Bert so many questions about being a rep, and he answered all them for me. I really admired Bert in the short time that I knew him because he would also be the leading spokesman for the reps in the field, always watching out for them and protecting their best interests. He was always one step ahead in ensuring we were always provided with the samples we needed to do our jobs.

Bert picked me up in the morning, and we were off to see some golf pros that Bert knew well. I was to observe how he transacted with them. More or less, it was a real live exercise in the dos and don'ts of the business.

At this particular time, reps in the field were engaged in selling woods, irons, and putters. A brand-new item was just introduced called the Karsten Punch golf ball, which featured a combination of orange and white coloration. We were selling them in a cone display that would comfortably hold six dozen balls. Bert wanted me to try my selling skills with each pro we met that day (we saw four) by introducing the new ball program to them. Every one of them placed an order. As I said before, I was there just to see how Bert would communicate with his customers, our accounts, and see how he could better serve them. He had so much energy stored in his 5'10" frame that he was always beaming with excitement over selling the PING brand.

After our last appointment, Bert took me to a restaurant near the airport because I was going to be catching the last flight out to take me back to Phoenix, and we chatted some more. I believe I asked him how he managed to work the entire state during his early years.

He said he would have a few cars parked in key cities. He would fly into the major airports, then work that area for a few weeks at a time, then fly home and repeat the process. I guess that would be the way to do it. Today, five reps are servicing the hundreds of PING accounts in California.

The new rep number that I was assigned to was #43. Every time an order was generated in my territory, the number 43 would appear under the sales rep box. Pretty neat.

I believe I got the most out of this exercise shadowing Bert on that mid-September day because I was only 23 years old, and I was dealing with gentlemen twice my age and sometimes three times older. I was able to hold my own with all them. I realized that we all shared one common passion, which dominated our industry back then: it was the love for golf. It was truly a great time to be in the golf industry.

14.
THAT FIRST LONG ROAD TRIP

The next day, after coming back from a quick training session with Bert Read, I was gathering up my things at my desk when John came over and said, "Let's go for a ride."

"Where are we off to?" I mumbled back, as it was still mid-morning, and I was a little tired from my travels to California.

"We need to get you set up with some credit cards."

It hadn't dawned on me, but I did not own a credit card at that moment in my life. I guess the folks on campus at ASU trying to pitch credit cards to young inexperienced students never worked on me. I was not strapped with any debt, and college was all paid up because going to a state college back in the day was very inexpensive.

We got into John's white BMW and went into action. I just assumed that John loved foreign cars from Germany, most likely due to their engineering prowess. His dad also enjoyed them, and for years he would drive to work in his classic white Citroen from France. He was also driving a white BMW at that time. White was a prevalent color for cars in Arizona due to the extreme temperatures in the summer months.

The first place we visited was the regional headquarters for American Express, just off Lincoln Avenue and very close to the Arizona Biltmore shopping district. We walked in, and in less than 30 minutes, I had a blue AMEX card. To this day, I still carry the card, and it has proudly stamped on it "member since '82." When I am with accounts who are dear friends, I sometimes take it out to show them when I first got started in the business.

The next stop was the Arizona Bank to get a VISA card. That only took 20 minutes, because when you are with the big man himself, things get done pretty quickly.

Shortly after we got back to the plant, we were off for lunch with the office manager and John's executive assistant. This would be my last time spent with company personnel for the next four months.

We went to a very nice fish market restaurant that was only ten minutes away from the plant and close to the Black Canyon freeway, which for locals is the main highway artery that can take you to Flagstaff if heading north. While there, we went over some tips on where I should stay and how to keep track of expenses. I was going to be gone for four months and needed to keep track of many things; at that moment, I was not even sure where I would end up working. Lastly, I was informed to check in with the marketing department a few times a week so everyone could see how I was doing out there.

I gathered all my sales samples I needed for the fall run and put them into my still relatively new car with the odometer reading only around 10,000 miles. Boy, was that about to change. I said a final goodbye to all my fellow workmates at the company and told them that I would see them again just before Christmas.

After arriving home, I started to pack up all the clothes that I would be using and the other essentials. We all had an excellent final family dinner, including Marcus, who was not eight years old and just starting second grade. Everyone was so excited for me but also a little sad as I was heading away from home for the very first time for an extended period.

I also had a chance to talk to Dad a little more about the job I was going to do. Earlier in the week, I had received some printouts from the marketing department about recent sales and orders in my new territory, and I showed them to him. I shared some actual sales numbers with him and emphasized to him that I would get a 10% commission on all sales in my designated sales area. He was awestruck.

The most he ever made in the United States Navy was nothing compared to what I would make in my first year. But I could sense from his mannerisms that he was immensely proud of me and happy. I still remember how he would always show me how to do everyday fix-ups around the house like installing wallpaper or putting in new carpet. He was so good at it. I always told him, "Dad, I really appreciate you showing me all this, but one day I will have such a great job that I will not have to do this as I will be too busy and would gladly pay someone to do it." Well, that day had come. He also knew that, and I could tell he was profoundly proud of me for reaching my goal.

Have you ever driven 800 miles in a day? I am sure you would say "not lately," but that is precisely what I did for the next three days—nothing but driving and steering my car to the northeast. The only problem I had was that while my car was considered a sports car and got around 24 miles to the gallon, it did not come equipped with cruise control features. My right leg was getting very tired by the end of each day, but I drove on.

On the fourth day, I reached my destination, finally arriving in upstate New York around 5 p.m. Earlier in the week, I had called the current rep and told him when I would be coming to town. The plan was for him to work with me for a few days and get me up to date with all the accounts in my new area. He was married at the time, as he and his wife had also traveled from Arizona after he worked in the plant for a few years. I believe it was Wednesday when I arrived at their home in Clifton Park, which was a lovely small town just north of the capital of Albany. I would stay with them for the next few days before they started their new journey to Indiana.

The plan was for me to rest up on Thursday, as I had just driven over 2,800 miles in three and a half days. On Friday, we would see a few key accounts in the area, and my new career with PING would finally begin. Exciting times for sure.

15.
NOW THAT'S WHAT I AM TALKING ABOUT

It was now Friday, and we were in the second week of September. The temperature was hovering in the low 80s, still slightly cooler than the weather back home in Arizona. The former area rep and I would call on a few key accounts in the southern part of my new territory this day. We left early in the morning, as we had a full day ahead of us.

He was driving to save us some time. The first place we visited was the Duchess Golf & Country Club in Poughkeepsie, about 90 minutes south. This was an old-school golf course nestled just off the main road in a city that employed quite a few IBM'ers. This was considered one of their main hubs for business development and had a vast factory just down the road in Fishkill manufacturing mainframes. We met Fred Lux, Jr., the head pro at Duchess, following in the footsteps of his father Fred, Sr., who was also in the pro shop when we arrived.

Fred Jr. was about the same height as I at 5' 9"; tall with light black hair and medium weight. He was charming to talk to, and we discussed how PING was doing in his golf shop, which was very good from his report. He very much liked the way PING conducted its business practices by supporting the green grass clubs like himself and staying away from the golf shops found in shopping centers. Fred was old school in many ways, and he liked that attribute of our company. This meeting was just a meet and greet, and I would reunite with Fred again in a month to work with him on a potential Spring '83 golf club order.

The next stop was the Blue Hill Golf Course in Pearl River, which was in Rockland County and less than one hour from New York City. We were in the southernmost part of my area, which was also one of the more lucrative in the state. We met head pro

Jimmy Stewart. Jimmy was a little less refined than Fred, most likely due to the Big Apple's proximity and closeness to New Jersey. He was straightforward in his actions.

As the previous rep introduced me to Jimmy as his new PING rep, a large brown UPS truck arrived in front of the pro shop and the driver was bringing in several large boxes.

"Excuse me for a moment," Jimmy said as he walked over to the driver to see who the delivery was from.

"This is that Wilson order I canceled a few weeks ago, not sure why it's here."

He said that he would give them a call and negotiate with them on the price to keep the order. In other words, he was going to use leverage with Wilson to get the price per set down to a level where he could make some money in return for keeping the entire shipment. From the looks of the boxes, it was a significant order.

Fortunately, PING didn't operate this way. That was a big lesson for me that day to see how differently we were viewed in the marketplace. This head pro, Jimmy Stewart, really liked the way PING controlled its distribution of product by having the allotment system. He always took advantage of this and did the maximum every month of his busiest time, which was April to August.

On our visit, we showed the pro the newest iron from the company, called the Eye2, which had just happened to show up at the current rep's doorstep two days ago. It was a great looking iron, and about 20% larger in diameter than the EYE model, which debuted two years earlier. I presented this new iron to the pro as well as the Eye2 woods and all our most popular putter models, including the ANSER and PAL bronze head models.

When we were all done, Jimmy had given me an order for his full allotment of irons, woods (all 1-3-5 combinations), and putters to start shipping from April 1983 through August 1983. This was really my first day of selling in my new role, and I did a little calculating in my head of what just transpired. The sales commission I was going to get on these orders would be plentiful, and I realized at this moment all the hard work I put in during my PING factory days was paying off. Now that's what I'm talking about.

I thanked Jimmy a lot for the order and told him it was a pleasure to meet with him and that I looked forward to seeing him again in the springtime. After I had closed on that big sales order with Blue Hill, I called the plant and spoke with Doug Hawken, my first boss at PING.

"Hey Doug, it's Stuart, and I just had a wonderful experience."

"That's great, Stuart. How's everything going so far?"

"I just made my first sale as a PING rep, and it was a big one. The pro bought five months of the full product line."

"That's fantastic news," Doug replied. "I could not be happier for you. You certainly have earned this opportunity."

After I hung up with him, I realized what my new role now was. I was brand-new at this, but I could see first-hand how what I did in the field was so important. My efforts to obtain the orders would, in turn, create the need for more workers at the factory to continue to churn out the product to fulfill the demand. It was the PING way. Everyone doing their part. It was simply magical.

16.

THE FALL RUN BEGINS

The main thing I can tell you that best describes my life in the fall of 1982 is pure panic and unknown. I was flying on the seat of my pants and learning as I went from day to day. When I said goodbye to the Indiana-bound PING rep and his wife on that Sunday morning, I was now on my own. But was I really? All I had was several maps from AAA, a car loaded with my golf samples, order forms, clothing items to wear for the next four months, and of course, determination. I went to work every day with the hopes of doing something great and would try to repeat this daily.

My new territory consisted of the central and northeast sections of New York State, Vermont, and the western part of Massachusetts. The only memories I have of this part of the country were when I was much younger, and my family on my mother's side would visit relatives in Salem, Massachusetts. I fondly remember swimming every day in my Uncle Miltie's fabricated above ground pool and soaking up plenty of sunshine in the process. I will never forget my Yaya taking live lobsters and tossing them in a huge pot of boiling water for dinner that evening. And, of course, our short two-year stint living in Rhode Island a few years later.

I started my new pilgrimage by heading up I-87, better known later as the Northway, a direct route to an area called the Adirondack Mountain Range, which spans over 9,375 square miles. My first destination was the Lake Placid region, better known for its quaint shopping and great skiing in the wintertime. It was also home to the famous Winter Olympics and its victorious men's hockey team only two years earlier. "Do you believe in Miracles?" became part of the history of this small town and put a young broadcaster named Al Michaels on the map.

After traveling for roughly two hours, I found a nice rustic hotel in Tupper Lake where I would spend the first of many road nights in this new career path. I had called the pro a few days earlier to set up what would have been my "first official appointment" for what would be called "the fall run." I had a terrific night's sleep, and after a quick breakfast at the hotel, I was ready to do my thing. The Tupper Lake Country Club was only a five-minute drive.

When I arrived, it was like a war zone. There was a large fire engine and several firemen scouring the area. Somehow, part of the clubhouse had burned down during a fire in the early morning. It also destroyed the golf shop. The person I was supposed to have had a sales meeting with was distraught and in no condition to meet with me. I was able to briefly speak to this individual and gave him my card and told him I was sorry for what just happened, and I would stay in touch. Not exactly how I planned on the first meeting to go, but sometimes things are out of your hands. With nothing to show for my first meeting, I was on to the next stop.

I just remember driving for the next two hours on a two-lane road that continued to meander through tall pine trees and oak trees and endless other forms of vegetation. This was God's country and simply beautiful to take in, and there was very little traffic on the roads. I soon arrived at the Potsdam Town & Country Club, a nine-hole semi-private club under the watchful eye of head pro Mike Rosenquist. He was terrific, along with his wife Nancy, who also worked in the pro shop.

Mike was a long-time fan of PING and even had a small collection of some of the earlier putter models that Karsten produced in the early '60s, including a few Scottsdale Cushin putters and the well-known PING 1-A model from Redwood City, California, that started the entire company. The noise made from this particular putter had a unique ring to it and thus the name PING.

Let me also point out that these earlier putter models that, as time would go on, would become sought after antiques were not made in Scottsdale as one might have thought. Just to be clear on what I am about to say about this topic, this is purely from what I had heard about during my early years at company headquarters. Karsten, who was so creative in every aspect of his being, put down a P.O. Box number with a Scottsdale address to avoid confusion with his putter brand and the other Phoenix-based BULLSEYE brand that was brandished by several top PGA pros, including Jack Nicklaus and Arnold Palmer.

I found myself in a terrific position with this golf pro having some knowledge of the company. At that time, Mike was in his early 40s and was very successful in the village of Potsdam, which was also the home to three very prominent colleges: State University at Potsdam, Clarkson College, and St. Lawrence College (in nearby Canton). The latter two were considered mini-Ivy League schools due to their reputations. In fact, Mike and Nancy's only child, Derek, was currently enrolled at Clarkson.

"Does PING still have its allotment on clubs to order?" Mike asked me.

"Yes, they still have the same figures," I responded.

"In that case, let's do the max I can get for both irons, especially this new iron, the Eye2, the woods, and putters. And let's do that for May, June, July, and August."

In taking this order of his full complement of product for four months, I felt like I just hit the lottery. I had to keep reminding myself that it was only day one. Mike also recommended a nice hotel for me to stay at and even had dinner with me. I would have to say my first day on the road was a success. I had to call home to say hi to the folks and let them know of my good luck. I also called my contact person at PING to share my early good fortunes.

As you can imagine, trying to get around a territory in less than eight weeks would require a lot of energy, conviction, luck, good driving skills, and innate ability to know how to listen to instructions to find golf courses. Without cell phones back then (or Garmins to direct you) and the ease to call for appointments in advance, my daily routine consisted of traveling to a golf course, introducing myself to the pro as his new PING rep, attempting to get a spring order (which, surprisingly, came easy), and then asking how to get to the next closest club. Just hearing that process is exhausting. But when you don't know the terrain or area, that is all you can do.

I just marched on. And on and on. Before I knew it, I was in the Green Mountain state of Vermont.

17.

THE FALL RUN
CONTINUES IN VERMONT

After I saw a few accounts in Burlington, I drove into spectacular Stowe, which was well known for its ski slopes and beautiful resorts that were summertime escapes for all the city slickers from Boston and New York City. They even had a famous tennis tournament on the Men's ATP Tour, which would annually visit Stowe at the Stowetop Inn then move on to nearby North Conway, New Hampshire (always playing on hard surfaces). This was part of the scheduling tune-up for the U.S. Open in New York City. Back during this time frame, living legends like Jimmy Connors, Arthur Ashe, John Newcombe, and newly arrived stars John McEnroe and Ivan Lendl would come to showcase their incredible skills on the court.

Every golf pro I met along the way to Stowe had treated me exceptionally well and had the nicest things to say about my company. The reputation of the product was outstanding. The only negative I would hear was the sluggishness on special orders. That was one reason most accounts would order their allotment in advance and mix up the color codes to help in the fitting process.

Also, back at that time, we did not have laptop computers. All orders were handwritten on order pads. Needless to say, I was writing a lot of orders. To keep things simple, at the end of each day, I would write up the orders. Each Saturday, I would send them to Arizona via FEDEX. All my orders I was turning in would keep the company busy in the winter months in preparing their designated spring shipments.

I met up with head pro Gary Bond at the Stowe Country Club. I could see from the account list that I received before leaving Arizona that this was the best account in the Green Mountain State. Like many other accounts I had already seen on this journey, Gary also took his full allotment of product from May to August.

After my visit with Gary concluded, his shopmate went out of her way to find me a room to stay in town at a reasonable rate. I ended up rooming at the Stoweflake Inn only five minutes from the course. I vividly recall it was Monday. After checking into my room, I drove a short distance to a local sports pub to have dinner and watch *Monday Night Football* on ABC. After working six days in a row, I would take Sundays off and devote that to watching football. That was going to be my escape to all that madness. As it turned out, that game I watched in Stowe, Vermont, on that Monday night was the last game for the next ten weeks as the players decided to go on strike due to contract disputes. This, too, pretty much put a dent into my planned schedule. "Turn out the lights, the party's over" is what then-ABC color man Don Meredith would say when a game was over. This is pretty much what happened after that game. Just a disappointment, but in hindsight, it was just fine. It accelerated my schedule, and I was working seven days a week, which ultimately made my first run through my territory a little quicker.

After Stowe, I traveled southeast to the town of Barre, which was just outside of the capital of Montpelier. This city took me back to the fifth grade of elementary school in Pensacola when my geography class would have a test on the United States' state capitals. This city was always a tricky one, but I somehow remembered it due to its odd name. Now I was very close to it.

Bill Ross Jr. was the head pro at the Country Club of Barre and was also an excellent PING account. He, too, was pleasant during our sales meeting and gave me lucrative spring orders.

Later that same day, I would also visit the Quechee Club and its well-known head pro Bob Lendzion. Bob was considered the best club pro in Vermont and most of New England. He would win the PGA Club Professional Championship in 1986 in La Quinta, California, considered the most important of all professional events for club pros. Bob, too, had a tremendous amount of respect for our brand. Due to his competitive success, he would be invited to play in some PGA Tour events and playing the product was only an added bonus. He, too, was an excellent account, and before I left the shop, my order pad had seen some action.

After finishing in the upper part of New York State and the clubs in Vermont, I was back in the capital region of Albany for a few days. I looked at the map to figure out my next move. I decided to travel west to the Syracuse area. I finished it in only three days, then drove back to Albany to attempt to finish up that part of the trip.

I talked to my mother, who told me that letters had been arriving from a bank and American Express for a few weeks. At the time, she didn't think much of it. Then one day, she received a phone call. That is when she realized the credit cards that had recently been issued to me were adding up and had not been paid. Having zero experience with credit cards, I was quickly reminded that even they needed to be paid. I called my contact person at the plant to inform him of this, and he took quick action. He told my folks to come down to the company headquarters with the bills and meet with him so the company could take care of everything. They would continue to do this while I was on the road. The problem was solved.

I worked the greater Albany area again that week. The strategy that I found to be the most practical when I was in a major market like Albany was to hunker down at the same hotel for the week and just go out and about seeing all the accounts, then come back to that one spot. This worked out well while I was working the golf accounts in Albany, as there were several. I was finding out this area would most likely make a good spot for me to settle in as it was pretty much right in the center of my new territory.

I was now past the halfway point of my fall run, and I was ready to visit my new accounts in Western Massachusetts. I just happened to be driving later in the day trying to get to the MASS Turnpike for the drive to Springfield, and I accidentally drove right by the entrance of the Country Club of Pittsfield. I quickly turned around and drove into the parking lot, and shortly I was talking to head pro Brad Benson. He was a great guy and a good PING account. After he gave me a large spring '83 order, I was on my way to Springfield. I was able to settle into a nice room and conducted all my business in four days again, staying in just one location and venturing out each day.

Things were progressing very well workwise, so I decided to take a much-needed break from the grind. I called my relatives in Salem and went to stay with them for the weekend.

Spending time with my two sets of aunts and uncles and a few cousins was also a lot of fun, and it was a great escape from all the work I had been doing. I showed all them the products I was selling and told them about my new job. They all knew from my younger days that I loved golf, and they were so pleased for me to find a new life working for such a great company as PING. I could sense they all knew I was in good hands and working for a fine organization.

I drove home back to Albany to finish up my last week. I also researched the area with the goal of finding a new place to live when I returned in the spring. I asked around for the best realtors. Somehow, I was told to see Bob Howard of the realty company bearing his name. I showed up at his office on Central Avenue and told him who I was. He was quickly impressed, as he, too, was a golfer and a member at nearby Albany Country Club. I told Bob that my predecessor had rented a home for the short time he lived in Clifton Park. Bob told me that Clifton Park would be a great place to settle and wrote down several apartment complexes to check out.

To this day, I remember giving him one of my sample PING putters that was in like-new condition as a thank you for his efforts. He was pleased as punch. I ended up driving over to the Foxwoods Apartment complex in Clifton Park and checking out all the options. I told the sales agent to reserve me a single room apartment with a move-in date on March 15th of next spring. I was now done working in this area and must admit I had a lot of success with the many accounts that I saw along the way. Having a place already lined up for the next year was just icing on the cake. The next step was a trip to Virginia.

18.
WORKING IN VIRGINIA AS A COMPANY REP

As I was driving down Interstate 90 from my new home of New York State, heading to the northern part of Virginia, I reflected on the feat that I had just completed. I was doing the math, and I was averaging around four to six account visits per day—roughly 20-30 per week. I had physically called on over 160-200 golf clubs. My closure rate on getting actual spring orders was very high, and I left my area feeling a great sense of accomplishment, as there would be a significant amount of product flowing into it come April 1st, 1983.

With the excellent help of the computer system the company had, they would have a spreadsheet created which would detail each account on exactly what they ordered and when it would ship, including all the dollar amounts so you could gauge how much product was being shipped into your territory at any given time. We were considered independent commissioned reps only, thus making a commission on all sales. However, we also paid for all our expenses. I racked up a lot of costs with hotels and gas during this period. But the reality of it all, and this would certainly sink in the next few years, was that this was my territory, and each of my actions would ultimately determine my fate and my reputation. In other words, it was all good.

While I was still at the factory during the late stages of summer, we all heard that the longtime Virginia PING representative had suffered a minor stroke and was not able to continue in his capacity. So, John Solheim wanted me to go there and act as a company rep and service all the active accounts, which of course, I had no issues doing. I figured the navigational driving skills I'd displayed recently would also prove worthwhile in the great state of Virginia, known as "Old Dominion," and one of the original 13 colonies.

It was now early November, and I could feel the crispness of the air as fall descended. The abundant trees that I found around me as I was driving were also changing their color to a light brown hue, helping to brighten up the sky. Fall was here. This also meant the days were getting shorter, and my time to see accounts was also closing. For these reasons, I continued to march on and work pretty much every day of the week.

My direct mission from the marketing and sales department was to focus only on the company's best accounts, and having a listing of all these clubs made it a lot easier to plan my schedule.

I started in the most northern part of the state and zigged and zagged around the hilly roads, as this part was the most elevated and home to several ski resorts.

I do remember calling on several prominent cities, including Harrisonburg, home to James Madison College but better known as the birthplace of Ralph Sampson. He went on to star at the University of Virginia before becoming an NBA stalwart with the Houston Rockets and getting labeled as part of the "Twin Towers" with fellow star Hakeem Olajuwon. I also visited Charlottesville, which was home to the University of Virginia Cavaliers. There was where I met up with a friendly young lady golfer. She was in the pro shop at the Farmington Country Club when I called on the account, and we started a conversation. She said her family was a member of the club, she played on the golf team for an area university, and she was home for a few days.

We really hit it off and she gave me her phone number so I could stay in touch and see her a little later on my trip, because I was going to be in the state for a full month.

I did leave the Farmington Country Club with a hefty order, as they were one of the best accounts for PING in the entire state. From there, I traveled to Richmond and worked in the area for several days because there were a lot of accounts.

Soon, I ventured off to the eastern part of the state, which brought me to historic Williamsburg, perched on the famous James River. Then it was onto the Newport News and Norfolk area, where I saw more water than I have in my entire life. Ultimately, I made it to Virginia Beach then continued south to Norfolk. My odyssey in Virginia continued onward as I turned the car northwest and headed back to Richmond, because that was where most of the state's bigger PING accounts were concentrated.

I was now three-quarters of the way done, and I started to think of some exciting things to do while I was still in the state. I'd recently visited the Country Club of Virginia, just outside Richmond, and I recalled the pro had told me that Vinny Giles was a member there. I knew that name; he was a winner of both the U.S. Amateur and British Amateur during his younger years. He was considered one of the best amateurs to play the game. I also knew he was a sports agent who ran a company called Pro's INC based right in Richmond.

For fun, I called his office and told him who I was and asked if he could meet me for lunch soon. Boom, we met up just a few days later. I entered one of the few high-rise office towers in the city to go to his office. We ended up walking down the block to one of his favorite eating spots for lunch.

"So, Stuart, how long have you worked for PING?"

"I started with them in summer 1978, so four years now."

"And you just became a rep for them recently?"

"Yes, in September." I told Vinny of my new area and that I was covering his home state as a company rep.

We were well into our lunch, and I was destroying the hamburger and fries that I'd ordered when Vinny said he had a great Karsten story to share with me.

Vinny appeared to me to be an older guy. Anyway, I remember him as being an old guy, which means he may have been 40. This was happening to me all the time, as being only 23 years old, everyone I was dealing with was older.

"I was playing in the Masters one year, and sure enough, Karsten came up to me to say hi and see how I was doing since I was putting with an Anser putter at the time."

Vinny continued with the story by adding, "I told him all was good but that I might have had a little too much loft on my putter; he took my putter and bent it right then against a curb on the cart path. I was shocked at what he did, but it did the trick. My loft problem was solved." That was a great story. We also talked for quite a bit about his new life as a sports agent, mostly with professional golfers, including his two best clients,

Ben Crenshaw and Tom Kite, PGA Tour Hall of Famers and past major winners.

I thanked Vinny for a great time and one that I would always remember. He wished me luck on my current trip and for a safe journey back home to Arizona.

It was now the week before Thanksgiving, and I traveled back to Charlottesville to see the young lady I had recently met. We ended up visiting Monticello, the birthplace of our third president of the United States, Thomas Jefferson. We enjoyed our time together, and we agreed to stay in touch. Unfortunately, they all had previous plans to visit family for Thanksgiving, so I was on my own. I stayed at the Holiday Inn in Roanoke and ended up having a nice family buffet dinner by myself. Not a problem, as I had become accustomed to being alone on this journey. After an excellent talk to the folks that day, I was ready to finish the trip and start heading home.

I decided to work right through the weekend, and after finishing up the Blacksburg area, I was on to Bristol. That Sunday afternoon, I made my last sales call for the year. I was now ready to go home.

19.

BACK AT THE FACTORY AGAIN

It was early Monday morning in the first week of December, and I was now on my way home to Arizona. I called ahead and made plans to visit my sister for a few days. I took the most southern route home I could, which meant driving through Texas again, most of the way on Interstate 20. I was so hungry to get home that I pushed it, making very good time. By my second night, I was up near Midland.

As I exited the town, I left behind what seemed to be dozens of round white silos of oil, as this was the famous Permian Basin. The oil deposits in these grounds stretched for hundreds of miles in southwest Texas into New Mexico. I was within a day's drive of my sister's in Carlsbad, New Mexico, located in the southeastern part of the state. It was in the region known as the "White Sands" due to its enormous sand dunes that were painted like bedsheets. My sister, Rheta, lived there with her husband, Bill, who was in the U.S. Park System and stationed at nearby Carlsbad Caverns National Park (known for its massive caves that house thousands of bats).

Since it was several years since I'd last seen Rheta, I decided to spend three good days with them to catch up and relax. I did just that. I also visited the park and checked out the caves. Along the way, I did see my fair share of live bats, all hanging upside down. Creepy for sure.

I was only 400 miles away from our home on W. Joan De Arc, and I was there in about eight hours. It was so lovely to be home. I was gone for over 14 weeks or three and a half months, and the odometer on my fairly new car now had well over 20,000 miles on it (double what it had when I set out). The folks were excited to see me, as was little Marc, who had grown quite a bit since our last time together. I believe it was early in the week when I arrived home, so I called up the head of the marketing/sales department, and we agreed to meet up in a few days, allowing me to get organized at home. I came into the main plant on W. Desert Cove Drive, and it seemed like I'd been gone for years. Everyone said hello to me and welcomed me back. It was a great feeling.

My first order of business was for the head of marketing and me to go through all my expense reports and sort everything out. I told him and John that I'd selected New York to be my new territory. The company had paid all my credit card bills while I was gone, so you can just imagine all the accounting that needed to be done to sort everything out. We ended up taking three days to categorize it all. I paid for all the costs during my time in my area, and the company gave me my commissions for all sales I'd generated during that time. Then the company paid me a salary for the time that I was in Virginia, and they paid all the expenses for that part of the trip.

I can tell you the company was very impressed with my book-keeping skills, and I also sensed they were pleased with my ability to get through such a large swath of area so quickly and effectively. My sales were solid in both areas, which was good for the firm.

With all that done, John had told me previously that he wanted me to work at the plant during the winter months, or while my territory was dormant. I would return in mid-March to start the new season. He helped me out financially with this winter jobs program before I was self-sustaining in a few years. I was, for sure, on board with this plan.

Christmas and the winter holidays were close now, and I could sense the cool air that seemed to always appear in the Valley of the Sun during this time frame. It wasn't like real cold east coast weather, but it was a nice change of pace from the normal hotter temperatures. The new year came, and it was 1983. With that came my new job.

John Solheim wanted me to work on an enormous project that dealt with our Tour department, which was growing exponentially at that time. I was in charge of helping to configure a new system for properly paying our current staff players on all tours based on their performance and the well-being of each tour or how much their total purse offerings were for the season. This was only going to be for the male players initially, but it would eventually apply to the women.

This was a colossal project, as at that time, there were several tours in operation. There was the PGA Tour, which was still considered the front runner of all tours globally, the growing European Tour, Australian Tour, South African or Sunshine Tour, and lastly, the Asian Tour.

The first thing I did was visit with an employee in our media department, which handled our advertising and marketing departments. This employee also dealt with all the print magazines sent to the company each week from all the world's major golf publications, including *Golf Magazine, Golf Digest, Golf World,* and *European Golf World.* I needed the last two because they concentrated on covering most of the tournaments played around the world and in the U.S.A. She had a particular room where she would keep all the older copies, and I was going to need all editions of the 1982 season to get the most updated info I could find.

I liked this stuff, as I always liked probing into the unknown. It was a great discovery opportunity for me, and my research would help pave the way for a new money pool for all the PING pros on tour. It was an exciting time for sure.

The only way this could be done was by doing each major tour one at a time by detailing every event on the circuit for that year and also noting the purse. Just for added information, I also put down the winner's share, which was usually 18% of the pot.

Since I was dealing with five major tours, I would be able to surmise all the info for each tour in about three days. Still, it would ultimately take about a week to do each tour, because I was summoned from time to time to do some other projects around the plant.

I also had to attend my first ever PGA Merchandise Show, which is always at the end of January in Florida. Back then, we would have a sales meeting the day just before the show's start to get together as a big team. Then, we would attend the show. That year, it was held in Miami Beach and not its usual location in Orlando (the new convention center was under construction).

I vaguely remember rooming with the rep I'd replaced in New York, and we were in one of the older hotels in the area since I was a brand-new rep. Accommodations at significant events like that were usually booked out a year in advance. We got through the show and watched the Super Bowl in our room since it was played during the show's third day. The show was done on Monday, and I was home on Tuesday.

Just as soon as we returned, I had the pleasure of being asked by John Solheim to caddy for him in the Phoenix Open's pro-am, which was still contested at the fabled Phoenix Country Club right in the heart of the city. I knew this course very well, and I knew I could help John navigate the narrow fairways and sloping greens.

In 1978, while a student at Glendale C.C., I had the pleasure of caddying for a then-rookie on Tour named Jack Renner in the same Phoenix Open in the final round. It was just luck that this happened, but rain had postponed play on Sunday and Jack's caddy, who I believe was his cousin, had to go back to Palm Springs for college. We just happened to be talking near the putting green on Sunday, getting to know each other, and he asked if I could help by looping for Jack. That was a great opportunity, and I seized the moment. Jack was very tall and very frail, but sure hit the ball fantastic. Donning his trademark Ben Hogan cap, he would fire a final round 67 or four under par and be low pro in a group that also included Tom Watson and South African Bobby Cole.

As I look back on that round, I had no idea that I was in the company of future greatness; Watson would go on to win eight major championships. Having an opportunity to shake his hand at the end of the round was priceless. Jack finished in the top ten for his first time by tying for sixth place. My childhood idol Arnold Palmer finished one stroke better in his best performance in several years. Jack gave me a crisp $100 bill for my efforts and all the Hogan golf balls he used for the week. He was so pleased with my efforts, he hired me in advance to caddy for him in the 1979 Phoenix Open. Now that was pretty neat in itself.

After my day of caddying and getting plenty of sunshine, I returned to the factory and continued my winter project. I found it fascinating to see all the places that the tour players were playing and, for some of the tours, how little money they were competing for compared to the rich PGA Tour. The main reason for each tour's documentation was that it was tied into the pool as it would be merit-based tours documentation and indexed upon the overall purse. A little confusing to me, but that did not matter. I was just doing the groundwork, and then the powers that would map it all and make it a reality.

Some time near the end of February, I finished this task, and I surrendered my final report to John. He shared it with the company's PGA Tour rep, who worked closely with all the players. From what I could remember, there were well over 100 players who were playing PING products on all these tours. From what I recall, you had to play a minimum of 11 clubs of our brand to be considered a staff player, and you had to play the putter. If you chose to play all 14 clubs, you would get maximum points. I was not privy to exactly how the player pool worked. I had heard things along the way, including that a player would get points based on various criteria such as qualifying for the event (during this time, if you were not in the top 60 on the money list you had to qualify to gain entry to tour events), making the cut, their finish in the event, and winning the event. I believe points were doubled in the four major events of the season. There would be a set amount put into the money pool for each given tour.

That was pretty much what came out of my project, as those players who made the most points would grab the lion's share of the pot. The thing to remember is PING (at that time in their early beginnings) did not have endorsement deals for players, unlike most of our competitors. We had the money bonus pool system, and it worked for many years. I am just glad I had a hand in molding it into existence. Karsten always believed in supporting tour players, and I remember him saying one day that "it validated his product" when the best players used it. Looking back on this time, I also believe that those players who decided to play on PING's staff did so because they knew they were going to be playing with the best equipment, which would allow them to succeed.

20.
HEADING BACK TO NEW YORK

I celebrated my 24th birthday on February 11th, 1983. At that time, I started making early preparations for my return trip to upstate New York to begin my first full season as a PING field representative. As I said earlier, I was designated sales rep. #43. I was one of 50 reps. In fact, during my time at the factory that winter break, the company announced a new representative for the Virginia territory that I'd just serviced. I met this individual when he came for some training.

This new hire would be joining his father and brother, who were also reps in nearby territories. The company had several of these family combinations in action throughout the country.

Also, around that time, there was a new rep named to cover northern Ohio. This was the same individual who was my immediate supervisor when I worked in the front office just after college. At this particular time, I was the youngest sales rep in the force, and I always considered this to be an honor as my career with the company progressed.

During the time back in Arizona, I took my Datsun 200 X sports car to the dealership to have the cruise control feature installed. That would for sure make the journey more bearable.

March was now just around the corner. I planned to leave just after the first week, which would allow me enough time to drive north but also to stop and see my new lady friend in Virginia again. We continued to write and speak on the phone after our last visit in Charlottesville. She had since transferred schools and was now a Lady Tarheel golf team member at the University of North Carolina in Chapel Hill.

I met her there, and we hung out for a few days. She gave me a tour around the campus, which was unbelievable and more of a natural country setting than ASU. She even took me to the recently constructed Dean Dome, which was the basketball arena named in honor of their long-time coach Dean Smith. Future NBA legend Michael Jordan was gracing its court, helping the Tar Heels win the NCAA Title in 1982. It was great to see her again, but we both knew we were both young and doing our own things, which made it impossible for any long-term relationship to develop. We left on good terms, and again it was this great game of golf which allowed us to meet in the first place.

Soon enough, I was back in Clifton Park and checking into the first apartment of my young adult life. I was just getting settled in that first week, including spending some time at a local rental store. I had never done this before, but since the apartment housing would be a temporary thing for me, I decided just to rent my furniture. I knew very well that I would be spending a significant amount of time on the road, so I only got the essential items: sofa, bed, some table stands, and at first, a TV, until I had the time to buy one to keep.

It was now around the middle of March, and I was just starting to plot my account visits for the spring run when I got a call from the gentleman at the factory in charge of us sales reps.

"Hi, Stuart. I trust you made it safely back to New York."

"Absolutely, all's good. I'm just settling into my new apartment."

"That sounds good. I have some news for you. John wants you to go to Germany."

I replied, "Germany, really, what may I ask for?"

"As you know, the gentleman Burt Lancaster who ran the distributor there for Karsten passed away over a year ago, and his wife Cora is still running it but needs help." He added, "We were all so impressed with your ability to cover so much ground last fall that we know you are the best man for this job."

I was stunned that they would even consider me for such an elite assignment. I was going to Europe again. When I was only ten, my mother took my sister and me to Greece to stay with our yaya, who had a home in her birthplace town on the island of Samos just off the Turkey coastline in the Aegean Sea. I remember we visited there in the hot month of June and were gone for only 30 days, but it felt like a year when we returned stateside. I was wondering if this trip would feel the same.

The plan was for me to make a quick trip through my territory, focusing solely on my premier accounts and letting them all know that I would be out of the country for a while and not call me but to call the company's 800 number for all their needs. I had about five weeks to do this as my ticket to Frankfurt, West Germany, set my departure in late April.

21.

THE TRIP TO GERMANY

Since the golf season doesn't officially start up in the northeast part of the country until all the snow is totally absent from the courses, the actual start date varies from year to year. I was able to begin engaging with my account base in the third week of March. I started in the southern part of my territory, and the pros were all in the pro shop by then. Many of them were even open for play. I ended up doing my spring run in record time, again only seeing my best-performing accounts. I was done in five weeks. My plane ticket to Europe was set for the last Friday in April.

I had met my new neighbors across the way from me in the apartment complex and told them of my upcoming trip and how long I would be gone. All the necessary things to make sure my dwelling was safe for a lengthy departure were now done.

My first leg was a quick one-hour flight from our local Albany airport to John F. Kennedy International, better known as JFK. I had not been at this airport in a dozen years or so, not since the time we visited Greece when I was only ten. I thought it was a super big airport then, and it had grown quite a bit. I was going to be flying on TWA (Trans World Airlines), which at the time was popular for international flights (it was acquired by rival American Airlines in 2001). It was also the same carrier we used for my trip to Greece.

All international flights to Europe leave at night, so with the five- or six-hour time change, you arrive there at the beginning of the next workday. I remember our flight leaving around 10 p.m. The plan was for me to fly into Frankfurt airport, and John Solheim would meet me there.

I brought a lot of paperwork to do on the flight. I had delayed writing many orders, planning to do them on the plane. I had no idea how many there were, but I ended up spending close to four hours getting them completed and stuffed into envelopes. I asked one of the flight attendants if she could mail them for me when she returned stateside, and she said they were not supposed to do that, but after explaining my situation, she agreed to do so. Mission accomplished.

I was getting ready to turn all my attention to Germany. My job title was Sales Liaison between Lancaster Sports in Germany and PING in America, and that title was on the business cards they gave to me.

When I deplaned and headed toward the luggage area, I saw John. He greeted me and asked how my flight was. We got both of my bags, as I needed some clothes for this journey, and hopped into John's rented BMW. During the 45-minute drive to Heidelberg (precisely 79 km away), where the distributorship was located, John explained what my job was going to entail.

"We need you to go to as many golf courses as you can and just let the golf pro know that Lancaster Sports is still functional, and they are open for business," he said (or something similar). And the ensuing conversation went something like this or as close as I can remember.

"What am I supposed to do, John, when I see the pro?"

"Cora (acting president of the distributor) is going to help you make up catalog packages that you will leave with each account to just fill them in on our new products like you are doing in your territory."

"I can do that, but what about the language?"

John said that since Germany was still considered a new country for golf, many of the golf pros came from the United Kingdom and naturally all spoke English. I was instantly relieved when I heard that. Communication problem over.

John also added, "Cora has an older Mercedes Benz car that Burt used to drive that she's going to want you to drive, but it's manual. Can you handle a stick shift?" My sister Rheta drove a Carma Gia when she was in high school. I remember it had a stick shift, and I didn't want any part of that.

"Actually, no, John, I never have and don't want to," I remember firing back at him.

Before we got to Cora's place, we drove out into the countryside to see things and found a nice area where John would teach me how to drive a stick. His BMW was manual, and I tried to do my best. I failed miserably. John said we would figure something out.

In a flash, we were at the headquarters for the PING operations in Germany. John introduced me to Cora Lancaster and to her long-time assistant.

We spent the next few days going over all the information sheets they had. I compiled over 100 folders for my upcoming account visits, along with price lists and my business card stapled on the outside cover.

We had some free time, so we all went into the center of town to visit historic Heidelberg, which is best known for its venerable university and the Heidelberg Castle overlooking the historic city, founded in the 14th century. It is, for sure, a destination for global tourists. When we were walking the cobblestone streets, my first thought of the city was just how old it was. However, it was vibrant with springtime visitors. John and I had the wiener schnitzel for dinner in one of the street-side restaurants, and it was quite good.

It was now Monday, the first of May, and John told me of the next plan. He said we would take a train ride south into Switzerland to visit with the distributor there, then he would be off to South Africa for more business. I would return by train to Cora's place to begin my adventures.

We boarded a super looking passenger train and traveled three hours or so to get into Lausanne, Switzerland (a smaller town just north of Geneva). This is where the distributor for PING for Switzerland lived (again from my best recollection). From what I could recall, PING was selling their product in over 30 nations.

The distributors met us at the train station and then swiftly drove us off to a restaurant just on the town's outskirts. It was a top-notch restaurant where the ambiance was very relaxed, and the food was fantastic. Expensive, I am sure, but hey, I was not paying for it, so that made it even more enjoyable!

After dinner, our host dropped us off at our hotel, which was overlooking Lake Lausanne. I had never been on a business trip with John before, but to make things simple, he booked us in the same room. It turned out to be like a suite, and it had lots of room. We would only be in town for one night.

"How much do you think this room costs for the night?" I remember asking John.

"I don't know, but I'm sure it's a lot," he answered.

After a restful night, the distributor picked us up and took us to their main office to see the lay of the land and learn more about the state of affairs of their distributorship. After a nice lunch nearby, we made the long trip to the airport in Geneva, where John had a direct flight to Johannesburg, South Africa, to work with the distributor there on PING business.

You can see the responsibility John had in helping to run one of the most successful golf companies in the world. Before leaving, John wished me luck and then said, "After you're done in Germany, we'll make arrangements for you to visit our factory in northern England. Then, you'll have a meeting with Karsten to go over your findings, as he will be eager to know." That new information motivated me to do a great job on this assignment. I was ready.

22.

TRAVELING IN
SOUTHERN BAVARIA

I was back on the train the next morning, heading back to the PING HQ in Heidelberg. I arrived in the early afternoon and began final prep work for my first trip to Southern Bavaria. Cora Lancaster knew that I was having issues with driving a manual car. I told her I was being paid to be there for the job, so I would simply go down to the local AVIS store and rent a car if need be as "I am not going to drive that car anywhere," (referring to the older automobile that her late husband Burt drove).

I knew right then that she would have empathy for me. Cora was a woman in her early to mid-60s and was an American who met Burt while living in Alabama. She was short in stature, had a foreign dialect, and was quite regal in appearance. She was strong-willed, but she was also fair. Cora then said to me, "I understand. Stuart, you're so right. You can drive my car instead."

Cora then showed me her white Mercedes-Benz station wagon, which was parked in the other part of the garage. When I saw this fantastic vehicle, I simply gave her a big hug and said, "Thank you very much." Whatever concerns I had quickly vanished.

At this time, there were roughly 120 golf courses in all West Germany. I had about five weeks to see as many as I could, which meant I would be on the road constantly. To test the waters and get my feet wet, I would be gone for only five days for the first trip. Cora gave me a lot of cash (or deutschmarks, Germany's currency) to pay for all my gas, lodging, and food. I vividly remember that first day as I was heading straight for Bavaria, which is in the southern part of this vast country. I had a Shell travel guidebook with maps for where I was heading plus a small beige book on where the courses were located with directions. The travel guide was in English, and the course finder book was in German, but I could still make out most of the key words. I was very fortunate to have found three courses that first day without too many issues.

Once I found the golf course, the routine was to simply head straight for the golf pro shop. Ninety percent of the time I did this, there was a sign on the door in both English and German stating the pro was on the range giving a lesson and back in one hour. I would find the range and then pick a good moment to briefly interrupt the lesson, indicating who I was, and the pro told me just to wait a short time and he could meet with me. When we finally met, I proudly introduced myself and handed over the packet of information for the club to retain. I told every account that I was just representing the distributorship on behalf of Karsten in the States and that Cora was still in charge, which would calm all of them down since they were all concerned since it had been about one year after Burt had passed.

My goal was to take that worry away from them and let them know that they could still deal with Cora and the current arrangement with confidence. I did show those who needed to see product the new Eye2 series of irons and woods and some of the more popular putters. I also took a few orders along the way. Occasionally, I sold a pro some putters out of my car stock for cash. In the golf market, PING was considered a premium brand, thus carrying a hefty price tag for the member who wanted to purchase a set. As Germany was a country that exported some of the best and most expensive automobiles in the world, this did not seem to be a damper on the company's sales there.

It was summer, and the days were stretching out long and straight like the nearby Rhine River. I felt a sense of accomplishment at seeing three accounts, but I was also showing some anxiety about finding my first hotel room of the journey because I wasn't quite sure how to find it. It wasn't like looking for the green lights of a Holiday Inn or Ramada.

Cora had told me to look for signs on the buildings that said *Gusthauffs,* which means "guesthouses." I was trying to avoid hostels and larger hotels, which would be out of my price range.

I found a spot, and it seemed to work. I saw the attendant at the front counter and asked for a *zimmer,* which is German for a room. I gave them the cash and got a receipt for my records. I remember getting these odd skeleton-shaped keys and sharing a bathroom/shower at the end of the hallway. It didn't matter. I had made it through my first day.

Unfortunately, that first night I did not eat well since I was unfamiliar with my settings. I grabbed a Snicker's bar and some chips when I filled up for some petrol (as they called gas over there) just before getting to the small inn. I had time to call Cora to let her know I made it through the first day, and she was happy for me. I saw one more club in the München (Munich) area first thing in the morning, then made my way southwest.

I never even came close to seeing the city of Munich, which was okay by me as I was already overwhelmed with all the travel. I saw the pro in Eurach then headed to Garmisch-Partenkirchen, a famous resort town best known for its winter skiing. In early May, you could still see plenty of snow perched high in the local mountain range that encircled it. This area was also home to a large American Army base, which was great as it made me feel a little more like being back in the States.

This would be the first of several military installations I would visit on this trip, since during this time frame, there were thousands of U.S. military personnel stationed in Germany. This particular golf club was also a good PING account, and I remember writing up some substantial orders to ship shortly. The local pro set me straight on finding a nice reasonably priced room that had a restaurant. I had my first delicious meal, and it was your basic hamburger and fries.

The next morning as I was heading to my next account, I remember having to drive in some mountainous conditions, which made me a little nervous, but I managed. Then suddenly, I was confronted by a man in military garb saying something foreign to me.

"Excuse me," I said back to him.

"Do you have anything to declare?" he shouted back to me.

"No, sir, I am an American golf sales rep just going to my next stop."

After showing him my passport, he was convinced, and I was off. I was entering Austria, albeit for only a few minutes, and could see street sign markers showing how far Innsbruck and Vienna were. Not long after that, I was back in Germany.

I would then see golf courses in Ofterschwang, Lindau, and Kempten. The pro at the Kempten course gave me some great advice on where to stay as well as some suggestions on future courses on my next leg to visit and avoid. He was very friendly, which ended up being very useful and saved me valuable time on the trip. I would use this strategy in the future in different regions of the country.

On day four, a Friday, I visited a course in Freiburg, which is just on the edge of France in the most southwestern part of Germany. I then visited the golf course in the town of Hechingen-Hohenzollern, then a course in Gutach. I was in a region called Sonnelapp, which for the natives was considered another common vacation destination. It was a beautiful area with endless fields of grass and colorful strands of flowers popping up everywhere, like being in the movie *The Sound of Music.*

I was now very close to a region called "The Black Forest," where Mercedes-Benz would test all its vehicles. I never saw this area in person, but it was very close to where I called on a golf club in Baden-Baden, which translates to "resort town." Again, this is another favorite tourist spot. I ended the day by visiting the one club in Stuttgart, which is the home base for the Mercedes-Benz brand.

It was now Friday night, and I was finally back in Heidelberg. I had stayed for four nights and was able to see 13 accounts, so I was on a good pace. My residence while I was near HQ was a lovely quaint hotel.

Cora had arranged for me to meet up with another golf sales rep in the area and his family on Saturday for lunch. I drove with her to their home in a town called Schwetzingen, which was considered the nicest suburb of Heidelberg. I then met Douglas Stonehouse, the distributor for the famous Titleist golf ball brand, and his charming wife, Elizabeth. There was another couple I greeted that day, the local golf pro at the Royal Air Force Germany Golf Club in Schwetzingen and his girlfriend.

We had a terrific lunch, as the food in Germany was excellent. A lot of meat and, of course, *spraggle* (what we know as asparagus). We agreed to play some golf the next day at the Army golf course. Please see photo of me next to the golf course club entrance.

I drove over to the course and met several golfers who had known Burt Lancaster, and they were all delighted to meet me. Doug and

I went out to play a round of golf with two other members who instantly befriended me. After the round, we all gathered up and had some local beer and started to talk like most men do after a round of golf. I was new to the party, so I did most of the listening.

I followed Doug back to his home, and we ended up talking for several hours about work-related things. He told me how well Titleist was doing in the country with keen competition from both Spalding and Wilson on the golf ball fronts. He complimented the PING brand on its reputation for both quality and playability.

Doug also gave me an excellent road map for the courses I should visit in the future, and I made some very good notes. We even talked about working together on the road and visiting the one American golf course base in West Berlin in East Germany. After meeting up with Cora on Monday and filling her in on what happened during the past week, she gave me some more money as I would be gone on this trip for at least two full weeks. I told her how well the car was performing and how dependable it was. I could sense she was relieved and felt more comfortable with me out on the road. I was also keeping a separate journal for my future meeting with Karsten, so I was taking notes on my essential account visits for this journey.

23.

GOING TO EAST GERMANY AND DENMARK

Week two of my assignment in Germany saw me venturing off to the country's mid-western region. I still was only seeing about four to five accounts per day due to the length of travel between courses and the uncertainty of the account's availability for the sales call. Most of my visits did result in face time with the pro at the club, which was a crucial part of the operation. On this particular week of travel, I visited courses in the following towns: Wiesbaden (which had three courses), Hennef, Duren, Gerhausen, Monchengladbach (which was the home to Royal Air Force Base Bruggen), Duisburg, Essen, Nordkirchen, Issum, Larsbruck Air Force Base, Dusseldorf (which had three accounts), and lastly the capital of West Germany, Koln (spelled "Cologne" in America). After this week, I had seen around 25 accounts.

As I look back on this experience, all I can say is I drove a lot, got lost more times than I can count, spoke to a lot of golf pros about the PING story, and wrote the day's results in my journal. At least twice a day, I would get club orders for at-once delivery, and I would write them up at night and mail them once a week back to Cora in Heidelberg (she'd given me some envelopes and stamps).

I remember vividly having breakfast every morning at the inn I was staying at and having a hard-boiled egg, toast, coffee (always strong), and occasionally some bacon. Rarely did I have cereal. I was up early and on the road by eight each day trying to canvas as much ground as I could. My youth factored mightily in my favor to allow me to do what I was doing. I have to say the golf pros I met were the kindest people, as they always helped me navigate to the next golf course. Exactly how I'd operated on my maiden voyage in my territory a year earlier.

I remember it being Sunday, and Doug Stonehouse had rung me (that is the European way of saying "calling on the phone") the day before about planning a trip to East Germany. He was going to meet me near my present location, and before we ventured out on our trip to the then-Communist occupied territory, we would play some golf in Holland, which was less than an hour drive to our west.

Doug also drove a white Mercedes Benz station wagon, just like the one I was borrowing from Cora. After all, he was the Titleist rep and had to have a lot of room to haul all those balata balls around with him and some DTs for the higher handicap golfers since his brand was by far the most played ball on the major professional golf tours. He drove us over there, and we played a beautiful golf course. It was a scorching day, but a cool breeze helped us get through the round. It was just great to get out on the links again. We ended up having lunch right at the club, and it was so neat because they had Heineken beer on draft since it was brewed not too far away. I just remember how strong it was, but it was so refreshing also. On the way back, I spotted the local police. It was so cool that they were driving around in Porsches wearing racing helmets. You do not see that every day of the week.

Doug's and my plan was to drive our cars Monday morning from where we were, which was right in the middle of the country on the western side, to a spot where we could then just take one car. We ended up in Hannover, and after transferring some club samples and materials, we were off. We were going to go see an American military installation in West Berlin, East Germany. Doug had made an appointment in advance with the course manager, which made my job so much easier. I remember Doug saying the trip would take about three hours, as the speed limits were very low, and the roads were heavily monitored by soldiers of the East German Army. He said not to talk if we were stopped. Since he was fluent in German, he would speak. We were fine, and when we entered the country after showing our passports, we were free to continue our trip, which brought us to West Berlin. As our history classes taught us, this was the land granted to the U.S.A. and its allies just after World War II in 1945.

I remember it was close to dark when we arrived, and we checked into the hotel room and had dinner right in the basement as most hotels also had taverns. We met a few of Doug's friends, and we had a wonderful time and an enjoyable meal. Doug took care of the dinner tab as well as the golf trip we went on. He was enjoying my company and taking care of a stranger in his home country.

Doug had his meeting first with the gentlemen at the club (one of the region's busiest golf courses), and I went second. I remember getting a very sizable order, as this club was one of the best accounts for our PING distributor. We were back into West Germany by the end of Tuesday. We both went our separate ways and would not meet up again until the following week.

I would also call once a week to the States to give the marketing manager at PING updates on my progress. He was pleased that I could find a friendly travel companion in Doug Stonehouse, especially considering the challenges that we faced going to East Germany. I also got word from Cora that our England operations manager found out about my presence and wanted me to go to Denmark to represent the distributor during a golf tournament. This new assignment added more to my plate with not a lot of time left.

It was now Wednesday of my third week in the country, and I decided to go north to Hamburg, the largest city in West Germany, with a population of well over a million residents. It is also the country's largest port area, sitting alongside the Elbe River, which flows directly to the North Sea. I am sure there are many popular European cars of today that are being exported from this port city.

In the metro Hamburg area, there were seven golf courses, and I was able to visit half of them as I was making my way up to the most northern part of the country before the weekend (as that is when I was needed in Denmark). I visited courses in Lubeck, Timmendorf, Kiel, Eckernforde, and finally, Glucksburg, which was right on the coast and another favorite tourist attraction.

I arrived in Denmark later on Friday and immediately drove to meet with the country's distributor, who was also the golf pro at the course where the event was going to be played. He had arranged for me to stay at a local hotel, which in my opinion was not like the smaller hotels I had been staying in while on my journey thus far. I knew that KARSTEN UK was financing this portion of the trip, so I wandered a bit and found the center of the city right near the water's edge, where there was a very nice modern hotel. I asked the front desk how much it was for a room, and she said 300 Kroner or something like that. I asked how much in American dollars, and when she said around $50, I asked her to book me a room. I was confident no one would have any issues with that.

I represented KARSTEN UK, which provided all the equipment for the golf course that was conducting this event and all the golf pros that were contending. The event was an individual event for most of the region's best customers, so it was a limited field of about 32 players and would be contested over the weekend. I greeted all the players and let them know that I had samples of the new Eye2 irons and woods with me along with a few new putters from PING for them to check out after their round. The event went well and was over on Sunday night. I remember being in the hotel by myself that night having dinner when I overheard some of the players who had also played that day. They saw I was by myself and invited me to join them. We had a lovely conversation about golf and PING and things in-between. They even asked if I would join them for a brandy nightcap, which is a drink I'd never before had in my life. Since they were buying, I had one. It was excellent, and I made a mental note that I should try that drink again sometime when I had something to celebrate.

24.
FINISHING UP GERMANY

It was now Monday of the fourth week of my trip, and I had a few more courses to visit. I started in Cuxhaven, the first course I saw when I got back across the border with Southern Denmark. I proceeded to work my way south through Oldenburg, Osnabruck, and, my last stop of the day, another military base in Bremen. I was done for the day and got a message from Doug Stonehouse that he wanted to meet up for dinner.

It was around 5 p.m., and Doug wanted to meet up in a hotel nestled just on the outskirts of Koln (Cologne), which meant I had to drive right through the center of the Ruhr, which is considered the principal industrial region of the entire country and is the headquarters of the famous Bayer brand. Only one very large problem. It was 300 miles away.

I strapped into my wundercar and took off. I remember it was a straight shot for me on the Autobahn A-57 route, which brought me very close to my endpoint. To this day, it was one of the greatest driving experiences of my life. I was driving over 120 miles per hour on average, non-stop for three hours. Can you even imagine that? Don't forget I had been driving in this country for several weeks now and had my fair share of driving on the Autobahn highways before since they are connected throughout the country (similar to the American interstate system). No speed limits for the most part. When I was there, I never witnessed an accident. All I can tell you is the exuberance I felt was unlike any I had before. This particular segment of the Autobahn was just two lanes, and I always had to pass larger transport trucks. Still, at the same time, I had to be aware of my surroundings as faster cars like BMWs, Mercedes-Benzs, and Porsches were always coming up in the fast lane at speeds of over 150 mph.

I arrived at our hotel right around 8 p.m. It was still light outside. I was so jacked up with adrenaline that I was bouncing in the air as I approached the entrance, or at least, I felt that way. I came to the front desk, but no one answered the bell. I started to walk down the hallway calling in a slightly higher volume to be heard but not too loud to disturb anyone: "Stonehouse, oh Stonehouse… where are you, oh Stonehouse."

A few seconds later, I heard the door open with a familiar voice: "It's about bloody time you got here."

"It's good to see you too, Doug," I said back.

"Let's have dinner," he said, and we were off to the tavern.

We then had one of the best meals I had on this journey and one of the most relaxing since I was with good company, and my task was 90% completed. We both had the wiener schnitzel and a few pints of the local beer while we talked all night about golf and the golf industry in general.

Doug told me I was a lucky man being a sales rep for PING. He said that PING was a company on the rise and what we were doing with our products' design and performance was setting the industry on fire. I could tell he was profoundly happy for me for my good fortune of hooking up with a company with solid morals and products.

The next day, we both started our way back to Heidelberg, and I got back to our headquarters after being away for well over two weeks. Cora helped me with my laundry, as I still had a few more days of work here before heading off to England. I was very close to running out of deutschmarks and was completely sold out of product, as I was selling items along the way. The plan was to work for three more days before my flight to London the coming Sunday.

Doug came by the showroom, and we both drove off to the Frankfurt area in separate cars. Doug introduced me to a long-standing PGA pro at the exclusive private Frankfurter Golf Club, but he was German and did not speak English very well. After our introduction, Doug also helped translate to the pro while I was showing him some new product. After all the English-speaking accounts I had seen so far on this trip, this was the first and only time I needed someone to help with communication.

After that meeting, I went my way, as did Doug, but we agreed to meet up on Saturday at his home in Schwetzingen for a final gathering and celebration of my departure. I finished up this day by visiting courses just west of Frankfurt, including Wiesbaden, Saarbrucken (where Ford had an assembly plant), and Neustadt. I would end up my last overnight stay in the town of Darmstadt. On my last day, I visited courses in Kitzingen, Bamberg, and my last official visit was at another military base in Nurnberg. This was a U.S. Army complex, one of the biggest in the country, and a good PING account. This was the main reason for my visit.

I tried to find this base for about an hour with no luck, but I had to get there. I just sat alongside the road in hopes of seeing a military truck. Sure enough, only after 15 minutes waiting, I saw one, and I followed it right to the base. For the record, I would have never found my way there if not for that strategy. After meeting with the general manager of the pro shop and securing some orders, I was off. I had about an hour and a half-long drive back to Heidelberg, but I thoroughly enjoyed the ride home as I was soaking up the road for one final time. In my four solid weeks in Germany, I saw about 80 golf accounts, roughly 70% of all the clubs there. They were all quality visits that I felt good about. My mission was to let them know that the local PING distributor was intact and open for business.

When I arrived back at the warehouse, Cora was there and greeted me with open arms.

"Stuart, I can't thank you enough for what you did for me and our distributor. I have heard from many of the pros you visited, and they are all so pleased with your communication with them on our situation. They are looking forward to dealing with us in the future."

"That is great news, Cora. I really can't believe I did what I just did, but I am so glad it's now over." And I truly did mean that.

I started to pack my belongings to get ready for my trip to London on Sunday, just so that would be done, and I could enjoy the day of fun at the Stonehouse's on Saturday.

I drove that white Mercedes Benz one more time over to Doug's home and arrived around three in the afternoon. The head pro at the Heidelberg Golf Club and his girlfriend were there, with several people I had met earlier at the club. We had a lovely dinner together, and we drank some of the locally brewed beer which Germany is famous for. We all just celebrated our friendship in the short time we had together.

When you are in a country so far from home, it helps to have people around you who care for you and make you feel safe and secure while you are there. That is how I felt around Doug Stone-house and his family, and I told him as we were leaving for good.

"Thank you again, Doug and Elizabeth, for having me over and for the great time you've shown me. I will always remember this time in my life."

"It was sure great meeting you too, Stuart, and we only wish you the best when you get back to the States. We know you're going to knock it out of the park with PING sales in New York."

After some sincere hugs, I was back to my hotel for one last time as I would be off in the morning for my next journey—a meeting with none other than Karsten Solheim himself.

25.

MEETING WITH KARSTEN SOLHEIM

It was early Sunday afternoon when I arrived at Heathrow airport in London. After clearing customs with no obstacles, I had to find my way to the subway system (better known as "the underground"). I realized I was now in a country where English is the common language and asking for directions would not be an issue. After finding my way to the main ticketing area, I was able to get my ticket for my travels to Gainsborough in the county of Lincolnshire, the home base of operations for KARSTEN-United Kingdom. I was told it would be a solid three-hour train ride.

I was starting to feel a bit tired from the air travel from Germany, and I napped a little on the train. I did get an excellent chance to see England's countryside and its vast amounts of green rolling hills and thick forests.

Before I knew it, I was there. I was told that a gentleman who was an executive for the operations would be picking me up at the small train station. The county of Lincolnshire lies on the coast of the North Sea. With a population of a just over a million, it was the 18th-most populated county in the country at that time.

I heard a voice say, "Hello Stuart, welcome." It was Glen, who was an "elderly" gentleman (probably in his late 40s) with short black hair, a medium build, and an intellectual disposition.

"I'm Glen and will be driving you to our operations center."

"Hi, Glen, so glad to meet you and finally make it here; it's been a very long day so far."

"I bet it has. Come on then, and let's get you ready for your meeting with Karsten."

When we arrived, Glen took me directly to a local hotel to settle in since it was getting a little late. He did have a quick light dinner with me, but all our business would be conducted the next day.

I finally got a chance to call home to talk to my parents and let them know everything was okay and that my trip to Germany was over. I then told them that I'd just arrived at PING's factory in England and would be meeting with Karsten himself the next day to talk about my trip. They were all so relieved that I was safe and doing well and wished me luck for my meeting. For some reason, I was not nervous about my one-on-one meeting with the Founder, President, and Chairman of one of the fastest-growing companies in the golf industry. From my speech communications class at Glendale Community, I'd learned that the most critical ingredient in making a speech or a presentation was to know your subject matter better than anyone. If you can do that, you have nothing to worry about. That night, for final prep work, I had outlined an excellent summary that included the key points I wanted to make.

Morning arrived quickly, and Glen came to pick me up and bring me to the place where all PING's golf business in Europe was headquartered.

"Are you going to drive today?" I heard Glen ask.

I thought I was getting into the passenger side, but the passenger and driver's sides are reversed in England.

"Sorry," I said. "No, I'll let you do the driving, Glen."

"Are you ready for your big meeting with Karsten?" Glen asked me.

"Absolutely, I have been preparing for this since I got to Germany four weeks ago."

"Good for you and good luck."

I entered the main building and was greeted by a taller, thin gentleman, who was the managing director of the entire facility, and a few of his assistants. They told me Karsten was in discussions with the main plant in Arizona and invited me for a quick tour of the facility. Glen also came along.

During my earlier years when I worked in the front office, I had become somewhat aware of how the European operations worked. And again, this is from what I recall on how things were done and not necessarily exactly how things did operate. To describe it simply, the PING plant in America would send shipments of loose iron heads and putter heads several times a month by boat or plane. This operation would then assemble the sets and the putters for final delivery to all the other distributors in Europe. The PING woods would come fully assembled from the States. The iron sets still needed to go through the normal steps of color-coding, and the putters needed to be checked for final loft and lie measurements. It was a complete operation, for sure.

The director of operations mentioned that Karsten was done with his call and was ready to meet with me.

I remember seeing this man again, so distinct with his silver hair and the trademark white patch of hair on his chin. I did not know it then, but I later read that the hair on his chin was to cover up a scar that he had received during a bad car accident in India several years before.

We shook hands and greeted each other with formalities. We went into a small conference room, just the two of us.

"So how do things look for us in Germany right now?" he asked.

"Everything is looking very good for PING with all the accounts that I visited."

"How many accounts did you see?"

"I was able to see around 80, or close to 70% of all the courses in the country, and I did see our best customers."

Karsten was not a man of many words, but I remember him praising me for what I'd done for his distributor.

I told him that golf in West Germany was growing and that there was also a growing need for the premium product that PING produced, as voiced by the many club pros I'd visited. They were pleased with the product, and their members were delighted with PING. They did express a desire to get some of the special-order custom sets quicker if possible. That was, for sure, something Karsten could investigate. I told him the putter line was doing exceptionally well. It certainly helped to have European stars like Seve Ballesteros winning major events, including the 1979 Open Championship and the 1980 Masters, while brandishing the ever-popular ANSER model. Add to the mix the American Tom Watson winning the Open Championship, first in 1977 (with the A-Blade), and in 1980 and 1982 with the PAL model. Near the end of our meeting, I told him about my experience meeting several club golf pros in Denmark and how they all expressed support of the PING brand from their respective clubs. I could sense that

Karsten was pleased with all the news I was telling him, and with the meeting in general. I was so relieved when he said, "Job well done, let's play some golf now."

I didn't expect to hear that, but that is what we did. Glen came up to me to ask how the meeting went, and I gave him two thumbs up. We all went out to the Gainsborough Golf Club, and, with borrowed clubs, I attempted to golf my best with the man himself. Unfortunately, that did not happen. I was a little intimidated by playing with Karsten, but I started to enjoy the moment after I settled down. The course was only nine holes, and Karsten liked to play fast.

I remembered back a few years to when he would come to visit us at the 19th Green Driving Range. He would knock out a bucket of 45 range balls in five minutes, thanks to the automatic tee machine he'd designed.

The round only took 90 minutes, even with us all walking and carrying our bags, but we had fun. I even hit a few good shots that got Karsten's nod of approval.

I remember we all had fish and chips for dinner that night. As the youngest person at the table, I remember just taking it all in and speaking only when asked. I thoroughly enjoyed listening to Karsten speak. It didn't matter what it was about. Just being in his company was special.

Now that I was officially done with my work in Europe, I also realized that working for the PING company was a family affair. After my accomplishments in Europe, I truly felt more a part of the family.

26.

HEADING HOME & LEARNING THE TRADE

The meeting with Karsten had gone as well as I could have anticipated. With that now over, I could finally let my hair down and do a little relaxing before returning to the States. It was Tuesday, and I was on the return train to London for my flight home on Thursday, so I had a few days of R & R and maybe some sightseeing. That afternoon I checked into the Holiday Inn in the Chelsea neighborhood, where there were many things to do.

I checked in with the concierge about the possibility of seeing a play or theatrical act. I was in luck as two major productions were going on at the same time. I chose to see a play the first night titled *Children of a Lesser God,* which had made its Broadway premiere in 1980 and, due to its popularity, was now playing in England. At the same time, I booked a seat for the other show using my American Express card for one of the few times on that trip. I also got my ticket for the next day on one of those tourist buses that would give me a full day of sightseeing in all local tourist spots.

I was part of the 9 a.m. tour, and it pretty much took me to everything I could see: Buckingham Palace, Tower of London, Big Ben, The Tower Bridge, and, of course, Piccadilly Circus. I got back to the hotel to freshen up and pack since I had an early flight home to New York. Next on tap for me was to see the acclaimed award-winning theatrical performance of *EVITA,* the musical composed by the great Andrew Lloyd Webber that concentrated on Eva Peron, who became the leader of Argentina. The main theme song "Don't Cry for Me Argentina" is one of my favorites to this day. For both shows I attended (since I was going solo), I was able to have great seats, both not very far from the stage.

When I was out and about as a pedestrian in London, I had to continue to always look for cars going the other direction as there they do drive "the opposite way." This was an obstacle that I needed to overcome, and for the most part, I was successful. I walked to both performances since they were within minutes of the hotel, but I did need to keep my focus while crossing the roads.

My taxi got me to the airport in plenty of time, and I was now on my TWA flight to JFK in New York City. The flight was quick, too. I only had a short layover, and my flight to my new home in Clifton Park was just over an hour. I got another taxi to bring me to my still very new apartment. Around 8 p.m. or so, I was finally home. The trip was a once in a lifetime experience, but I was so glad to be back on American soil. I made my first phone call to Mom and Dad and little Marcus to let them know I was home, and everything was great. I was now ready to resume my role as a PING field representative in the northeast.

As soon as I arrived home, I told myself to take a week off to get acclimated to being back in the United States. I went to the store to buy a few essential items to carry me over for the week, and sure enough, as soon as I was on the highway, I found myself going 70 miles per hour in a 55-mile zone. That was the Autobahn effect, which I quickly ended by getting back to reality. With some groceries in tow, I went to the post office to grab all my mail, of which there was plenty.

When I got back to my one-bedroom apartment, I gave the marketing department at PING a call to go over the European trip. This gentleman stated before I left that I would be paid a salary for the four weeks I was working in West Germany as a sales liaison, and all my expenses would be paid for by the parties I was helping. He was going to get a check processed for me and mail me all my essential mail for the past month, including all my sales reports and commission report for April. The company would send me that check in the same envelope as the new check for my work overseas. A little complicated, but what it meant was I was going to get some money to help me offset my expenses while I was gone. The relaxing time was also going to allow me to recoup from my whirlwind adventures and set my course for the remainder of the summer months. This was still totally unfamiliar territory for me, and I had a lot to learn and do. Of course, being brand new, I also knew that everything I did was going to be a learning exercise that would ultimately make me the best at my job. All I ever wanted to do was represent the Solheim family and the PING brand the best I could.

If I could do one thing over about my time abroad, I would have had someone save some newspapers of some of the significant events that took place in the world during that five-week span I was gone. When I was in Europe, I had no clue what was happening because I did not watch TV or read any newspapers. I am convinced to this day that some events took place that I will never know about.

The following week after I got home, I was back on the road to go and call on my roughly 250 accounts. I had made the first run through the territory in late March and early April, seeing all my key accounts. Now I was going out to see the rest of them.

This was about when I realized that doing a lot of driving was going to be par for the course, and if you didn't like driving, you were for sure in the wrong profession. I did not have any issues with it. My only complaint was that I continued to get lost a lot, but that even improved. The summer months flew right by. I stuck to my routine of being out on the road Tuesday through Friday and trying to stay out overnight no more than three nights at a time. I did not have much of a personal life, but I sort of knew that would be the case going into this. The only thing I had right now was the job that consumed all my being. The company had an 800 number and a bevy of customer service reps to handle all special-order requests. When I would get my weekly sales report, I could see where all sales were taking place. That is sort of when it hit me that I wasn't the only salesperson there; all my accounts helped sell my product to their members for me. That is a winning formula for sure. Each week, the sales report got a little better, and my commission reports at the end of the month were also getting larger. I was on an excellent sales trend that might allow me to double my sales volume for the year, which only added to my excitement and enjoyment.

I would call home frequently to say hi to everyone and even check in with the marketing department to let them know all was going well. I could sense that everyone was very pleased with my performance. After my season ended in mid-December, I was also told that

John Solheim wanted me back for the winter break to again work in the factory for him on a particular project yet to be determined.

With the fall run about to begin, it was reassuring to know that I had a place to work again in the winter while I was on my winter break.

The "fall run" is that time of the year just after Labor Day that we sales reps (in seasonal areas) will go see an account for the very last time of the season and attempt to secure a "spring order," which the company would then ship in the springtime of the next year (usually in April). Many people don't realize that this time of the season is our busiest we are and the most productive. The orders that we were writing kept hundreds of workers busy back at the factory in the winter months. These orders are a crucial indicator of how your year is going to look when the snow melts and golfers return to the links in the spring.

On this particular fall run, I was also able to start to see which golf clubs throughout my large territory were shaping up to be my "star" accounts or showing the most promise for future growth. It was a lot of fun, for sure. Most accounts were taking in their full allotments of our top three product lines: irons, woods, and putters. The company also just introduced its first carry bag model, called the L-7. I was now able to sell a full complement of premium products to all my customers. You could just smell the excitement in the air.

In Vermont, where I started my fall run, I had continued success, booking spring orders with what was turning into my A-1 account list, including the Quechee Club, Stowe Country Club, and the Country Club of Barre. Crossing over into New York, I had a nice run with Malone Golf Club and Potsdam Town & Country Club. Then I headed south to Syracuse, and the Drumlins Golf Club was turning out to be the best account in this area along with the Yahnundasis Golf Club.

In Binghamton, the bright spots were Binghamton Country Club with the older gentleman Bob Klink running the show (we called him the Colonel due to the popular TV show *Hogan's Heroes*), and Vestal Country Club.

The Albany market, which was my backyard, was led by the Northway 8 Driving Range, which happened to also be in my hometown of Clifton Park. In the Poughkeepsie area, we had Fred Lux at Dutchess C.C. and Ron Jensen, the wily fox of a pro at public golf course McCann Memorial.

Lastly, in the Western Massachusetts region, we had the private clubs of Springfield Country Club with Harry Mattson, Jr. guiding the ship and Longmeadow C.C. with Richard "Dick" Stranahan calling the shots. All these gentlemen were older than me, some even three times my age. They were all loaded with experience, and you could just see it pouring out of them when they spoke. I was brand-new to them, but I was holding my own and getting the job done. At this particular time of my young selling career, I could not have been more pleased.

27.

FAREWELL PROJECT AT THE PING FACTORY

It was now a brand-new year, 1984, and I was still only 24 years old. I was back at the PING factory. This would turn out to be my final year ever working within the confines of its all-white structures. The head of the marketing department had a task for me which would take several weeks to do. The company had made an executive decision to raise prices across its full product line for the 1984 season, but this raised some concerns. There were a tremendous number of orders written during the fall run in the Midwest and northeast parts of the country, and the company's top management group wanted to make sure they were exempt from the new prices for pre-book orders up to a specific month. I believe the cutoff date was May 31st.

I had to analyze hundreds of orders to make sure the pricing was correct for the orders shipped in March, April, and May, and allow the new higher prices to kick in on all orders starting June 1st. It was a monumental assignment, but I was up to it (just like I have been for any other task the upper echelon assigned me at the company).

Occasionally, there would also be time for me to do some other errands. Every once in a while, the Tour department would need someone to drive out to Moon Valley Country Club to drop off some clubs for a PING player to try out or to pick up a player who just finished testing some equipment. PING's Tour department was considered one of the best among all golf companies in the golf industry during this period. They did a fabulous job. The department would travel each week to the PGA Tour event and attend to all the staff player's needs.

The Tour players were considered the best players in the world, and each player had their own set of specifications for their clubs. The tour personnel made sure they were all pleased. They were always accessible to any player in the field that week. There were countless players who were not on the PING staff that needed something, whether Nick Faldo or Tom Watson was looking for an adjustment to their PING putter or someone needed a one-iron or an Eye2 sand wedge. The putter's constant presence on Tour undoubtedly hastened the rise in the popularity of the putter and its usage among amateurs. If the best players on the planet were playing the PING product, spectators on-site for the event and millions watching on TV would see that and hopefully become PING customers; that was the goal.

In between times of working on my project, I also attended my second PGA Merchandise Show at the end of January, returning to Miami, Florida, for a second year. I partnered up with another PING rep during the show, and we ended up staying at a charming hotel—The Doral of Miami Beach. By staying there, we would have playing privileges for the famed Doral Country Club, better known as the "Blue Monster," which was home to a PGA Tour event every March.

The Show would start on Friday, and back then the three-and-a-half-day event wound down on Monday. We both arrived late Tuesday afternoon, which allowed us to play the courses on both Wednesday and Thursday. We would only have to pay for the carts each round, so we fit in 36 holes each day. The club had three courses, so we got a chance to play all of them and were fortunate to play the Gold course which was simply called the "Blue Monster" due to its many holes with two water hazards. That was really the course we were most interested in competing on and it indeed was a monster of a course to play.

The show went well for me with lots of orders written to help pay for all the extra amenities I partook of on that trip.

I had to admit it was great being back in Phoenix again for the winter months and not in the cold back in New York. The weather in Arizona from January to March is always the best. This is the main reason why they have so many snowbirds who flock from the Midwest states and Canada. I also had some time to see my beloved Phoenix Suns play a few NBA games.

It was early March, and the project was nearly done when I stopped by to see John to discuss another matter. I was waiting for him, and next to the desk of his personal assistant, I happened to notice a golf club just resting against the desk. I could tell it was a fairway wood with a metal head, and it also had a graphite shaft. It was from TaylorMade, an upstart company in the golf market that was created in 1979 by Gary Adams and was the pioneer in the fast-growing "metal wood" market.

I remember grabbing the club and shuffling it around a bit and saying to John's assistant, "Look at this, a metal wood with a graphite shaft. This is the ultimate weapon." I looked at the shaft band and, to my amazement, it said "The Ultimate Weapon" by TaylorMade. I showed that to this individual (who was not a golfer and didn't seem interested at all), but even she shouted out "Stuart, you were for sure meant to be in this business." Which I took as the ultimate compliment.

I then met with John Solheim, and he told me he was very pleased with my recent job. It was now time to start preparing for my return to New York, in which I would end up staying year-round. My days at Karsten Manufacturing were over.

28.
ATTENDING MY FIRST MAJOR

I remember by first time attending a men's professional golf event as a spectator. I remember my first-ever time doing this. It was in Pensacola, Florida, and most likely would have been the 1973 Monsanto Open played at Pensacola Country Club.

When I was 12 years old, I sent a letter to Arnold Palmer, claiming that I was his number one fan and included a bunch of clippings of his results in recent events. On November 19th, 1971, when we were living briefly in Rhode Island, Mr. Palmer sent me a letter thanking me for my letter and the clippings and even gave me his "Handbook on Golf" book to read. He closed with his best wishes to me and, of course, that famous Arnold Palmer signature. That was nice of him, and I stayed a fan of Arnold's for the rest of his playing career. This made me want to go and attend a Tour event as soon as I could.

What struck with me the most about my first Tour event was how the golf ball flew on the iron shots the pros were hitting. It was precisely like hitting a wiffle ball, which I would do from time to time around my house, trying to emulate the swings of the players

I saw that day. I would stand right behind one of the greens on a par four and could see every group hit their approach shots, and the ball would start low then accelerate to a great height before just dropping out of the sky and landing softly on the greens. Years later, I would find out that the golf balls were doing that because of the dimple design of the ball itself. I was way too young to know who they all were, but I remember watching Gary Player hit a tee shot on a par three. The ball hooked at least 20 yards, but it still came to rest close to the hole. I also remember being very close to one of the tee areas, where I saw the mannerisms of Bruce Crampton from Australia: very little emotion and no talking between the players in his group.

After a player's round, many of them would go to the driving range. They paid for their range balls back then. Their caddies would go at the end of the range side by side and shag the balls for their players. No one ever got hit by mistake, as even way back in the early '80s these tour players were remarkably accurate.

I liked the event so much my folks let me go again the following year, and that was when Lee Elder won and became the first African American pro golfer to qualify for the Masters golf event in Georgia. You could say I was a part of history. From what I could recount, I don't remember seeing too many PING bags in the tournament, but back then, I was not paying much attention to details like that. I do recall seeing many HOGAN bags, well over 25.

In my second full year in my territory, I attended a major men's professional golf event? Well, it was about to happen for me in my second full year in my territory.

Spring was drawing to a close, and the great Capital District area had just set a record for rainy days. It had rained for 12 consecutive weekends in a row from mid-March to Mid-June. Everyone's yard was as green as a meadow in Ireland, and no one had to even turn on the hose to water the grass. I know the golf neither the course operators nor the members were too pleased about that or the members. I had just joined a country club myself that spring, called The Willows due to all the willow trees. The club was considered private, but it was not rated among the elite in the area. That was just fine with me, as all I wanted was a place to play some golf when I could in-between all my work responsibilities.

The Connecticut sales rep for PING, who also covered the MET Section, which included two of the wealthiest counties in all the U.S.A, Westchester (NY) and Fairfield (CT), reached out to me to see if I wanted to go to the U.S. Open in mid-June.

Without hesitation, I said, "Of course." It was to be played at the famous Winged Foot Golf Club in Mamaroneck, New York, which lies in the heart of Westchester County and is only a 40-minute train ride into New York City. We agreed to meet at the will-call station on opening day.

I remember that day as if it was yesterday. It was brutally hot, with temperatures in the low 90s, and the humidity was relatively high too. The threat of thunderstorms was imminent and forecasted for the entire 72-hole event.

I saw the Connecticut rep at the will-call. We got our badges and secured them to our persons, and it all began. My first-ever major. I was excited. So were all the other 40,000 spectators who flocked in to watch their favorite golfers play. They were all there.

This event is called the Open for a reason. The USGA, who conducts this event, has a qualifying system for this tournament that covers the entire country. Every year, well over 15,000 entries vie for roughly 50 to 60 spots. It is, without a doubt, the hardest but fairest major to qualify for. The rest of the 156-player field gains access by fulfilling other exempt status requirements.

The list of players for this U.S. Open is too long to mention here. Still, the best players were present: Jack Nicklaus, Tom Watson, Greg Norman, Johnny Miller, Curtis Strange, Hale Irwin (who won this event in 1977 at this venue), Lee Trevino, Fred Couples, Seve Ballesteros, Gary Player, and Raymond Floyd.

The other rep and I agreed to watch some of the players putting on the nearby practice green before heading out on the course to see the real action. We got separated for a short time, and when he did't return, I got a little concerned. I happened to be near a white tent there for medical emergencies, which was where I found him. He was 25 years older than me (almost 50), and he had suffered a heat stroke. He became dizzy and needed to get some help. About an hour later, he was released, and—aided by a large water bottle—feeling better.

He didn't want to ruin my day, so he encouraged me to go out on the front nine and watch a group play. We would meet again in a few hours. I went out and followed some groups. I just wanted to get a lay of the land so when they would show this event on ABC Sports on the weekend (they had the contract then with Jim McKay behind the microphone), I could identify the holes better. I encourage any golfer going to any type of professional golf event to walk the entire course. It will only add to the excitement of watching it on the tube later on.

I came back in to see how my fellow rep was doing. He was much better, and he was up for trying to go out on one of the holes on the back nine and finding a nice spot near the putting green so we could watch all the groups come and see many players up close. As I said, many big names were there.

The afternoon sun was still relatively high at around 5 p.m., but it was time to leave and start my trip to Clifton Park. My felloe rep was heading back to the Danbury, Connecticut, area. We said goodbye but agreed to meet again soon to play some golf. This was the first time I had spent any real time with him, and I really got to know him better and enjoyed his company very much.

That weekend, I watched the playing of the 84th U.S. Men's Open Championship on ABC, where I saw Fuzzy Zoeller tie with Australian great Greg Norman after 72 holes. Fuzzy ended up winning the next day in the customary 18-hole playoff. I thoroughly enjoyed witnessing a major event, which would be the first of many more to come in the years ahead.

After a few weeks back on the road servicing my accounts, I was ready to attend my first-ever women's professional major golf event, the U.S. Women's Open. The event was held at the Salem Country Club, which was in nearby Peabody. My mother was born in Salem and grew up there before moving to Arizona. I still had a lot of relatives living in that area, and I was able to stay with them and visit them while attending the event.

Hollis Stacy ended up winning the championship, which was the last of her three U.S. Open crowns. I vividly remember the crowds were so much more manageable than they were at the men's event I saw a few weeks earlier. It was great to follow a group around the entire round. Now it was back to selling those PING clubs again!

29.
STARTING TO SPONSOR SECTION EVENTS

The remaining years of the 1980s saw many changes in both my professional life and my personal life. My relationships with my accounts were improving in such a way that I had a solid core of business associates who were also my friends. We would play some golf together or have dinners when I visited to service their accounts.

In late 1985, there was also a territorial realignment affecting three areas. The Connecticut rep was relocating to southern Florida. I would be taking over a portion of his area in Connecticut and taking on the lucrative New York City accounts. Former PGA Tour player Michael Brannan would be getting the "MET" Section area, along with Long Island. Another rep would be taking over the Central New York area that I was surrendering. I would still have the same number of accounts and my road travel would be about the same. However, my new area would provide more income for me over time.

Also, as I started to settle more into my territory, I approached the Northeastern New York PGA Section about sponsorship opportunities. For years, the local Freihofer Baking Company had an umbrella sponsorship package with the section which gave the company title rights to all the major events during the year. Freihofer was being bought out by a large conglomerate and they suspended all their sponsorships, which freed up things. I jumped at the opportunity to be the main sponsor of the Section Championship, which was viewed by all as the most prestigious event that the club pros participated in. With the support of Karsten Mfg. back in Arizona (we would split the costs 50/50), the Section event was now known as the PING Stroke Play. We would sponsor it for the next decade or so.

My feeling at the time was that PING was doing very well with sales in the region, so this would be a great way to show our support to the same club pros who were supporting us. It was a win-win situation, and over time, I believe we did more business due to this sponsorship.

During this time period, I was also fortunate to be invited to partake in four professional pro-am events as PING's guest.

In 1985, I played in the Senior PGA Tour Round-Up event in Sun City, Arizona, which was played in late March. It gave me an opportunity to fly home and see my family again. The greatest thrill of my entire golfing life was to have my whole family—Mom, Dad, and younger brother Marcus—in the gallery to watch me play on the second day of that two-day event with legendary golfer and former Masters champion Gay Brewer. I had a blast, and so did the three amateurs with whom I played. I played on my own ball in the best ball format, which was one of my best rounds ever. It was just a delight to have the family with me, as over the years I have played hundreds of rounds of golf—but never like that. It was such a treat.

The first day we played with left-hander George Lanning, a PING staff player who'd joined the over-50 circuit a few years earlier. He was a pleasure to play with, too. It was so nice of the Solheim family to invite me to play in that event. The memories of my family watching me play this great game of golf remain with me to this day.

I also attended the 1985 U.S. Women's Golf Championship in Baltusrol, New Jersey. In July of that year, I even attended the Sammy Davis-Jr. Greater Hartford Open in my new territory of Connecticut.

The following season, PING again invited me to participate in a pro-am. This time, it was an LPGA circuit event in Corning, New York. This was a good three hours' drive south of me.

I got into town the night before the event and had dinner with my long-time friend (and former classmate at ASU) Lauri Merten, who was now in her third full year on the tour. Our group played with Deb Richard, who at the time was a very good up-and-coming player out of the University of Florida. I still have a picture of all the players we played with in my basement office. I had a bucket hat on that day, because we played in a steady drizzle. Once again, it was a lot of fun to play, and I give my thanks to the Solheims for the invite.

On a personal note, my family made a giant decision to move back east during this same summer. They started looking for places in the New Hampshire area, but ultimately settled on a place just 20 minutes north of me in Malta, New York. Malta is very close to Saratoga Springs, best-known for hosting the ponies at the Flat Track in the month of August. It was a new experience for me having them so close, but it was great.

Marcus was now 12 years-old and in the sixth grade. He was playing a little golf by then. I, too, had recently moved out of my apartment and into a nice two-bedroom townhouse only fifteen minutes from my old place in Clifton Park. It was in a brand-new development, and I had bought the home the previous fall while it was still being constructed. I finally moved into it in April.

All the new homeowners decided to throw a block party for the entire neighborhood, and we had the party on a Friday night during the second week of June. It was there that I met someone. We would go on to date for the next 18 months. It was my first relationship since I'd moved to New York. It was so nice to have Nancy in my life, and we slowly started to do more things together. It sure helped me get through the summer, which was quite hectic with work and with my family there in New York.

Upon coming home after working in Connecticut during the fall run in mid-October for three days, I had several messages on my answering machine at home. They were all from my mother. Her voice was so distraught as she let me know that Dad had suffered a seizure at home and tragically died. I raced to the hospital in Saratoga to greet my mother and Marc.

My father had tinnitus, most likely from being around aircraft in his Navy days. He'd been taking some new medicine which we found out years later was improperly prescribed.

To put it mildly, our world would be upside down for the rest of 1986 and for most of early 1987. It was a very hard time for my mother, as they had just moved into their new home a few months prior. My sister and her husband Bill flew out for the funeral. We received cards, and the Solheim family sent flowers for the wake.

We lost my father, Paul Myers, way too early at age 50. Thankfully, we had so many good memories to keep us going during this tough time. Nancy also showed support during this time, but I had to give more attention to my mom and brother, which she understood.

Marc, especially, was going through some tough times at school since he was the new kid in town, and he was being bullied. My mom was still a wreck and just could not deal with him constantly getting into fights, which would end with her summoned to see the school's vice-principal. I finally stepped in and went with her to the elementary school to meet with the vice-principal. It was my dad, who earlier in my life told me to never start a fight but to always finish one if suckered into a confrontation.

Here's what was happening to Marcus—each time, a different kid would induce a fight with him as the bullies were taking turns on who was being disciplined. My brother, however, was taking the fall for every encounter.

I asked the administrator to try something. I asked him to let my brother defend himself next time, but to only discipline the instigator. If you let my brother beat up this person with no repercussions, I said, this thing will end quickly. That is what we agreed on, and ultimately that is what happened. Before you knew it, the bullying, name calling, and fighting quickly stopped. I was Marcus' older brother, not his father, but I know Paul Myers would be proud of the steps I took that day for his youngest son.

30.

ARNOLD PALMER
WATCHING ME

Somehow, we got through the rest of the year, and we were all looking forward to better times in 1987. Everyone in my family was doing much better, and my sales with PING continued to grow. The Eye2 iron model was starting to take off, and we also had just come out with a newer carry bag called the L-8. It was doing very well, especially with all the private clubs who would opt to have all these bags customized with their club logo on them. We were also selling apparel during this time, which quite a few of my accounts did very well on. My personal life was as good; Nancy and I were still a couple.

I was still calling on over 250 accounts then, and it sure did require a lot of time. I was also seeing my New York City accounts every month. Usually, at the end of each month, I would book a round trip ticket on Amtrak, which would take me from the Albany station directly to Grand Central Station. I would see my three accounts, allocating each one a few hours. I would usually arrive at my first account by 10 a.m. and catch the 6 p.m., getting home by 11 p.m.

My NYC accounts included the World of Golf, the New York Golf Center, and the Richard Metz Golf Studio. A routine day for me while in the Big Apple was to just walk to my first account, which generally would be New York Golf Center since they were the furthest south. I would work my way north from there. After making my sales call to Mr. Rhee and getting my fair share of orders, he would always take me to a nearby Korean restaurant, and we would have lunch. Sam (as he wanted me to call him) would always order for us. I was trying so many different types of food, and it was always enjoyable. I sure enjoyed our conversations. Sam also had two younger sons, who would join their father in the business several years later.

Next, I would take a 20-minute walk and pass right by the New York City Library and the famous Grace Building, which had a unique design to it, on my way to see the World of Golf. Each year they would do the most business with me overall. In my opinion, that was due to their excellent and plentiful sales staff. Every time I was there, the place was buzzing with customers who were always being helped by a sales associate. They did an excellent job of promoting and selling the PING brand. My last stop of the day usually was Richard Metz Golf Studio. He was the consummate golfer and connoisseur of golf. We always worked together on our orders while a few golfers were getting some golf lessons from the teaching staff.

The train station was only 15 minutes away, and I used the time wisely on my return home by writing up all the day's orders on the order forms (we still did not have computers). After a day in the city, I would just stay in the office to catch up on paperwork and catch my breath because going down there took a lot of energy, and I needed a little time to recoup. I just know from looking at past notes and sales reports that being a field representative for a major golf equipment company such as PING required a great deal of time and devotion. In looking back on these times, I had both attributes, and it created a foundation for me that exists to this day. I was a rep who cared about his customers and provided the absolute best customer service possible.

Again, I have to go back to my younger years when I was working hard for Mr. Pickett in Rhode Island or helping out my dad around the house or to my job as a carryout at Smitty's in Arizona. I guess I was raised that if you are going to do a job, just do it the best you can. That is how I did it during my PING days. I also did quite a few personal things between workdays, including attending the 1987 GHO Hartford PGA Tour for the second year in a row.

The highlight of my year was being invited by PING to again play in a pro-am on the senior tour. It was late July, and one of my fellow PING rep friends was also invited to compete in this awesome event known as the NYNEX/Golf Digest Commemorative held at the prestigious Sleepy Hollow Country Club in Scarborough, New York. This was another two-day pro-am, which was fantastic for us amateurs as it allowed us to play with two different senior tour players. The first day we played with Doug Ford, who early in his career won the Masters title, and the second day we were paired up with Howie Johnson, a lesser-known player who still had the game to compete on the senior circuit. While playing with Howie, I experienced the highlight of that event.

We were waiting on the eighth hole for the group ahead of us to hit their second shots on this short par-four when the pro-am group led by the King himself, Arnold Palmer, came striding up to one of the earlier holes.

"Hi, Arnold, how're you doing?"

"Great Howie, how are things?"

"We have some horses as we have a couple of PING reps," I remember Howie saying to Arnold, and as I recall, I don't believe Palmer had a response.

At that time, Palmer was associated with Pro Group, which was part of the Arnold Palmer brand, and he was competing in the same space as we were. Their teeing area was very close to ours, and since we were ready to tee off, Arnold's group had to wait until we all hit.

Howie hit first and it was my turn. Back during this time, I never used a tee when I was hitting my Eye2 three-wood. I simply tapped into the ground and propped up some grass to act as a tee, because I wanted to hit the ball crisply to get it to propel with less height and get maximum distance. To this day, I can still remember the moment and the feeling I got—pure panic, as I knew the King was watching me. I could feel his presence as the hair on the back of my neck was rising with anticipation. Woosh. I hit it as straight as can be and as good as I could. I was so pumped and relieved that it was over. My fellow PING partner would go on to snap-hook his tee shot using his driver.

As we started to walk down the fairway, I said to him, "Could you feel the pressure?" referring to the presence of Palmer.

"Why do you think I snap-hooked it so badly?" he replied. We both laughed it off and marched on with our round.

A few weeks later, I also attended my first ever U.S. Girls' Championship, held at one of my best accounts, The Orchards in South Hadley, just a short drive from Springfield, Massachusetts (home to the National Basketball Hall of Fame). The head pro was Bob Bontempo, a legend among club professionals in the region and one who I'd gained a lot of knowledge from in my early days of being a golf rep. Bob also bought some of the valuables pouches that we were producing to have as logo items for the players to buy as souvenirs. Michelle McGann from Florida won that event and went on to have a remarkable career on the LPGA Tour.

I also had time to squeeze in some more competitive golf rounds for myself before things got too busy with the fall run. I played at the Mohawk Golf Club in August for the qualifying round for the New York State Mid-Amateur (you had to be over 25 to play in this one) and birdied my last three holes to shoot 77 and easily make it in. I didn't fare so well in the event in mid-September, which was played at The Drumlins in Syracuse, but it was a lot of fun to compete at this high level as I saw all the elite players in the state at this event. As it turned out, this would be my only time qualifying for this event and playing in it. The year before, I attempted to qualify for the New York State Amateur for the third time, and I successfully made it through to play at Knollwood C.C. in Westchester County, New York. That also would be my last time competing in this event since work was increasingly demanding more of my time.

I would round off the year by joining forces with my new colleague to the south, Michael Brannan, and PING to become official title sponsors of the Connecticut Section Stroke Play Championship, held each year at Ellington Ridge in the state's north-central region.

Michael was also a past U.S. Junior Boys' champion, winning in 1971 as a 15-year-old, becoming the youngest winner. Michael would come up for the final day of the two-day 54-hole event to help hand out the trophy and the check to the winner. This was a new partnership that would also last for several years. Connecticut was still new territory for me and was further from my home, so I always liked the idea of sponsoring an event as it made the pro's decision a little easier when it came time to ordering product. When we were involved in this sponsorship, from what I can recall, 90% of all the private clubs in the section stocked their shops with PING custom carry bags.

I continued to do well with my fall run, seeing, on average, four to five accounts a day—close to 20 for the week. At that time of the selling season, I would only focus on the most productive accounts, which were plentiful.

Also, my 18-month relationship with Nancy ended in mid-November. It hit me kind of hard, but I guess it was just not meant to be. That is how I looked at it. In the end, we were just arguing over the littlest of things, and it just didn't make sense to stay in something that wasn't working. We both agreed to end it, which softened the hurt somewhat.

My work was still my focus, and of course, helping Mom and Marcus was vital as we were preparing for the holiday season without Dad for the second time since his passing. On a brighter note, things with PING continued to trend upward as I was just finishing my fifth full year as a rep.

31.

HAVING DINNER WITH KARSTEN IN HAWAII

At that time in my career when I was starting to get some years under my belt in my profession, my year was comparable to that of a school teacher. I worked nine months and had three months off. A rep in southern states like Florida, Texas, and California would have to work year-round. I would start up my year around mid-March and conclude around mid-December, leaving me with three full months or 12 weeks to do whatever I wanted to do. As I said earlier, I spent my first two winters back in the home office, but I was now at a point where traveling around the states was becoming more common for me. It was a great way to escape the cold winter months of New York but, more importantly, a great time to relax and recharge the batteries for the next season.

The only obligation we had to the company was to attend the annual PGA Merchandise Show in late January. We would be responsible for paying all our expenses, but PING would have a great booth set up for us to conduct business with our customers who attended. In the early days of being a rep for PING, I always had a successful show since a large contingent of my accounts would always participate. It was a great escape from the frigid weather. The commissions I would earn during the convention would, by far, offset the costs of attending.

This particular show of 1988 was also a special one for me. My sister and her husband had moved to Florida. My brother-in-law Bill would be a park ranger at the Seashore National Park near Cape Canaveral, where the Space Shuttle missions were launched. After another successful show, I would drive my rental car about an hour northeast to visit them and stay for a few days. We would continue with this tradition for the next several years while they were living in Florida. It was a great way to unwind and do nothing while seeing my older sister.

When I got back up north, it was super cold, of course. I did as much as I could to stay indoors. Since I wasn't from the area, I wanted to avoid the colder weather, which made my next decision so much easier.

While I was at the show, I arranged with the same PING rep that I'd played golf with at Doral to fly to Hawaii for a full week and a half of relaxation and golf. I had never been to our 50th state before and thought it would be cool. So, when I was in my townhouse in Clifton Park making the arrangements for where to stay with my travel agent, I heard from John Solheim that his parents would be over there the same time I was, and that I should call Karsten up to have dinner with him and Louise. I was petrified but also tempted for sure. I said, "Of course, that sounds great."

I learned from reliable sources that Karsten and Louise would go every year to attend the Hawaiian Open on the PGA Tour, usually held the second week in February. My friend and I started our journey on Maui, playing courses like Maunea Kea and Kapalua Bay Course as the Plantation Course was not built yet. It was the beginning of the week, and I finally got enough courage to call Karsten about potential dinner plans. I called the Hilton hotel right on the property of where the tournament was being played. To this day, I can pretty much sum up what was said.

"Hi Karsten, this is Stuart Miller, I'm your sales rep in New York State. I'm over here on vacation, and your son John told me to give you a call about maybe having dinner one night this week."

We spoke about what night would work better for them, and he said Thursday night would be best. I told him I only had casual attire, too. I just remember this from Karsten as the call was about to end.

"Okay, Miller, see you in the lobby this Thursday at 7 o'clock."

I caught an island hopper flight from Maui to Oahu and got a room for the night. I arrived at the hotel in my rental car right around 7 p.m., and as I was driving up to the front entrance, I spotted Karsten. He was wearing what they called a "luau shirt" (a flowery Hawaiian shirt), which made him look like a tourist in a very relaxed atmosphere. I was wearing my new golf shirt with the famous Kapalua logo and my Sansabelt pants with FootJoy street shoes. Back then, I did everything to emulate a PGA Tour player. When I think back on that moment, I wished that I, too, had worn one of those luau shirts.

The only thing I remember about that night was that I drove us to the restaurant, which was one of Karsten's favorites. We had a wonderful dinner, and I was so blessed to be with two wonderful people. It was an honor. When it came time to pay, I remember saying, "May I take care of this?" and Karsten replied, "No, you may not." I pretty much knew that I had to offer. I know he and Louise appreciated the gesture from me. I knew they also were grateful for my company and for me doing the driving that night. This was a great night for me having dinner with the founder of PING and the company I was representing. It was one of those moments you do not forget.

This moment has also stuck with me over the years. I cannot remember the exact year, but it had to be at the time I was working at the factory in my early days, so around 1979 or 1980. I was asked to caddy for Louise in the pro-am of the LPGA Tour event that PING was sponsoring, which was played at the Arizona Biltmore. I remember the round went great, and we were going to have dinner outside with plenty of seating, but a huge thunderstorm was moving in. They had to get everyone put into one of the maintenance buildings, so things were bunched up. I was sandwiched between Karsten to my left and another person to my right with no wiggle room with my hands.

I only remember this because the main course was ribs, and for some reason, I was afraid I might drop one on Karsten. I just know he was thoroughly enjoying his ribs, which I too should have, but I just didn't want to cause a scene. I guess you could say that was the first time I had dinner with Karsten, but the Hawaii moment was better. That was priceless, for sure.

32.
ATTENDING ANOTHER U.S. OPEN

Once I was back on the mainland in New York, I started to sort through all my orders from the PGA Show a few weeks earlier in Florida. I just wanted to make sure I had all my top accounts covered for their spring orders so everyone would have plenty of product when the season opened in early April.

I was beginning my sixth season on the road in the spring of 1988, and due to my tremendous fall run and success at the PGA Show, my spring bookings were my best ever. The product pipeline I was selling was solid from the popularity of the Eye2 irons. Their square grooves were a hot topic in the golf industry and were being discussed by the USGA. I will not go into any details about this matter, but there was a lot of talk about this club during this time in the golf industry.

As Karsten had introduced several popular putter models back in the early part of this decade, including the stainless steel Anser 2 (1981), the manganese bronze Anser 3, and stainless steel Anser 4 (both in 1982) along with the already-popular models of the time, my putter sales were the best ever. It seemed each week on both the PGA and LPGA Tour, players were using the PING putters in route to victory. I was one of about 40 PING reps who were out on the road representing the brand and giving the hundreds of employees back in the home office plenty of work to do to keep pace with the high demand for the products during that time.

In the spring of that year, I moved into my new home because my former residence was too small for all the things I needed for my job. I found a terrific place in Clifton Park, just one more exit north on the Northway (Interstate 87). It was only a few years old and was also owned by a single professional who had to move for his business. Before I moved in, I had a team of professionals come in and redo all the hardwood floors on this two-story contemporary house's main level. I was quite pleased with it, as were my mom and my younger brother, who were now even closer to me.

I continued to be a golfing member at The Willows, because I still wanted to keep playing this great game of golf. I would slowly start to unwind my competitive career as an individual, but I would participate in several team events. I still got a lot of joy out of the game, and I felt it helped my overall business by still being in the spotlight from time to time.

One memorable moment happened at my club in June, shortly after moving into the house was one of the early team scramble events where we had an excellent field participating. I happened to play exceptionally well that day to help my team finish at the top of the leaderboard. We finished a little early, and after we had a bite to eat, my team of three other members quickly vanished. For some reason, they thought that any ties would simply be split. They were—except for first place, as it turned out.

I remember the pro coming into the clubhouse and telling me there would be a sudden-death playoff to determine the winner. I had to tell him my team of three other members had already gone home.

He said, "Well if you want to go for the win, you can do it yourself." In all my years of playing this game, this would be the first (and only time) I would attempt this. I told the other team, "Let's do this."

The first hole was a reachable par-five of about 485 yards. I hit a lovely tee ball. My four opponents picked their best drive and then knocked one of their shots on the green about 30 feet above the hole. The only defense this hole had was a green that sloped from back to front, and you had to keep the ball below the hole to have any shot at two-putting and making a birdie.

All four players hit their first putts well by the hole, and they were left with a lengthy ten-footer up the hill with some break. My approach shot had ended up 20 feet short of the pin, and I putted it to tap-in range and made a four for the hole. I watched each player narrowly miss the cup, and before you know it, I was the victor. To this day, it is one of my best stories to share. I remember walking back toward the clubhouse area. Several of the members wondered what had happened, and when I raised both arms in victory, a giant roar broke out as I had beaten the opposing team of four players by myself. It was a good story, indeed— and I did it with 14 PING clubs in my L-8 golf bag.

After this triumphant event, I was off to Boston to attend the U.S. Men's Open at The Country Club in Brookline. This would be my second time going to this grand championship. Due to a tight schedule, I only went to Friday's round but saw plenty of action. Attending golf events like this is always exciting as you see all the best golfers in the world. Since this event was also open via different qualifying stages, I happened to run into longtime friends of mine at the event. I collected several badges from the major championships I attended, including this US Open in Boston.

Mike Swartz from Phoenix, Arizona, got into the field via the qualifying, and I saw him on the driving range along with his older brother Dave, who'd played with me on the Glendale C.C. golf team. It was so neat to see them there. They came over to the ropes where I was and shook hands. Dave and I chatted while Mike was warming up for his round. Mike had a very accomplished college career, playing at the University of Arkansas under coach Steve Loy, who has since become Phil Mickelson's manager. I would go out and follow their round for a few holes.

The golf at the U.S. Open is not always the best, as these golf courses are set up to be as hard as they can be. Often, you will see the worst in players. The course just beats you up over time. We amateur golfers have all played challenging courses in our careers and know exactly how it feels to get beat up like that. You do the best you can, but most times, you are just outmatched. That is what happens to even the best players in the world during this championship. It always brings out the best player in the end. This tournament saw Curtis Strange go on to claim victory by beating Nick Faldo in an 18-hole playoff.

Also, in 1988, the company started to keep records of the best-performing salesmen in the categories of golf balls, apparel, golf bags, wood covers, putters, and woods. At the end of the year, we would get a report showing our percentage of sales only in each category. The names of the top ten reps in each category were also revealed kind of like an honor roll list. It was very nice to see my name on this list, more for personal pride than anything. That year I made the list in five of the six categories, which made me feel very proud. My peers could see this as well. Despite my young age of only 29, I was still trying to be the best—and it seemed to be working.

33.
DINNER WITH KARSTEN & JOHN AT U.S. OPEN

One time, I was just finishing up with an account at the end of the day. I was in my car, and I saw a bunch of construction guys gather and jump into a truck, most likely heading to a nearby tavern to have a cold one and relax after a long day. Whereas when I got back home, I still had to prepare several boxes to ship via UPS the following day. At that moment, however, I also realized that I was working super hard so one day when I got older (which is right now) I would have something to show for it financially (and I am proud to say I do).

Nothing comes easy. There is usually a price to pay for it. Despite all the hard work I was doing, I loved every moment of it. I am proud to say that I had and still have the dream job. The most important thing that I've realized when working for PING and now for myself is that you are your own boss. Your sole responsibility is to represent all your companies with the utmost pride and professionalism, and to do this day in and day out. If you do that, you cannot fail. Failure is always just around the corner, but if you put in the work, you will not lose. So, I do the work and try to do it correctly the first time. The reality is that you can always do better. Even back in 1989, I for sure sensed this and tried to do better each day.

I was now at that point in my career where I honestly can say I had this job figured out. I was (in my opinion) now efficient in every capacity of my occupation. There was nothing I could not do. I was just oozing with confidence. I didn't know it at the time, but outsiders would call it ignorance or cockiness. I just didn't see it that way. I am sure I was guilty of all that, but what always secured my success in life was my work ethic and dependability.

In the golf business, that really means a lot. Whatever shortcomings I had—and looking back I am sure I had a few—I got a pass due to my work ethic and my generosity in sponsoring Section events, as well as doing my part to help with local charity events.

I felt that life had been very good to me, considering my wonderful job, and I just wanted to give back. Over the years, I supported many charitable endeavors.

There was another major championship that I was fortunate to attend. Sometime in early May, I got a call from the PING communications director who informed me that I was invited to attend the 1989 U.S. Open at historic Oak Hill Country Club in Rochester, New York. As a bonus, I was also invited to have dinner with the Solheim family after the first round.

The Rochester area was serviced by another representative. Thus, I had never traveled there and had no business ties in the area. Nevertheless, I knew where I was going to be in the second week in June.

It was a good three-hour drive for me to get to the tournament site, but I had a ticket to get on the grounds, so I took advantage of it and arrived mid-morning to watch the first day. Heavy rains had been in the area early in the week, and the course was very wet. It was also somewhat difficult to navigate. I tried to hunker down in places with a good view, and I just watched as many players as I could see. This was my third U.S. Open in the past six years, so you could say I was getting spoiled with opportunities to see all the great players in person.

Among those I saw were Jack Nicklaus, Lee Trevino, Nick Faldo, and Greg Norman (to mention a few). For diehard golf statistics fans, Curtis Strange ended up winning his second straight Open while wielding a PING Zing 2 model to victory. After that first round was over, I ventured over to the restaurant where I was meeting the Solheims.

I don't recall the name of the restaurant, but it had the word "Wheel" in it (maybe "The Cover Wheel"). I believe it was in the town of Penfield, another nice suburb of Rochester that was not far at all from the golf course.

I arrived at the restaurant and told the hostess at the stand which party I was waiting for. They suggested that I just wait at the bar.

Then, a few minutes later, I remember the general manager coming over to me. I will never forget what he said.

"Karsten wanted you to know that his meeting with Jack Nicklaus was just finishing and he will be here shortly."

You don't hear those words every day. I would later learn that Nicklaus was meeting with Karsten about a patent that the McGregor Golf Company (which Jack was involved with) may have been infringing upon. As Tom Hanks famously said in *Forrest Gump,* "That is all I have to say about that."

The family did arrive soon after. Accompanying Karsten was his wife, Louise, the communications manager for PING, and John Solheim, whom I had become better acquainted with over the years. That made for a table of only five, including me.

Boy, did I feel special. It has been many years since this night happened, so I don't have any recollection of what meal I ate, nor do I remember much of the conversation. I do remember Louise asking me how my personal life was going, and I mentioned that I had recently met a nice woman from Mechanicville and had hopes of that blossoming into something special one day. I believe I asked Louise how she met Karsten, and she told their story.

The only takeaway I still have from this night was that it was an honor to spend a special night with the Solheims. That marked the second year in a row that I had the privilege of having dinner with both Karsten and Louise, but it would not be the last.

It was only about 10 p.m. when we finished dinner. I was still a young sprite, so I climbed back into my car and drove home that night, finally arriving around 1:30 in the morning. I knew my adrenaline was also pumping due to the day's events, so driving was not a problem.

34.
A DARK DAY IN AUGUST

I was still excited about my dinner with the Solheim family at the recent U.S. Open in Rochester. As I mentioned earlier, there was a lot of talk there about the PING Eye2 iron model. In a *Golf World* magazine (June 30, 1989) in their "Bunker to Bunker" section, they mentioned that this would be the last U.S. Open for which the USGA (golf's ruling organization) would allow the use of PING's square-grooved clubs. And from a sales angle, since the Eye2 model was introduced, sales in my territory were going up exponentially every year; just a testament to how good the golf club was.

Shortly after returning from the U.S. Open, I received some good news from our communications department. Typically, when I heard from them, it was an invitation to play in some exciting event. They did not let me down, as I was extended an invitation to play in my second LPGA Pro-Am. This one was in the Boston area during the second week in July. For this invite, I was granted permission to bring with me a player of my choosing. I chose my travel agent and fellow member of The Edison Club, Ed Finkle, to join me.

We made the trip over together and played on July 19th, 1989. Our pro that day was a rookie named Sarah Ann McGetrick. Years later, I learned that her husband was Mike McGetrick, a nationally known PGA instructor. My team played great that day, and due to our stretch of 12 consecutive birdies in the Scramble format, we ended up in the top three and received some pro shop merchandise.

After a few weeks of getting back on the selling trail, I was also invited to join the Solheim family and some other PING reps at a special meeting that the USGA had set up in New Jersey, not far from their Far Hills headquarters.

From what I can recollect, it was mid-August when I drove myself down to New Jersey for this meeting. All the major club manufacturers would be present, along with representatives from the U.S.GA. When I arrived, I was with a small contingent of other PING reps, including one of my newer friends Michael Brannan. We were sitting near the back. Karsten was there, and so was John.

Despite these uncertain times, life did go on for me. In just over a week, I was in Arizona attending the company's annual sales meeting. The meeting week always went fast, but it was a great time to reconnect with far-flung friends, remember stories of the past, and create new memories.

Upon my return to upstate New York, I was present for the playing of the Stroke Play Championship for NENY Section, The Vermont Match Play in September, and the Connecticut Section Championship in October. These were the events that PING corporate and I were sponsoring together.

Once I was done with all the section sponsor's obligatory duties, my colleague to the south, Michael Brannan, and I united for one day to play some of the greatest golf courses ever created. We'd started this tradition three years prior, shortly after he became the PING rep in the MET PGA Section. We would typically meet the second week in October when golf courses generally started to see less play and we could get tee times more easily.

In 1988, we played Winged Foot, then we battled Quaker Ridge. In 1989, we tackled the Country Club of Fairfield and The Patterson Club where Mike was a member. In 1990, we treated ourselves out on Long Island by teeing off at Shinnecock Hills in our morning round, then spoiling ourselves a few yards away at National Golf Links, finishing just as the sun was fading over the sound. These annual pilgrimages to great golf courses would have gone on but for the fact that the Brannan family was suddenly summoned west. The Northern California region was opening, and Michael, with wife Shelley's blessing, opted to take it, leaving Connecticut in August 1991. It seemed my time playing America's most outstanding courses would have to take a short hiatus.

35.
THE CREATION OF THE LOU TORRE EVENT

To this day, I am not sure who it was that mentored me, but I have concluded it was something I just learned along the way. When I was working inside the factory, I witnessed firsthand that PING sponsored many tournaments and other endeavors. I am sure this played some part in my philanthropic ways. The simple thing, if you stop and think about it, was the fact that I could. I was so blessed with a job that enabled me to do many kind acts during my career.

Sometime during the latter part of 1988, I was putting together a rough concept for creating and sponsoring an amateur golf tournament from scratch. It was going to be named in honor of Lou Torre, a long-time local golf writer whom I had the privilege of knowing and dealing with on several occasions.

I started to talk with the golf pro at The Edison Club, Rick Wright, about my event idea and he loved it. Not only that, but he said, "It would be an honor for our members here at The Edison Club to host the event for your first tournament." That was only fitting as this gentleman was also a recipient of the club's Hall of Fame award. I also spoke to a fellow member of the club, Ed Finkle, an educator at one of the local school districts, to see he knew who Lou Torre was. Ed said that he had been introduced to him at a couple of golf events he played in but never did play golf with him. Ed was on board immediately to help with the event. Please see photo of Rick and I at the inaugural event in 1989 on following page.

It was now out of the bag. The Lou Torre Champions' Cup was soon going to be a reality. My company, Karsten Mfg. Corp., and I would be the main sponsors. I would be the Executive Director. Lou was the golf writer for *The Schenectady Gazette* for several decades and covered every tournament you could think of in the Capital District during his career. He was a sweetheart of a guy and fun to be around. I first spoke to his widow Nancy about the concept, and she was on board.

The event's name told the story of the championship. We would invite all the club champions (men and women) from all the clubs in the greater Albany area who had such events. The first event took place on Friday, September 8th, 1989, at The Edison Club. We ended up having 43 golfers attend with 31 clubs represented. I have to say it was a good start.

In the program, on the very first page, this was printed:

IN REMEMBRANCE

With gratitude and respect, the Capital District community dedicates this tournament to Lou Torre for a job well done.

Since Lou was so instrumental in reporting and promoting golf for both the amateurs and the professionals, this tournament is a tribute to his efforts. All proceeds will go into the Lou Torre Me-

morial Scholarship Fund to assist outstanding young golfers in their college endeavors.

The first thing that I did as the Executive Director of this new event was to select a committee that would help me get this project underway and make it successful. I also had a conversation with my contacts at PING to make sure that I had the company's blessing for the event, with them (and me) being the sponsors. It was going to be a win-win for everyone.

In the program that every golfer received at the award ceremony, I also recognized the committee, including Rick Wright and his staff and the members of the host club. My mother, Elayne (who acted as my secretary), was also instrumental as her primary role was contacting all the players to invite them to the event. Mom would go on to add, "I must admit it was quite a busy time in contacting the many golf courses for the names of their men and women champions along with the follow-up phone calls. However, their happy voices about taking part in this wonderful tournament made all the work worth it."

Before the tournament commenced, I would also sell sponsorships, which was the primary way we funded the scholarships. I also sold tee signs for $100. We displayed these on tee ground areas on the course or even around the practice putting green.

I became quite good at asking for money. We got an overwhelming response from the golf clubs themselves and specific individuals and business owners I knew. Even my fellow PING colleagues helped with the cause. That very first year, I sold 41 of these "premier sponsorships." Every sponsor was recognized in the program as well. A $25 patron sponsor would be mentioned in the program guide. I was able to get 73 of them. After the event, we were able to raise close to $6,000.

After the golf event, we had a luncheon for the players and recognized our champions with a trophy displaying our event's logo. We also gave out several other golf products from PING for top finishers, all with the event logo on them. We also had a charming "tee favor gift" for every player that waited for them when they got to their assigned table for the awards giving ceremony.

My mother also added, "All the players who won a prize, which was PING merchandise, were all so pleased and appreciated the great care displayed as every item was decorated with the event's logo." My committee made the entire golf experience for these players for this first event to be as good as it could be so that they would be talking about this for years to come. Everyone seemed very pleased. When it was time to go, every player came up to me personally thanking me and my team for putting on such a lovely day for them.

Now for the fun part of doling out the money we'd just raised. The committee and I determined that the $6,000 we raised for our first event would be used for our first class of scholarship winners. We would select a group of students from the class of 1990. We sent out the qualifications for the scholarship to all the schools that were in the districts of the clubs represented and set a deadline for applications to be sent in. As I mentioned earlier, one of our committee members was Ed Finkle, an educator in one of our local school districts, and he played a leading role in setting up this program. Once all the entrants came in, our committee met and made recommendations based on each student's credentials and merits. This was done in the latter part of the school year. Once our four winners were chosen, we sent them a congratulatory letter letting them know they won. We then invited them to a reception at The Edison Club to celebrate their achievement in the first part of summer. Their parents were invited along with their golf coach or favorite teacher to add to the celebration.

Here are some of Ed's feelings to share with everyone on what this event meant to him as a person involved in educating young people: "Stuart organized and brought together the entire concept of the fundraising and the management of a golf tournament that he funded. Additionally, Stuart provided incentives and awards to encourage people to participate. It was a huge success and provided a great monetary return for the scholarship program."

In the first year, we were able to grant four scholarships worth $1,500 each with the event's money. The committee decided that a fair way of giving this money to the winners was to hold the funds in an interest-bearing account at one of the local banks that was also a major sponsor, and after an official transcript was sent to the committee from the applicant's college showing successful completion of the first semester, the money would then be sent to the applicant's parents. All the trophies, tee favors, and other items given to the top finishers were all donated by myself with PING giving me the best price they could on all the things selected. Not one dollar we received from our loyal patrons and donors was used for any other reason but the scholarship fund.

My mother Elayne had a comment to share with everyone: "Helping my son Stuart with his sponsoring the Lou Torre Championship golf tournament held for eight years were the most rewarding and memorable years while working as his secretary. I am so proud of Stuart for his many efforts to raise the money from these events to offer the financial scholarships to the local high school seniors for their college careers. Lastly, it was such a joy to hear their grateful words of appreciation when accepting the award."

In the end, we would hold the event for eight years. Over that time frame, we would have had 555 players participate. We would also invite senior men and women champions to participate, and well over 50 of the area golf clubs be represented. The following golf clubs in the Greater Albany, New York area, supported the event the entire duration by purchasing a TEE Sponsor sign; without this constant financial support we would not have been able to conduct a successful mission: Albany C.C., Colonie C.C, Country Club of Troy, The Edison Club, Shaker Ridge C.C., Normanside C.C., Mohawk Golf Club, Cronin's Golf Resort, Hiland Park Golf Club, Pinehaven C.C., and Wolferts Roost C.C. and many other clubs that were outside the Capital District area. Please see photo on next page of image of the large Advertising Board that showed all of the TEE Sponsors and flanked by Jim and Lauren Tureskis then head pro at Wolferts Roost of host club for 1995 event.

The most rewarding aspect was that we gave out 40 total schoarships totaling over $66,000. To this day, this project was one of the best accomplishments in my life and, by far, the most fulfilling.

36.
A NEW DECADE BEGINS

The year was now 1990, and my fifth decade on this planet Earth was upon me. Great things waited for me in this new decade. When looking back, I feel that it was one of the best periods in my professional life.

Things got off to a great start when, on January 27th when I was present for my 8th PGA Merchandise Show in Orlando, the company had reached an agreement with the USGA on the groove issue regarding the Eye2 model. That was great news for all our sales reps because this topic was in the past. The PGA Tour situation continued, but as history would have it, that too ended in early 1993, and before you knew it, the engineers at the company were working on new products for us to sell one day.

A few weeks after returning home to New York, I was invited by the home office to attend the Nabisco Dinah Shore LPGA event in March in Palm Springs, California. I was joined there by another fortunate PING rep who also got an invite. It was a quick trip with some golf watching, a few rounds on the links, and special dinners.

Whenever I would go to one of these functions, I was always representing the PING name. By that time, I had gotten entirely used to the responsibility and had no issues in doing so.

Up to that moment, I had attended ten professional events in person as well as five pro-ams. I guess it helped to be associated with a major golf company.

I switched country clubs and joined The Edison Club in spring of 1989. The head pro, Rick Wright, had told me a few years prior when I was a member down the street at The Willows that he would see me there in a few years. Well, that time had come. The Edison Club was the perfect new club for me to be a member.

It had 27 holes, which meant you could play at any time with no issues. If the club was having an outing, you could always play the open nine. I was still very consumed with my work with PING and would try to play at least once on the weekend, sometimes both days depending on the time of the year. There was always more time to play the game from Mid-July to the end of August. This was the time I could pretend to be on tour and sometimes play five days in a row for a few weeks. I was always invited to play golf somewhere, as I had parts of four states in my territory. I often found myself playing with my best competitor rep and friend Steve Sormanti in his home state of Massachusetts and when he was visiting our area.

This brings me to my next topic which was the creation of yet another tournament. The aforementioned Steve Sormanti, who was the Wilson sales rep, me, and golf professional Ron Beck of Crumpin-Fox Club in Bernardston, Massachusetts, about 45 minutes north of Springfield met up one day in late spring. It was while we were having a few drinks in a sports bar in college town Northampton that the S.P.I.T. event was formed. This title was short for the Salesmen Professional Invitational Tournament. Ron had said they had one of these events in his home state of Illinois and he thought it would be a success there. We all agreed to do this, and with the Connecticut Section's blessings, we had our first event at what we would simply call The Crump in mid-September on a Monday when most everyone could come play. The first year, we had a good-size field. We would utilize the best two balls of the foursome format. Only one score could count from a team composed of two sales reps and two club pros. It was a lot of fun to compete, but the comradery of the occasion was what stole the show. On this day, we were not opponents on the battlefield of market share or any of that stuff, we were simply golfers coming to have fun with one another. And we did. At the end of that first event, Ron, Steve, and I all raised our glasses and toasted to a job well done.

37.

KARSTEN INDUCTED INTO EDISON CLUB HOF

For some reason when I was younger, I thought I might be married by the age of 30; more specifically, I had concocted a time frame from age 28 to 32 for this to happen. By this time, I was 30 and there was no Mrs. Miller in the future.

Ever since getting transplanted into my new sales territory back in 1982, I had pretty much been married to my job. I did have that one very serious relationship with Nancy, but nothing since.

Sometimes I wonder what it would have been like had I stayed in Phoenix after college and worked in the front office for a longer period. I may have met someone there as I had befriended many people while working in the office. I know several of my fellow PING reps who also started in the factory met their future wives while residing in Arizona, and they parted together on new adventures. But at the same time, I was able to get started in this sales career so much younger than most people, and it had certainly accelerated my learning curve. This allowed me to achieve more during that time frame.

One of the things that I'd learned about this job was that it could certainly be solitary at times, as you might expect when spending over 60 nights on the road during the season is required in order to adequately service your account base. So it's a great deal of time behind the wheel driving, as in most years you are putting in around 35,000 miles in a nine-month period. The saving grace in all this, of course, is the relationships you develop over time with your accounts.

While on the road, I had dinner with many accounts and in some cases with their wives and families. It really made life on the road bearable when I had nice distractions like this. To some degree, my account holders and their wives became an extended part of my family and vice versa.

My job has also given me access to many different activities. Attending many professional golf events and playing in several pro-ams added so much fun to my life. Being a big sports fan, I also attended many sporting events in my life as a PING rep, which was great.

One of the greatest benefits of my job was that I was my own boss for the vast majority of the time. It was up to me to manage my territory the best way I could. The only consistent ingredients needed were effort and time.

This was also a great time for my mother and I to spend time together. Like clockwork, she would make the 20-minute drive to my home every Monday, and we would spend at least eight hours together. She would write checks for me, file paperwork, help me prepare shipments to UPS, sometimes iron my clothes for me, and take care of whatever items I needed for my work. She was a godsend for sure. And I would also find time to play golf with my younger brother Marc, who was now 16 and playing on his high school golf team. PING, Mom, and Marc were my life in a nutshell.

I mentioned that, just a year earlier, I joined The Edison Club as a golfing member. The club was originally formed in 1904 and was owned by General Electric, who had a very big manufacturing plant in Schenectady and made the course available for its employees to relax and enjoy. Since Thomas Edison was also associated with GE and was the inventor of the light bulb which GE still sells to this day, it was only fitting to name the club after him. For many years, including the time I was a member, tee markers at the club were made in the shape of light bulbs. With over 300 golfing members, the club was doing very well in the community.

Karsten Solheim worked for General Electric for many years prior to starting his golf empire.

When doing some research on Karsten, I found that he came to New York State on several occasions to work on special projects for GE. He started in Ithaca in 1953, then it is written that he designed his first putter in Syracuse shortly thereafter. Three years later in Redwood City, California, the 1-A putter was first created, as well as the name "PING" due to noise that putter made after contact with the golf ball. Karsten was then sent to

Schenectady, New York, in the summer or fall of 1959 to work on another special project for GE. It was while he was here in my new home that his first putter, the PING 1A, began to get buzz from the press.

Despite the fact that Karsten himself had not lived in the area for a long period of time, he had certainly left his mark on the game of golf there and everywhere with his creation of the PING golf company. Former and longtime Head Golf Professional Rick Wright, when asked for his opinion on potential 1990 inductees for the club's Hall of Fame said, "First person I thought of was Karsten Solheim. Due to his employment with GE at that time, he was indirectly a club member, so he was eligible." Rick would go on to say, "I brought the idea up to Stuart Miller, an Edison Club member who was the local PING Sales Rep. He aggressively got involved. He was able to talk to Karsten, and he agreed to have himself inducted into the H.O.F."

At the time, despite my being such a new member of the club, Rick had rapidly become my best green grass account in my entire territory due to his unwavering desire to be the best merchandiser in the section and his willingness to continue to offer the best fitting methods to his members. The club for sure had many PING-playing members. This would only make the induction ceremony that much more rewarding.

Rick would go on to add, "Stuart was responsible for having Mr. Solheim become one of the most recognized members of the Hall. Karsten and his wife showed up for the induction party in front of an overflow crowd of over 300. Thanks to Stuart, one of the most memorable events in Edison Club history took place."

I get choked up just hearing those words again from Rick, who retired from the Edison Club in 2009 and, to this day, is one of my best friends in this world.

We were able to work out all the logistics of the timing for this grand event, as Karsten, despite his age of 79, was still a man on the go and traveled a great deal. The best timing for his induction would be in late September upon the Solheim's trip to England.

Even to this day, having Karsten come to my golf club and be inducted into its Hall of Fame is one of the most memorable times I had with him and Louise. I was put on the presentation list to speak that night, and for those brief minutes I was at the podium, I felt pure delight. I remember telling the abundant crowd, including my mother, Elayne, who was my plus one for that evening, how honored and proud I was each day to be a representative for the greatest golf company ever.

Edison Club
Golf Hall of Fame
INDUCTION CEREMONIES
September 23, 1990

I shared my story—how when I worked in the front office, I would greet Karsten every morning with "Good morning, Karsten!" and he would bellow out, "It is a good morning, isn't it!" The audience loved that moment. After I said a few words, Rick Wright followed and then Karsten came up and accepted his award. He gladly thanked the club for the honor, and before we knew it, the night was over.

I agreed to pick them up in the morning for breakfast and then take them to the airport for their trip to Phoenix. I took them to the Blue-Ribbon Diner and treated them, with which Karsten was fine. The Blue-Ribbon Diner was owned by one of the members at the Club, and he stopped by to say hi to Karsten and Louise. He, too, was present the night before at the ceremony.

Unfortunately, there was some new commission program going on at PING that caused a delay in the sales reps being paid. Michael Brannan knew Karsten would be in town, and he told me to represent all us reps and put in a word to see if this could be solved. I really wasn't comfortable talking to Karsten about it, but at the airport, Louise had asked how everything was going for me in the field. She was always good at asking about my work. So, I told her about the commission thing, and before I knew it, she was asking Karsten about it. He said he was aware of it and would get it done. I apologized to Louise for bringing that up, but she assured me it was fine and that all would be good soon. Just like that, they were off back to Arizona. My commission check arrived within a week and the problem was solved for all.

It was time for me to get back on the selling trail, as my "fall run" busy season was about to start.

38.
FAIRWAY ADVERTISING
IS BORN

As I entered the year 1991, my life was all over the place. I was entering my ninth year as the PING rep for my area, was preparing for the third annual Lou Torre Champions' Cup, was still seeing my accounts regularly, and I was still seeing my New York City accounts once a month. I was playing golf with my younger brother, Marc, as much as possible and his game was getting very good. I was playing at the club on weekends, and for a bonus, I started an advertising company.

Now, why would I do something like that? I guess you could say I had given it some thought, and since I had all this energy, I wanted to give it a go. Of course, I cleared everything with PING headquarters first by telling John Solheim that nothing I did with this new venture would interrupt my PING requirements. Once I got that out of the way, Fairway Advertising was launched. We were going to solicit area businesses to advertise on golf carts in the Capital District area only. Our slogan was "Putting your business on the right course." I went to a patent attorney and got a service mark registration for my company name and that phrase.

My immediate target was heavily trafficked public golf courses. The golfers at these venues were part of the demographics these companies were targeting. I remembered all these buzzwords from the advertising courses I took back at Arizona State. I always loved advertising, but as a golf rep, I was enamored with marketing and, of course, selling techniques. I utilized all these in abundance as I was finding my course locations early on. We ended up going to Stadium Golf Course in Schenectady, The State Park Golf Course in Saratoga Springs, and the Western Turnpike Golf Course in Guilderland. I pretty much had the three most played golf courses in the area covered, thus giving my advertisers plenty of places to view their logo. I would guarantee each golf course owner a set amount of money that they would earn each month from May to September, as this was the busy season. I was responsible for putting all the signs on the courses and ensuring the ads' appearances were maintained correctly.

I was working exclusively with a special marketing company, who also assisted me with my PING job and was vital in putting the program together for the Lou Torre event. He also helped me out and bought several ads at all three locations. We put together package deals and tied golf terminology to them like "birdie" or "eagle" package. We were having fun with the experience and making some headway as business owners opted for our medium.

The last selling feature I offered was what we called "The Tournament Fleet." This was all tied to one of the local golf cart operators, who made his living by renting golf carts to local country clubs when they had large outings and needed the extra carts. This experience would allow us entry into the private country club market. We could also charge a little more for these ads as they were hitting a different demographic. It seemed to be a bit complicated, but it wasn't. The main thing I was doing with each advertiser was maximizing their exposure. To do that, they had to buy a certain number of ads. We would then calculate the best price for them, and the deal was done.

I even bought several spots to advertise for PING, as I knew many golfers who would see these ads were also looking for golf equipment during the season. The ads we put on the side of the golf carts were finished with a vinyl exterior, so they were easy to clean and were also great in the varying weather conditions. They were straightforward to put on the carts and removing them did not damage the paint. The hardest thing and most consuming part of the venture was putting the ads on the carts. Since this was a one-time-only task, I would do most of this prep work on the weekends. It never interfered with my PING responsibilities.

The local weekly business publication, *The Capital District Business Review,* also featured me in July, putting me right on the front cover. It was very thrilling to have my image on the front cover with a story detailing my company's mission.

I was quoted in the piece as saying, "The way I look at it, it's an extension of outdoor advertising, with a targeted, captured audience."

Please see the photo of myself on one the golf carts upon which we advertised.

Companies that signed up for this advertising experience included banks like Union National Bank and Ballston Spa National Bank as well as Appolo Heating and a local cellular company. Of course, I had my **PING** ads, which I could deduct as a business expense for the year.

The primary purpose of this type of impulse advertising, which I was able to implement with each business operator, was to help establish long-term brand identification to acquaint a consumer with a company or a product. That was our mission from the outset, and it seemed to work. An economic recession forced us to call it quits after three years.

"This is the first type of advertising medium that would be the first to be cut," I said in that article. I am so glad I undertook this venture, as I always wanted to dabble in advertising. Just like that, this enterprise was over. Back to selling **PING** products exclusively again.

39.
WINNING A $28,000 CAR

Golfers have that common goal of giving it our best and attempting to get around the course in as few strokes as possible each time we go out to play a round. We all know that you can't beat this great game, but you certainly can do a few neat things that bring a smile to your face.

According to a 2019 *Forbes* article by Erik Matuszewski, the National Golf Foundation found that there were over 24 million Americans who teed it up on a golf course in 2019. The vast majority of these golfers play the game solely because they love it. Like clockwork, they go out and test their skills with their friends or business associates, and along the way, they can have a little fun during their round and maybe do something special that brings them back for more. I know in all my 50-plus years of playing golf that striving to hit that elusive shot or two during the round always keeps you coming back for more. Most of us would be happy to make a few birdies and a handful of pars, as we all know that that dreaded double bogey or more is just looming around that dogleg. For those of us who have played the game for a long time and even may have been pretty darn good at one time as I was as a two handicap golfer, you may even have experienced the ultimate in golf by getting that elusive hole-in-one.

There are many ways to get a hole in one, but for the most part you need two things: a good shot to get the ball on its intended target line and then, most importantly, LUCK. For the golfing gods to allow your golf ball to enter that elusive club, you ultimately do need some luck.

According to a 2021 *Golf Magazine* article by Jessica Marksbury that cites the National Hole-In-One Registry, there are, on average, over 128,000 of these each year. Only about 1-2% of all golfers will get one. Forty percent of all holes-in-one are made with a seven-, eight-, or nine-iron (14% of these with a seven-iron). The average handicap for golfers who get a hole-in-one is 14 (someone who shoots in the mid-80s). Most aces (57%) are made by mid-handicappers (10-19). These are all the most up-to-date stats from 2019.

It was the late summer of 1992. I was participating in the annual Big Brothers Big Sisters charity golf outing at Crumpin Fox Club, where the head golf pro was Ron Beck. A few years earlier, Ron had invited me to participate in this pro-am event, where the team would have a club pro from the Connecticut Section PGA playing with a team of four amateurs. Club pros from Vermont were also invited since the state line lies less than 30 minutes from the golf course. I gladly accepted his invitation, as it was a great cause, and it would also allow me to be in the company of a lot of my accounts. I remember having lunch just prior to the 1 p.m. shotgun start with Mike Bailey, the then-head pro at Wethersfield Country Club in Connecticut. We had a wonderful time. For some reason, this got me into the spirit of the round a little more than usual.

This particular golf course was a gem of a layout, as it was designed by world-renowned golf course architect Robert Trent Jones Sr. Each hole had its own set of obstacles to tend with, but if you hit the ball straight and true and found the fairway, there was always a clear path to success at this venue. The majority of the greens had a lot of tilt or slope from back to front, so if you were able to keep your approach shots below the pin, you would have easier access to birdies.

My pro member for the day was Dave Phaffenstein, who was working out of Crown Point Country Club in Vermont. He brought three members with him, and I rounded out the team of five.

Most of the time when I play in events like this, I am, of course, trying to do my best for the team, but I am also representing PING. I always like to conduct myself in the best manner. I never go out there expecting to play well, but if that should happen, it is only a bonus.

From what I can recall, our team was doing okay in the event. I, too, was doing about average. However, things were about to change in a very big way.

We approached our 15th hole, which was a picturesque par-three with a good 140-yard carry over a pond that was required to get to the green. I remember the moment like it was yesterday—this particular hole had a very nice automobile parked just behind the tee area. It was a maroon Buick, the Roadmaster, which was the biggest model that company made. I was not familiar with Buick cars, because I had been driving Mercury Cougars for the past six years, and just this past year I'd bought my first-ever Lincoln Continental. The local Buick dealer had set up his cars on two of the four par threes on the course and granted a car for any golfer lucky enough to ace one of those holes.

I believe I was the last person in our group to tee off. I remember hitting my ZING #7 iron on this 160-yard hole as well as I could. ZING irons were so special because they were designed to go straight. This eliminated my normal right-to-left draw. This shot never left the pin. It was going straight for it.

I also will never forget hearing these words from my pro, Dave, when the ball was halfway to the target: "Well, there goes your LINCOLN!" He was referring to the new Lincoln car that I'd just bought. He'd noticed it on my last trip to his club in spring.

The pin placement that day on this hole was on the very front portion of the boomerang shaped green. When the ball hit the firm surface, it was only ten feet from the cup. After it bounced one time, it started to roll like a putt. It was in line with the pin, which made it very eerie as no shot ever looks like that unless it is THAT shot. All a sudden, the ball dropped. It was a hole-in-one. And it was for a car.

As you can imagine there was a lot of celebrating going on, with a lot of high fives and fist pumping between everyone in the group. I had just won a $28,000 car. My mind was racing, for sure. I was excited, no doubt, but it was a good excitement, not too melodramatic.

As I have often said, my life was so blessed—to be working in this great game for a wonderful company that I had achieved so much with already. I was happy more for the pure pleasure of making the hole- in-one than I was for winning the car.

For the record, this was my fourth ace. I had one when I was only ten, a short three months after I started to play the game back in Pensacola and got another one on the same course when I was 12. Then, I had to wait another 18 years to get my third. I got this ace when I was playing with three PING workmates at Camelback Country Club resort in Arizona in August 1989. I only had to wait three years to get my fourth, but this was my big one. No one was going to forget that moment.

We all celebrated when I took the ball out of the hole. I could barely get enough energy to finish the last three holes, as I was emotionally spent. I knew I was also going to spend a lot of money on drinks at the reception for this accomplishment, but I had no concerns. It only took about ten minutes for everyone on the property to hear of my achievement. My hole in one was even covered in an article in the local paper (*The Greenfield Recorder*).

MILLER SCORES HOLE-IN-ONE

I was congratulated by so many people at the conclusion of play. We freshened ourselves up and then went to another venue for the reception and prize giving ceremony. As it turned out, there was an open bar for this tournament, so I was off the hook there.

There was also a special auction to raise money for the cause. Bill Sandri, the facility owner, also said a few words and congratulated me on winning the car. Several nice items were up for grabs in the auction, so I put in a winning bid for a staff bag signed by numerous PGA tour players. I bought it for $500. It was the least

I could do, considering what had happened to me earlier. I still have this bag today.

It took several weeks before I could finally pick up that car and take it home with me. I was going to be sent a 1099 for tax purposes. I believe the claim on the vehicle was just north of $21,000. I was never going to drive this car, as it was not my style, and I already had a very nice car. I sold it to one of my local accounts for the said amount of money. I remember taking that money—less the amount I would owe on taxes—and putting it into a special account at the bank.

I used that money solely for travel vacations for the next three years. By winning that car, I also lost my amateur status due to the amount the prize was worth. The USGA, years later, did change that rule. It took me three years to get my amateur status back, but I will always have the bragging rights to professional golfing career money winnings of $21,000. This is not too bad for those keeping stats, and I still joke about it with some of my accounts today.

40.

A THRILL FOR MY BROTHER

I will mostly remember 1992 for that magical hole in one at "the Crump" in late summer, but I will also not forget it for a few other neat events that occurred. I would have to go back to springtime, just after my brother Marc had graduated from high school and where he was a top player on his golf team for the last two years. We were playing another routine round of golf at The Edison Club when it happened. For as long as I could remember, my younger brother's only mission in life (or so it seemed) was to beat me on the golf course. Well, it finally happened.

I vividly remember him having an excellent round going up to the 12th or 13th hole. I believe we were tied at that time. I remember saying something nice to him, but he would have nothing to do with it and stayed focused. As it turned out, he shot a two-over-par 74 compared to my 75, and he beat me fair and square for the first time. I couldn't have been happier for him.

At that time in our lives, we certainly had played a lot of golf together. He was a member at Ballston Spa C.C., not far from his home in Malta, and I would often play with him during the week. He did not play a lot with me at my club as he was still doing lots with the golf team, but he made the best of it on this day. We both told Mom the same time, and she was ecstatic too that Marc finally beat me. Even head pro Rick Wright got wind of what happened and offered a hearty congratulations to Marc. As it would turn out, Marc would go on to play college golf in our adopted state of Arizona, first at my former college, Glendale Community College then at Grand Canyon College. For the record, he played in every tournament and earned scholarships at both colleges. We were all so proud of him for the excellent golfer that he had become. He would spend the rest of the decade playing professionally on the mini tours.

As I mentioned earlier, I used a ZING iron to win that car with my ace, and for my days on the road representing PING, this was our new iron. The Eye2 iron had a great ten-year run, and it was the most popular iron in history as far as sales go. That is what I heard. Even with the ZING as our new go-to club, I would still sell my share of the former model in addition to the popular wedges that we still marketed. I would have to say that the ZING iron might not have been the most appealing iron to look at. However, it sure was effective. PING would improve the visual appeal of its irons with the ZING 2 model in 1994.

As I write this story of my life, I must confess that I have intentionally left out many everyday things that a golf rep does in their day-to-day operations. I have come across many documents and notes and appointment books in researching my book. These documents basically act as a ledger of my life's travels. When I read some of these, I get dizzy from just viewing the many transactions that I did each day way back then. The only thing I wanted to say was you would not believe in a million years what golf reps do.

In the late '90s to the early part of the new century, we had some people from the factory visit the sales reps to see what we did. Over five years, I had four individuals from the Marketing Department come to visit me. I know Roy McMillin, my former college roommate, came to visit me one summer. He would go out into the field himself a few years later, and we would room together at the PGA Show each year and at our annual sales meetings in Arizona in August.

Everyone who came to see me told me how great of a job I was doing and that they were all surprised to know how much behind the scenes work is required to do the job. The purpose of the visits, in my opinion, were for these folks to see exactly what we do and, more importantly, see how our accounts are reacting to the products the company was making and the service we all were providing. Plus, it was an excellent way for my accounts to voice any management concerns that they believed needed addressing. Everyone at PING cared a lot about the accounts and just wanted to do everything they could to keep getting better.

Now getting back to my brother Marc. Early in the spring, I got an invite from our communications department to attend the 1993

Men's U.S. Open at Baltusrol in New Jersey in the second week of June. Marc and I drove down in my car on the first day of the event, and after driving for well over four hours, we arrived. After getting on the bus that transports you from the assigned parking lot (at this event, it was an old quarry mine) which has to be done at all major events due to the large daily crowd size, we finally got on the golf course.

I was very excited as this was my fourth U.S. Open as a spectator, and it was Marc's first. The part of the golf course we entered was very close to one of the closing holes—number 17, I believe, which is a long par five. The rumor of the day was that John Daly had just reached this hole of close to 600 yards in only two shots. For those who remember, Daly appeared on the scene in his early pro career by winning the 1991 PGA Championship at Crooked Stick while a PING staffer.

I still vividly remember this U.S. Open because we quickly ran into John Solheim after just ten minutes on the property. I had heard that he would be there along with Karsten and Louise and might need my assistance with something, so I was going to find him. It just turned out that we met up just like that. After introducing Marc to John, he said that he might need help with Karsten and Louise's transportation to the airport at the end of the day. I told him that we could do it with no problems. Just let us know. He said for me to just be around the clubhouse around 3 p.m. to check in with us. We had been there for only ten minutes, and we already had a potentially significant task to do.

Marc knew who Karsten and John were. He has been around me his whole life, and for most of that time, I worked at PING. He knew I am a PING guy and would do anything for the Solheim family. He would soon find out for himself what that role feels like.

Marc and I would go out on the golf course to see some action. I had already been present at this same golf venue as a spectator for the 1985 U.S. Women's Open championship. I was just in my third year as a rep for PING then, but my friend from younger days in Arizona, Danielle Ammaccapane, played in the event as an amateur from ASU, as did Lauri Merten. I went to show some support. I remembered a few nice holes that were good for spectators, so we went there. In the few hours we were there, we saw many of the Tour's top players, including Payne Stewart, Paul Azinger, Tom Watson, Ernie Els, Ray Floyd, Fred Couples, my college friend Dan Forsman, and eventual winner Lee Janzen.

It was getting close to the end of the day, so we ventured off to the clubhouse area. When we were close, I spotted Karsten sitting on top of the clubhouse's balcony with a perfect view of things. He was so easy to spot with his white PING shirt and the white goatee on his chin. I moved in closer, just under him, and I yelled up to him after I got his attention, "Hi Karsten, it's Stuart Miller, your sales rep in New York. John told me that you all might need a ride to the airport, so I'm here for you if you need me." I just remember Karsten telling me that it was good to know, and we will see you soon. At that time, I thought it would be best to hang around this area, which was still busy with fans, but somewhat away from all the action. Soon after, John appeared and told Marc and I that our services were not needed to drive his parents to the airport. However, John asked my brother if he could do a critical task for him. Paraphrasing the conversation from so many years ago: "I need you to watch over Karsten and Louise for us while Stuart and I go to get our car." My brother remembers the situation very well and shared his views on that moment 27 years ago:

"I just remember being around Karsten, and he was asking who I was, and I told him I was the brother of your sales rep in New York State. I felt bad that Karsten couldn't quite remember that as he would ask me again just a few minutes later." It was a scorching day, as we both recalled. Marc then said he heard some of the spectators saying, "Hey, look, that's the PING guy," referring to Karsten, whom many people would recognize due to seeing him in all the PING magazine ads that the company ran. At the time, Marc was nearly 19 years old, was six-foot-tall, and weighed about 220 pounds, so he was a larger presence around the much shorter Karsten.

Some fans asked Karsten for his autograph on a golf ball, and Marc remembered seeing Karsten's hand shaking a bit while doing this. After a few autographs, Marc intervened and said no more autographs and slowly walked the two of them closer to the front gate where John and I would soon emerge. I would later learn that

Karsten came out with a baseball-style card with his signature on it and would hand these out to fans starting the next year.

Marc concluded by saying the thing that touched him the most about this moment with Karsten was how nice he was during the entire time. John had parked his car just down the road from the club entrance, and it only took a few minutes for us to get it and bring it to the front. When we got there, he went to the back of his car and handed me a box of putters. He said these were new putters Karsten and the company had been working on, and he wanted me to hand them over to the head pro of Baltusrol, Bob Ross, who was very well known in the golf industry. He just said to give them directly to Bob, telling them they were from Karsten and asking Bob to let us know what he thought of them. They were so new that even I didn't know what they were.

Then, John and I went to find my brother and his folks. They were still there and still standing. Mission accomplished for Marc. We all said our goodbyes, and before you knew it, they were back to Arizona. I told Marc to wait, and I would be right back. I went into the pro shop and introduced myself as the PING rep from upstate New York. They went and got Bob for me, and I told him that Karsten had some new putters for him to try out. He thanked me and that was that. Our Baltusrol experience was over.

41.

MY REPORT FOR IMPROVING OUR LADIES MARKET

I remember being at a demo day at the Glens Falls Country Club in the summer of 1993, when demo days at private clubs were becoming more of the norm. The host pro liked to invite reps from the four most popular brands of clubs in his shop to attend. Fortunately, one of those brands was always PING, as we did well with the club's members. At the beginning of the four-hour demonstration, one of the few women who attended asked me for a "ladies' iron" to try out. I told her all that I had was a regular graphite club to try, and she immediately rejected that thought and moved to the next company. I felt terrible that I did not have a club she could try out—one that had more flex in it to serve her slower swing speed better.

At that time, we just didn't have a softer shaft flex that might benefit women and senior men whose golf swings have slowed down. For sure, this was a growing segment of the golf market and one that we (in my opinion) could improve with our choices in shaft flexes.

After that experience, I began to do some research on this matter and spent the rest of the summer collecting facts. I was curious to see how our company was doing specifically in the ladies' only market by asking our marketing department to find some sales figures for the past five years (1989-1993) to help me with my project. Not to reveal anything specific here, but the numbers did indicate a downward trend. I also asked several of my accounts what they thought of our presence in this market, and one account in Connecticut took me by surprise. In his 20 years at his club, he had sold over 200 sets of ladies clubs, and only four of those were PING clubs. The pro said to me he never considered PING a women's club "because steel shafts don't fit the women's profile and your graphite shafts are too expensive." He recommended that I relay to the company the following four tips:

1. Need to offer more shaft choices, both steel and graphite
2. Need to alter the cosmetic appearance of the clubs-hence different band color and color of the graphite shafts
3. Price needed to be lowered to be more competitive
4. "Women need to be in graphite, but PING's price is still too high."

I mentioned four other popular manufacturer's prices in my report. PING's prices were higher by a considerable margin. This pro went on to say that the Cobra brand of lady irons was priced quite a bit below PING's prices. Cobra had a very aggressive demo program with all their irons, including the ladies, which helped them gain a significant foothold in the category.

My last comment on this topic also came from another highly ranked club pro at one of the busiest private clubs in the Hartford, Connecticut area. This pro laid out a five-point approach for PING to take to improve their ladies market share:

1. Ping needed to build a ladies club with its own shaft characteristics
2. Need to have a softer graphite shaft than their current shaft (then called the 101) because 95% of the clubs he sold were graphite
3. Need to have demo ladies sets offered in the program
4. Should have softer colors for women's clubs
5. Lastly, he stressed that PING's current prices for women were still too expensive, and he gave me a comparison in costs of his two leading sellers at the time (Daiwa and Cobra).

At the end of my analysis, I pointed out that KARSTEN Mfg./ PING, according to a *Golf Pro* magazine publication (April '94), remained the top seller in irons in the industry.

I put all this information into a small binder report dfated May 12th, 1994.

During my career as a PING sales rep in the Northeast, I had offered up my opinion on several topics from time to time, especially on the subject matters that affected my sales and, ultimately, my income. However, this was the first time I had ever written up a paper like this.

I called John Solheim up in his office one day and told him I had some crucial things to talk about, and that on my next visit to Phoenix, I would like to have lunch and discuss these issues. I believe my brother had a golf match going on in the area, and I could see both John and my brother's event.

As John was driving us to one of his favorite Mexican restaurants, I recall saying these words in a rather dramatic fashion: "John, if we don't do something soon, I will never sell another ladies club in my territory."

John then looked at me a little strangely and asked me to explain what I meant. That is when I relayed the story of that demo day. I then told him about the paper that I had written.

We would have a lovely lunch, just the two of us. Back during this time frame, things like this were still possible. It was always so special to have time alone with one of the top figures of the company I worked for. Our relationship (in my opinion) was on solid footing that allowed for occasions like this. Since I had a captive audience, I highlighted some of my paper's major points. I told him that I had made six copies, and I handed him his copy during lunch. I then asked for his permission to hand out the rest to the following departments: communications, head iron foreman, and the marketing department where I derived all the iron stats to support my report. I can't recall the others, but they all needed to see my findings. I thanked John for lunch, of course, and he thanked me for the report. That project was over.

Fast track to late August and our annual sales meeting. I remember the iron foreman coming up to me during one of our discussions with various department heads and saying, "So that you know we are going to have a ladies club at the upcoming (1995) PGA Merchandise show" (in Orlando)."

He smiled his trademark smile, which I had gotten a lot from him over our 16-year relationship. I only interpreted that smile to mean that my paper may have had some impact on this decision. The key phrase being "may have had." That point did not matter at all.

The main thing was that a change was on the horizon. And for me, that was all that mattered. I believe that I stood up for myself by writing this paper and presented it, which is all that matters.

I was not looking for any credit. But if this did play a small role in this decision to create a new shaft series, I would be honored. The most important thing to take from this entire experience is that the company took the proper steps to ensure that they would continue to be a significant force in the overall irons market.

When we all got to the 1995 PGA Show and saw a particular area on the wall displays depicting these new shafts, I was so pleased. The company called the latest women's shaft the "U34." We also had one for the seniors. The ladies shaft had unique bright markings on the label area and said, "Ladies." The company even came out with a unique advertising campaign to support the new clubs. As far as I was concerned, I had only envisioned a new selling opportunity, but I was delighted.

42.

MY FIRST RYDER
CUP EXPERIENCE

The year was 1995, and after a very successful PGA Show, I just knew I was going to have another banner year with the company. While at the show that year, several of us PING people were also invited to come and check out the new company called The Golf Channel. It is based right in Orlando, as it was the vision of long-time resident Arnold Palmer. It was quite a treat to check out their new studio, and we were able to see a live segment being filmed. When done, one of the host announcers, Brian Hammons, spoke to us and took a team picture. I know that picture was displayed in one of the marketing department staff members' offices during that time period, and I wished I had a copy of it because it was a part of history since this company is so successful today.

At that stage in my career, I felt that what I was doing could last a lifetime, or in other words, that could be the only job I would ever have. It was that good. Like I have said so many times before, working for a family-owned company is truly special. Every day, when I awoke, my goal was to work as best I could and represent the PING name in the most distinctive way possible. I was now entering my 13th year as a field representative and my 16th year overall with PING, and I was still only 36 years old. That would pretty much be my theme going forward as everyone I interacted with was amazed at how long I had already been in the business despite my age. I always liked that, because it made me feel different and unique.

As we all know, when you are doing the same thing over and over, it can be somewhat dull. To break things up, I tried to see how I could regularly woo my customer base. I don't recall anyone teaching me that, but I did find from experience that trying to do my job better not only helped me keep my sanity, but it's also good for business. During this period, PING was very involved in apparel, and I prided myself on consistently being ranked in the top ten in sales for this category.

I used one approach to promote the brand the best I could— having a social seeding program with top accounts. For all my three New York City accounts, I would make sure to have the entire full-time staff of each store wearing the PING polos that we were selling. Their company logo would be on the left chest, and PING's name was on the left sleeve. Brand awareness was so important to me, and I took a lot of pride in outfitting many a club golf pro into our apparel. Depending on the year and what we had to offer, I would mix up what I gave to my accounts.

The longtime head pro at the Duchess Country Club in Pough-keepsie, Fred Lux, recently recounted, "You always gave us something when you came to visit. Whether it was PING score sheets or a shirt, you always took care of us." Fred would go on to say, "That is what made you stand out among all the other salespersons that came to see me. You always went out of your way to make us feel special." Fred also mentioned he could still remember when I gave him a unique item that acted as a briefcase but was made up of unique canvas-like material. We called it a messenger bag, and if memory serves me over time, I had to give out over 100 of them. Like anything, you had to budget things, so I would give out so many in a year, especially to accounts who were growing their business with me every year, and thank goodness there were many.

During the early part of summer, the communications department reached out to me with another invitation to attend a major golf event. I was cordially invited by PING to attend the Ryder Cup in late September, which meant a return trip to Rochester and historic Oak Hill Country Club. This would be the 31st edition of these fabled matches, which pitted 12 of America's best players against Europe's best 12. During the last five matches, Europe had prevailed twice, U.S.A had also won two times, and Europe retained the Cup with a tie (14-14) in 1989. I remember watching Bernard Langer narrowly miss an eight-foot putt in 1991 on TV to lose his match and thus give the Americans the win by one point in a tournament dubbed "The War on the Shore" on Kiawah Island, South Carolina. For me, that pretty much solidified how important the Ryder Cup had become important again and was now a must-see TV event. If you are fortunate (like me), you could be among the 40,000 or so spectators that roam the course during the three days of fierce competition. The company had given me a pack of tickets, so I went to the event on the first day and then again on the third and final day.

The first day, I traveled super early in the morning as it was a good three-hour drive straight west on the New York State thruway system. I went with David Nevatt, head pro at Albany Country Club, and his top assistant pro. After working under the guidance of long time Oak Hill golf pro Craig Harmon for two years, David was hired to be the Director of Golf at Albany Country Club in 1987, and that is when our relationship began. Prior to the beginning of his PGA career, David was the winner of the most prestigious junior golf event, the U.S. Junior Championship in 1974. I had mentioned earlier that one of my other good friends and fellow PING rep Michael Brannan also won the U.S. Junior in 1971, and David and Michael knew each other very well as young aspiring golfers since both hailed from the northern California area. Not everyone can claim to be friends with two former United States Junior champions!

David would then go on to play at Arizona State (my school as well) for only three semesters; he left there to go back home to California and compete at a junior college first then finish up college golf at Fresno State for only one semester. Then at 20, he turned professional and qualified for his PGA Tour card later in the year at Pinehurst, North Carolina. Finishing 12th of the 30+ qualifiers simply allowed him to become Monday qualifiers (Rabbits) on the '78 Tour. (The all-exempt tour came later in 1982.) He would do tour life for just one year then begin his PGA club pro career.

David and I would continue our working relationship at Albany C.C. until he left in 1998. He then went to start a unique project in the creation of the Saratoga National Golf Club. which officially began operations in 2001. And to this day that club, along with the Albany Country Club, are two of my best accounts as an independent golf rep. David is now living in the Philadelphia area running his own golf consulting business, and his long-time wife Linda works at the ACE Club serving as Director of

Golf; we remain friends, and I see them usually once a year at the PGA show.

So, I was attending my first Ryder Cup event with a decorated golf club professional in his own right. Spanning my long career as a golf enthusiast, I have attended over 50 "Tour" Events over the years, so I don't recall much of the first day of competition at Oak Hill. I know it was fun and challenging to see the golf that day. As I alluded to earlier, many fans are watching only four matches or 16 players during the morning matches on the first day. I knew that we were planning to see the main match of the day, which was the foursomes match of Corey Pavin-Tom Lehman versus Nick Faldo-Colin Montgomerie. The Americans won one-up.

In the afternoon four-ball matches, we hung out on one hole to watch all four matches come and see all the top players up close and personal, which is always a fun perspective to see. For the most part, we hunkered down in the massive hospitality pavilion, where you could grab something to drink and eat and watch the action on the countless TV sets. Before we headed home to Albany, we also checked out the equally gigantic merchandise tent to buy some souvenirs. I also took the liberty to buy several shirts for some of the folks back at PING—a small way for me to thank them for all they did for me.

The next day was special, as I returned to Rochester with my home pro Rick Wright and his accountant, best friend, and fellow Edison Club member Fred Mauer. We drove to Rick's parents' home in Webster, another suburb of Rochester, and very close to Oak Hill. We all had a lovely home-cooked meal at the Wright household, and we were ready to get to the course very early the next day.

I distinctly remember waking up before first light and heading over to the shopping mall, where we had to board a bus to transport us over to the course. The first tee time was scheduled for 9 a.m., I believe, and we were on the property a little past 8 o'clock. We all went straight to the first tee to find a prime spot so we could see everyone tee off. We could not get in the small spectator stand, but we found an area where we could see perfectly. All I could tell you, reflecting on that moment in time, was how much tension there was in the air. You could just feel it. If I was nervous, you know the players had to be feeling the pressure as well.

The sun's early rays were shining on that first tee area, and it was fully illuminated. The stage had been set, and the drama was about to unfold. U.S.A held a slight lead with a score of nine to seven. They would need to get to 14.5 points to win the cup back, while team Europe only needed to get to 14 points to retain the coveted cup they'd won two years prior in England.

After the eighth group teed off on the first tee, we decided to find another key spot to see the players. We ended up on a par four that was straight, and we staked ourselves right in a position where we could see the players hit their approach shots. I remember we were on the left side of the fairway and had a perfect view. We watched all 12 matches come through, starting with the first grouping of Tom Lehman and Seve Ballesteros. Shortly after that, we saw the Concorde taking off from the airport carrying Prince Andrew, who had come to support the European Team. We then saw Davis Love come by, followed by Brad Faxon. Then the Ben Crenshaw-Colin Montgomerie match, then Curtis Strange-Nick Faldo. After that match hit their shots, we decided to go back to the pavilion tent to watch the rest of the action. The matches were very close, but Rick made the call to head back to our car before potential long lines and delays. We ultimately listened on the radio to the final match. U.S.A would lose the 11th match, and the final score was Europe 14.5, U.S.A 13.5. We had lost on American soil, which was rare, but it did happen.

Since I was providing the tickets, I forgot to mention that I was spared from doing any of the driving to the event, and that was a bonus. Fred Mauer did the driving for us on this final day. Fred loved to gamble, so on the way home, we stopped off at the reasonably new Turning Stone Casino just east of Syracuse. We also had a nice dinner there and celebrated having all watched our first-ever Ryder Cup in person. This was by far the most exciting professional sporting event I had ever had the pleasure of watching. It for sure was everything the press had made it to be... and more.

43.

NEW FITTING SYSTEM LAUNCHED IN BOSTON

After finishing up my 14th PGA Show, I came home to the New England winter's bitter cold to compile my orders and ensure everything checked out. I was also getting ready to embark on what would become the best golf vacation of my life. My longtime golf account and friend Fran Kringle, the pro at Crestview Country Club in the Springfield, Massachusetts, had scheduled a trip for me and one of his best friends, Roger, to go on in early February.

We started in the northern part of California by meeting up with Fran's cousin. He ended up playing with us on the first leg of a 21-day golf excursion that would take us to some of the best spots on this planet. We wound up playing Poppy Hills, Spyglass Hill, and the Links at Spanish Bay, all must-see golf stops on the fabled Monterey Peninsula. The golf was fantastic despite the time of the year. It could be a little cooler than desired, but mother nature was on our side, and sunshine was plentiful. We rotated our play with some sightseeing. We drove over the Golden Gate Bridge. Unfortunately, the fog had set in, which prevented us from seeing the grand city of San Francisco at its iconic best. We did drive down iconic Lombard Street, which zigs and zags everywhere. I did the driving, and I would not recommend it to anyone as it was a pain just trying to keep the tires from hitting the curb since it was a tight road. We also took a tour of the well-known Muir Woods National Forest, where you would see petrified pine trees spiraling up to the clouds. We even spent a little time on the back of the 18th green at Pebble Beach, and it truly is a breathtaking view.

We gathered up our luggage and golf bags, left The City on The Bay, and headed directly to Hawaii's big island, landing at the Kona airport. We were scheduled to be in this tropical paradise for at least eight days, so we would do a lot of island hopping. I don't remember all the great golf courses and hotels that we stayed at, but they were all so spectacular in their way. I do remember playing at Waikoloa Golf Resort and Mauna Lani while we were on the Big Island. We also took a day to travel up to the most prominent volcano park in the state, and it was remarkable how cool the temperature was when you got to the top.

The next island we visited was Maui, the most known island other than Oahu, with Honolulu being the state's biggest city and capital. We played at the famous Kapalua Golf Course (the Bay Course, which was the only one at that time because the Plantation Course was being built as we were visiting). The views at Kapalua were very inspiring. We also played the Royal Kaanapali course, which was very close to Lahaina, where we ate most of the time while on this island. I just remember Fran saying every time we checked into one of the hotels, "This is fantastic. This truly is the best one so far." The famous movie *South Pacific* was filmed on the beach next to a Maui Sheraton property that we stayed at.

We were then whisked off on a 45-minute plane ride to the most northern island and the wettest and greenest by far, Kauai. I happened to know a former pro in Vermont who was the Head Pro at the Princeville Resort, and he was able to get us a little discount on our round of golf there. We ended up playing 36 holes of the resort's 54 holes in one day. We took the pro out for dinner and drinks that night. Just being in Hawaii was outstanding and a great time. We all had a blast. We would go to Honolulu just to board our flight back to the continental United States.

Our last part of our journey was playing a few rounds of golf in my home state of Arizona. Both of my travel companions had never been there before. We would play at two of the more popular venues: Camelback Resort and the Arizona Biltmore. I remember Fran marveling over the Mexican food we were eating each night, specifically how it tasted so much better than the restaurants serving it back home.

Our 21-day trip ended, and we were back home in the northeast. It seemed like we were gone for three months. It was a real treat. All the money derived from the sale of the car I won was used to pay for my portion of this trip.

That was my major trip for the winter. When I got back home, I was there for the rest of winter, which meant I would spend my fair share of time shoveling snow for myself and for Mom. We did have a professional snowplow removal person, but we still had to maintain our front porch area. That was fine since it was great exercise. I remember one year at my mother's home, I was clearing the pathway from the driveway to her porch, and the snowbank was as high as I was. Thank goodness that amount of snow only happened that one season.

I made my first round of travel through my territory, including visiting New York City a few times. I was also enjoying playing at the club and occasionally shooting good scores in the low to mid 70s. One day, I remember getting a brand-new set of ZING 2 beryllium copper irons sent to me as my sample set. I took them directly to the club, and as we were waiting for our tee time, I took off all the plastic wrappers and tossed them in the garbage can. I went on to shoot a great round of even-par 72 without ever even practicing with these clubs. One of our playing partners was so impressed that he went directly into the pro shop and placed an order for a set. I thought that was a pretty neat gesture on his part.

Shortly after that round of golf, I got another invitation from the communications department. This was a little different from all the other ones I had gotten in the past. This was an invitation to join John Solheim and Doug Hawken at an LPGA event in the Boston area where PING was a co-sponsor.

The company was discussing a new PING fitting format that would ultimately change the world as we knew it. I also joined them for dinner after the meeting. From what I recall, the company's area rep at the time had been talking with company officials about changing tthe fitting we had been doing for several years. I vaguely recall there were a number of PING accounts who were there in an informal setting expressing their thoughts on club fitting. I recall having dinner at a seafood place called Legal Seafood, and I had one of the best seafood meals I have ever had (including all that great food I had in Hawaii). I remember Doug also commenting on how good the food was there.

What resulted from those few days of discussions, and I am sure countless other shared information with upper management was the advent of what became known as the "PING Fitting Cart." It was officially launched in early 1998. It was an exciting time for PING and all of us who worked for this great organization. I remember thinking that even back in 1990, there would be that normal passing of the torch for the powers that be at this company. Deep down, I knew Karsten was aging, and I just felt it would make it all so much easier for everyone if a new change at the top would occur sooner than later. That is precisely what happened.

On June 1st, 1995, KMC had a stockholders meeting. Karsten remained chairman of the company, but John Solheim became the President for the first time. The passing of the torch had arrived. I just remember hearing of this through our internal memos from the marketing department. From that moment forward, I felt a sense of relief and comfort, knowing that John would have a stronger voice in moving this company forward in the years to come. And did he ever.

The new Fitting Cart system was the talk of the town. It would have 40 irons (all assorted lengths and lie angles) that would be contained in a cart that had wheels and was very easy to transport from the pro shop to the driving range. It would allow for a more thorough fitting experience. What the company did next is what made the new fitting system work. They would charge PING accounts a set fee to buy the fitting system and have them come to the factory in Arizona to be trained and view the various departments at PING. This was a very successful program and brought the company to new heights in the golf industry.

From what I can recall, each sales rep was allocated so many spots to place in their territory. In other words, we were the ones who would go out and find the best candidates to get this program off the ground. This was a straightforward proposition as for all those PING-supporting accounts we already had. We had more applicants than spots, so this would be something that would take time to implement fully. Since we could bring in only so many a year, I sort of had a five-year plan of finding my best fitters. As it turned out, they were all on board and just waited for their turn.

I believe the first golf account that I asked to be on the fitting system was Rick Wright of The Edison Club. In early 1998, Rick came out to Arizona for his training, as did a few other accounts from my territory and many more from around the country. These training seminars were planned mostly in the winter months, which is the best weather in Phoenix, but they were also offered in the fall season. That is when Rick attended, and I was with him on his trip.

It has now been 22 years since Rick was on that trip, but he wanted to interject in this book what being a PING fitter meant to him:

"One of the highlights of my professional golf career was attending the inaugural PING Account Fitting Program. Stuart Miller, my PING Sales Rep, invited me to attend the seminar. We met PING company employees for a three-day informational seminar."

Rick would say that he was able to see the complete process of manufacturing a set of PING irons, including the lost wax process of the iron heads at the company foundry known as "Dolphin." Rick also got a kick out of the design department, noting, "The area was filled with cubicles and computers and a design engineer. They were able to re-design iron heads, trying to result in maximum performance."

Part of the itinerary also included a day of golf at nearby Moon Valley Country Club, a place with so much history for me as that is where my high school golf team played. To top it off, the company had access to a private suite at the downtown arena that was home to the Phoenix Suns, and several of the pros who were attending the seminar had the chance to attend a game.

I had even better plans for Rick than earlier in the day. I took him along with my brother Marc, who was still in college in Arizona, to an Arizona Cardinals football game at Sun Devil Stadium. Then, I drove Rick to the basketball game. If that is not enough, I dropped him off at Sky Harbor International Airport. Rick caught the red eye back home to Albany, New York. Rick concluded by saying, "What a whirlwind evening and great trip. Thank you, Stuart."

All I can say to that is "Thank you, Karsten and John."

44.

VISITING OUR
CANADIAN DISTRIBUTOR

I was so fortunate to have been able to experience all that came to me. I was even experiencing some great success with the Sections I was working in, as in 1994 I was selected the winner of the Ernie Sabayrac Award, given to the top salesperson for the year in the Connecticut Section PGA. In 1995, I was presented with the Salesman of the Year Award for the Northeastern New York Section or my home section. I like to say I was very good to PING, and they too were very good to me.

I believe the year might have been 1995 or so... as I have already alluded to this was a wonderful year for me as well as for the company. I was at the PGA show in Florida and happened to spot another sales rep in the booth, but I had no idea who he was. Zero clue. So, when I was in between appointments, I went up to him and introduced myself.

For simplicity, let's just say this individual worked for PING as a sales rep in Canada. I didn't know much about how PING did its business in Canada. He would explain to me what he did up there and that he was anchored in the Toronto market, which was really not too far from my home operations in the Albany, New York, area. That is pretty much all we said that first year because before I knew it, another account came by, and I was back to selling again.

I guess you can never get tired of attending PGA Merchandise shows. For me, I was always busy with customers coming in and orders being written left and right.

One story I wanted to share is pretty remarkable, but for me it came quite easy. When an account would stop by and was ready to place an order, I would grab the order form I always had with me on my clipboard and find a table to conduct our transaction.

I would look at the pro and say, "Your account number is..." then blurt off a few numbers, and the account holder would say almost every time, "Yes, that is my number with PING. Wow, do you have a good memory." I would always return this line to that person: "I only remember account numbers for those accounts that are doing a lot of business with me and are very consistent." That would always get a smile from them and usually would get me a few extra items added to the sale. I took a lot of pride in remembering as much as I could about each account, and for me, at the show, I was just showing off. They seemed to enjoy it just the same.

The rest of the remaining years of the 20th Century went very well for me and for PING. In 1997, the company came out with its first-ever titanium driver, the TISI, and man, was it a beauty. It had a shaft hosel that allowed you to preset the lie angle of the driver head. Combined with variable loft options and shaft options, it was a winner from the start. All of us in the sales force were selling more drivers than we had in a long time. That same year, I also attended the PGA Championship at Winged Foot in New York with my brother Marc, who was at home visiting for a few weeks from Arizona.

Marc and I thoroughly enjoyed our day together, walking around this famous golf course steeped in so much tradition. This would have been the fifth men's major championship that I attended in my lifetime, but my first PGA. Marc was also with me four years earlier at the U.S. Open at Baltusrol.

As I mentioned earlier about how the new fitting cart was introduced, the company also launched—in perfect harmonic fashion—a new PING Clubfitter of the Year Award. They announced all the winners at the PGA show during a special breakfast function. Each rep would select a winner, and all would be invited to this ceremony. This tradition would start the following year in 1998 (to the best of my recollection). I believe that it was also at that '98 show that I met up with my new PING rep friend from Canada again. My roommate at these large events was always Roy McMillin. So, I asked our friend from the North if he would join Roy and I for dinner one night during the show.

He gladly accepted, but I am sure he regrets the offer. We ended up going to a pretty well-known seafood restaurant just off of

International Drive and not far from the entrance of the Grand Cypress Resort. We all had a wonderful time getting to know each other just a little better and attaining a better appreciation of just how things ran in Canada. Unfortunately, the next morning this gentleman was not feeling so well due to potential food poisoning from our meal the night before. I felt very bad for him, but I was glad I had made a new friend along the way. On the last day of the show, with him feeling much better, he invited me to come up for a quick visit to see their operations one day. I told him I would get back to him on that.

As it turned out, I was able to go up for a visit in early March since that was still my downtime, and I had more free time. I was told that there would be a very big golf show in Toronto at the Convention Center in early March, and that would be the best time for a visit. It has been so many years ago that this trip occurred, so from what I believe, I would arrive in Canada on Saturday, and the Golf Show was set for Sunday and Monday. So, I departed from Albany International on a Saturday late morning, and the PING team in Canada picked me up a few hours later at the Toronto International Airport and took me first to my hotel to settle in. I was staying at a Holiday Inn in the lovely suburb of Mississauga, which was only 30 minutes from downtown Toronto and ten minutes from PING's Headquarters. That was where I spent the next few hours getting to see the operation first hand.

This was a trip that I was paying for entirely on my own, but once I got to this great country, the rest of my expenses were taken care of by TEAM Canada. After the tour operations was concluded, we went to a restaurant owned or named after Canadian hockey great Wayne Gretzky. We had a great time. In total there were five of us taking part for this occasion. The one thing that stood out to me that night over dinner was how many questions my new friend from the North was asking me about PING. Not only my dealings in my territory, but also back at the factory. All good stuff, and I was happy to respond.

The next day was the first day of the golf show, and PING had a small booth at the Convention Center. There really wasn't anything for me to do so they told me it would be fine for me to go and do a little sightseeing and meet them back at the center around 5 p.m. So, I walked just a few minutes down the street and went up the famous CN Tower, named after the sizable national railroad concern Canadian National, which built it in 1976. I went straight up to the top of this 1,815-foot-high concrete communications and observation tower located in the downtown area. I distinctly remember at the very top it had a glass area you could stand on that allowed you to see all the way to the bottom. I never really liked heights, so I avoided this area and just looked out at the open skies, and I could see for miles.

For kicks, I just started walking back toward the heart of the city. I happened to come upon a theatre and saw in big bold letters that *Beauty and the Beast* was playing. I went to the counter and saw that a matinee show would be playing in less than an hour, so I bought a ticket. Being solo, I was able to get the best available seat in the house and I ended up only eight sections from the front stage. It was held at the Prince Albert Theatre, and it was a beautiful production. First Class. And it pretty much consumed my afternoon. I walked back to see how my PING friends were doing with their show. They all had a good show. I cannot recall for sure where we went that night, but we did go out for another nice time and great conversation.

Monday was the last day of the Golf Show at the Convention Center, and all went well from what I recall, and the show ended early. I wasn't sure what they had planned for me, then they hit me with it. We were going to an NBA basketball game at the same stadium they had baseball games, but of course they had the court and seats positioned to allow spectators to see the game more easily. So, we saw the Toronto Raptors play the Boston Celtics. I still have my ticket stub and it says Raptors vs. Celtics MON. Mar. 3, 1997, Sky Dome 4:00 pm. Over the years living in Phoenix, I saw my fair share of NBA games, but this was my first time in Canada. It was super. The company wasn't too bad either.

After the game, we all went to a sports bar for some drinks and a few more questions. I also asked my fair share of questions. As it turns out, Canada is vast in overall geographic size, but the population has always been small. Around 35 million, with over 14 million in the province of Ontario, where Toronto is located. One of the other reps chimed in to add that most of the golfers in the country also played left-handed due to them also playing hockey. The last count showed close to six million playing golf in the country, and close to 13% of them were left-handed.

I would be off back to my home on Tuesday morning. It was a quick trip, but everyone in the **PING** Canada operations treated me like a king, and I couldn't have been more pleased with my visit.

45.

DOING THE
RIGHT THING

Interesting new developments were on the horizon for PING at
the beginning of 1999. I previously mentioned my trip to Canada
to visit their operations due to an invitation from the individual
I had met a few years ago at the PGA Merchandise Show. This
person was also the acting General Manager of Karsten Canada.
When I was down in Florida in late January attending the PGA
Merchandise Show, PING would always conduct a day-long
sales meeting to get everyone ready for the show and a new year.
Guess who was announced right at the outset of the meeting as
the new Director of Sales & Marketing for the company? Yes, that
is correct, none other than the same person who previously held
the top job in Canada.

As I have pointed out earlier, I had befriended the company's new
executive several years ago at the same show by merely walking
up to him and introducing myself and starting a conversation.
Talk about a small world.

This promotion certainly caught a lot of the rep force by surprise.
I could only think that all those questions I had fielded from him
may have been his way of checking out things on this side of the
border. It didn't matter to me one iota, as I liked this individual
very much and looked forward to continuing to be a PING rep
under his new guidance.

For the record, this moment in time marked the beginning of
many changes for the PING company regarding its sales force,
changes that I had not seen in my first 18 years on the job. Good,
bad, indifferent, all that didn't matter.

During the 1997-1998 time period, the company had a slightly down year in sales and created the "Customer Appreciation
Program." This was a program that would show appreciation to

an account for how much their business grew in that one year, as measured by their end of the year sales. They would be eligible to receive certain PING products free of charge. It was an exciting promotion that had never been done before, and there would be a lot of accounts that would automatically qualify based on their sales.

The only problem was that several of my top tier accounts who usually did well had a down year in sales and didn't qualify under the program guidelines to win anything. Well, I saw that as a problem and wasn't going to have anything to do with it. So, I looked at all the items that were being doled out and bought a wide array of products ranging from a golf ball rug for the pro shop, a putter stand, a staff bag, and other neat items like a cool sign that acted as a clock but also had room for advertising messages to appear on it. I even bought smaller PING clocks that they could hang in the pro shop.

After calculating how many accounts I needed to give these items to, I had spent almost $3,500 because I knew this would appease my account base. I spent the first part of the year handing out all these items to my accounts and ensuring all the other qualified accounts got the things they were entitled to. Two months had passed, and for some reason, I still hadn't received an invoice for all these items I purchased. I called the person in the marketing department who was the leader of this unique project, and asked him, "May I ask when are you going to send me my bill for all this neat PING stuff you sent me a few months ago?" I could hear a little silence on the other end of the phone.

"You haven't been billed yet?" he said.

"No, I have not, and I certainly would like to be."

That is when this person opened to me and conveyed that since I had not come to him with this request, a bill would never have been generated. There was an oversight on the department's side, and a bill was never created nor rendered to me. I was thanked for my honesty and told emphatically that the company would not lose sight of what I had done. In other words, I had done the right thing.

We were in our new year with a new person in charge of the marketing department. Shortly after that, regional sales managers were created—four in all, representing the country's four primary areas. Then, a national sales manager was named. Everything that I had never experienced as a sales rep for PING was now happening before my eyes.

I am struggling with this specific part of my journey as a golf representative as there was a barrage of new developments. For so many years, I knew things only one way, from my experience working inside the company walls and then ascending to the sales arena and claiming the coveted title of a PING sales rep. I was proud to be considered one of the "original" PING reps in a field composed of many who joined after me. In the ensuing years, we would have many new reps who would come from within the factory and several who would come from outside.

Like I have said many times before, changes were upon us, but I was still a PING rep, which was still considered one of the best jobs in the industry. I was still doing my own thing of being responsible for a particular territory, but there were now new outside elements that were never present before.

This new layer of territory managers and national sales managers created a buffer between us sales representatives and the Solheim family. This was part of the new evolution from a family-run business to more of a modern corporate structure. I would evolve and find a way to fit in.

For my remaining years with PING, I never worried about my role with the company. I had proven to everyone my merits, resolve, and commitment to being a PING sales rep. But my primary motivation, which was instilled in me all those many years ago, was still to make the Solheim family proud and honor them. If you stop and think about it, what I have always loved about my job as a golf salesperson is the relationships with my accounts that I have created over the years. They are indeed an inspiration to me, which is why I do this job day-in and day-out and year after year. It is hard to describe, but there is a personal connection with a golf pro/account and a rep like me that is so important that there is such a friendly trust created. It is a very important part of my job that I would never trade. It is immeasurable. And for that reason, I march on.

After another successful campaign of selling PING products, 1999 was capped off by attending the 33rd Ryder Cup Matches at The Country Club in Brookline, a venue I was fortunate to play

18 years previous and view the U.S. Open 11 years prior. I was with my brother Marc, and we were lucky again to get the tickets from PING, and we attended just the first day of the competition. Heavy rains had been around the area for the previous days, and the golf course was very wet and hard to get around, so we only perched ourselves in a few places, so we could see the four-ball matches played in the morning and foursomes in the afternoon. Again, the crowds were massive. The PGA limited 30,000 spectators to each session, which created absurd spectatorship conditions on a course that was better suited to accommodate half that many onlookers. It was the most I have ever seen for a golf event. With only four matches going on in each session, you pretty much had to go out on the course and find a proper location and just wait so you could see the players up close, which is always a thrill. We could see Montgomerie, Garcia, Jimenez, Clarke, Westwood, and Harrington from the European side and Duval, Mickelson, Lehman, Woods, Love, and Stewart on the U.S.A. side. We would also spend a lot of time in the large Pavilion Tent to refresh and watch the action. We also visited the merchandise tent, where I bought my customary amount of logo golf shirts for the PING staffers back in Arizona. Things were not looking great for Team U.S.A. as Europe held a commanding lead of six to two after day one. As history would tell us, the Americans stormed back on the final day, overcoming the largest deficit at the time in Cup history (trailing by four points) to eventually win 14.5-13.5. It was great watching it on my SONY TV set since I could see everything. I would see many more major golf championships, but this would be my last Ryder Cup due to the massive crowds.

46.
MEETING A GREAT
GOLF AGENT

Welcome to the 21st Century, everyone. The year 2000 was officially upon us. I was soon to be 41 years old, with a birthday coming up in February. I would be entering my 18th year as a PING sales representative and 21st year with the company, or almost half of my life here on Earth. Everything was still going very strong as far as sales in my territory.

Unfortunately, we also got some sad news delivered to us that year: Our long-time leader, Karsten Solheim, had died on February 16th at his Phoenix home of complications from Parkinson's disease after several years of declining health. I could sense that he was not doing well in the last few years and had been preparing for this day. The entire golf community lost a legend and someone who completely transformed the game with his ingenuity and engineering prowess. I was so fortunate as a human being to have been able to do the many things I did with Karsten while he was in charge of the company. I flew to Arizona to pay my respects to the family and was present for his memorial service, which was witnessed by hundreds.

After the church service was over for Karsten, I would be on my way to California for the trip I had planned for the prior six months. I was invited by an ex-golf account of mine, Patrick Moynihan, to fly to California and stay with him and his family for a week in mid-February. They all had heard the news of Karsten's passing and expressed their condolences to me upon my arrival. I was now back in the state I was born in back in 1959 (ironically, the same year that PING got started). To give you a little background information on Patrick, he was hired in the late 1980s to be the head pro at the prestigious Longmeadow Country Club in the Springfield, Massachusetts, area and left there in 1998 to go work for the Callaway golf company in Carlsbad. I had the privilege of servicing his account all those years he was working at Longmeadow C.C.. Interestingly, you could say that our business relationship did not get off on the right foot. The very first meeting I had with Patrick went something like this: "I just want you to know that I really don't like PING. They take way too long on their orders, what's that all about?" Before I could say anything, he also added that he had always been a Ben Hogan staff member and would be inclined to push their product at his new club.

"I am sorry you feel that way, Patrick," I countered back, "but we do a lot of special orders based on fittings, and it does require more time." I would go on to let him know that we were always trying to improve our delivery times. That pretty much ended that first meeting.

Just a few days later, the phone rang, and it was Moynihan. "Hi, Stuart, I hope you're doing well. I need a favor. Can you find me a lady's set of PING irons as I have a member here who's looking for a set?" I hesitated for just a moment and told him I would certainly do my best. I did know of a location where I could obtain this set, but I was thinking back on our inaugural meeting and how it could have gone better. Then I thought that might have been just an act to see how I would react. It could've also been a test to see if I was up to the task of helping him out. So, I called Patrick up and said, "Yes, I found a set and may I drop it off soon?" Residing only 75 minutes from his club, I came by in a few days with the set and sold it to Patrick, and he gladly paid me with a check for the product. Not more than a minute after he handed me the check, he said these words which I will never forget: "I have been thinking about this for a few days, and I am only going to carry three lines of clubs in my shop this year, and PING is going to be one of them." I thanked him very much for his confidence and left his shop knowing I made a very wise move in helping him out with his request since it appeared our brand would be in his shop, which only meant more sales.

I remember Patrick picking me up at Lindbergh Field, which has now been renamed the San Diego International Airport. I believe it was very early in the week that I arrived, and the weather was delightful after coming from daily temperatures in the 20s and

30s. We shortly arrived at their home, about a half hour drive north up the I-5 Freeway and not far from where Patrick worked at Callaway.

This area has been a hot spot for golf equipment manufacturers, which include Callaway, Taylor Made (also in Carlsbad), Titleist in Escondido, Cobra Golf in Oceanside, and several more. I got settled in the Moynihan home as Patrick's wife Denise showed me my room for the week, along with a tour of the house. They had a beautiful home and family, which included three boys. I believe only the youngest was present because the two other boys were attending college in other states.

Patrick told me he was going to be busy at work for the next few days. He knew that part of my plan for the week was to attend the Anderson World Consulting Match Play Event, which was conducted at La Costa Resort not far from their home in the Carlsbad area. I went out on Wednesday to the resort since Pat granted me a ticket through his work.

The first thing I did was grab a pairings sheet so I could see all the scheduled matches for the first day. Generally, in an event like this, there are 64 of the best players based on the official World Rankings. To be the winner, you must win six matches during the week-long contest.

I searched the pairings sheet in hopes of finding all the PING players in the field. I wanted to focus on one of their matches. The one player I spotted quickly was Lee Westwood from England. He was going to tee off shortly, so I decided to follow his match. It has now been over 20 years, and I do not recall who his opponent was, but it was just great to be at my first ever match play golf Tour event.

The weather was somewhat iffy, as clouds had engulfed the entire region for most of the morning and there were predictions for heavy rain later in the day. I brought an umbrella just in case. I believe it was on the third or fourth hole that I spotted a person in the gallery who I recognized. I thought it might be Lee's sports agent Andrew Chandler, who everyone called Chubby. He was short but well-rounded with thin black hair and a grey beard.

I went up to him and his friend and said, "Are you Chubby Chandler, Lee's agent?"

"Yes, I am," he said back, "and this is Lee's coach Peter Cowan."

I then introduced myself and told them I was the PING rep in upstate New York, and they were delighted to meet me, as we had something in common. Chubby had a nice stable of players (all on the European Tour) under his guidance.

We were all following the match very closely. For the most part, Lee held a one or two up advantage in the match.

I remember Chubby saying this: "Boy, you PING people are tough" or something to that effect, meaning the player pool guidelines with club minimums and things like that. I stayed clear of that situation as it was not my department or my place to say anything about that topic. I just listened and Chubby added that Lee's arrangement with Titleist to play their ball, glove, and shoes brought in twice as much in endorsement money as the PING deal. Again, this occurred many years ago and I don't know exactly how much more he was referring to, but he was adamant that it was significantly more. But then he added, "But Lee loves PING and wouldn't have it any other way."

Those closing words were music to my ears, as I, too, really liked having a player like Lee Westwood represent the PING brand. He is a proven winner around the world and does a great job (in my opinion) in helping to sell our product. They all told me they would be more than happy to introduce me to Lee when the match was done, and that would have been great. The rain that was predicted did come, and it lasted for a while. The rest of the day's play was postponed to the next day due to wet conditions on the course. I was hoping to meet Lee, but the delay ruined those plans. Through my connections with both Tour reps, I was able to get Lee to send me one of the posters we had created for the European theatre only with his signature addressed to me. It is still on my office wall in my basement to this day.

I drove back to Patrick's home and told everyone about my experience on the course, meeting one of the greatest golf agents in the world and watching Lee Westwood play his match. They were all pleased that I had a lovely day on the links, and we all shared a delightful meal that Denise had prepared for us.

I believe it was on Friday night of my trip that Patrick made arrangements for us to attend a Major League Baseball game as the San Diego Padres were at home, and I believe they were playing the New York Mets. As we were driving over to the game in Pat's classic black Suburban (it was a beast in size), I was riding shotgun. The car (for some reason) just felt a little warm for that time of the day. It was a typical SoCal afternoon with temps in the high 70's and enjoyable weather—no clouds, only beautiful blue skies.

I was starting to get a little agitated. When I commented to Pat about the car being hot, he just burst out in laughter. I knew I had been duped. He had one of the cars that had heated leather seats with the ability to control each seat, and he was opting to raise the heat on mine all the way up to an uncomfortable level. The joke was on me. Pat commented that he couldn't believe I took that long to figure it out. I have been known to be gullible for sure. The weather conditions at the ballpark were so much better than in that car for those moments.

We also found some time to drive around the neighborhood that the Moynihan's were near, and it was very nice. In fact, on the way home, we saw Ely Callaway's Jaguar pass us. Patrick had pointed that out. We were in Rancho Santa Fe at that time, on our way to Del Mar to have dinner at one of the local fish markets. This part of California was, for sure, one of the more upscale and had a lot going for it.

This was one of the most relaxing and enjoyable vacations that I had been on at that time, and I had to thank the Moynihan's for that. As it would turn out, Patrick would end up taking a sales rep job with Callaway, and within a few years from that trip, would be back in my area representing the Callaway brand. We would now be competitors, but good, friendly ones for sure.

47.

HAVING TO GIVE UP NEW YORK CITY

The year 2001 will always be remembered for that awful day, September 11th, when evil came to our door. The bombing of the Twin Towers in New York City and the Pentagon in our nation's capital was a shock for all humanity. Things changed for many lives that day. This is one of those JFK moments where on this day at that very moment of the first attack, you will always remember where you were and what you were doing.

I happened to have started early in the morning for my three-day, two-night trip to work in Vermont as my "fall run" was underway. It would be the 19th rendition of my fall run, which is the hardest four-month stretch of work I do all year long. I was listening on the radio about a plane attacking the World Trade Center, but I didn't think too much about it. Then, as I brought in my samples to show my first account at the Haystack Golf Club in Wilmington, Vermont, I could see on their big-screen TV the actual scenes that have stayed with us since then. It was just sad to watch and so emotional. I did my best to get through the appointment, but then I still had a lot of work ahead of me.

Shortly, I got a call on my cell phone (which were still very new back then) from one of the staff workers in the marketing department to see how I was. I was still the rep for New York City, and the company just wanted to make sure I was safe. I called home to speak to my mom, and told her I was fine and would continue with my work.

The next few days were hard on everyone, but we managed to get through it. I continued to have another successful selling season despite what was going on in the world, which ultimately did affect travel as a lot of people were just afraid to fly again after what happened.

Also, for the time being, I did not go to visit my three accounts in the city for several months.

To break up the turmoil going on in the world, we had our annual S.P.I.T. tournament at Crumpin Fox. This particular year, my team ended up winning the event. I remember the day was overcast and the threat of rain was imminent. It ended up pouring on us for the first four or five holes, then it stopped and we ended up shooting something like five under par, which was not that great, but due to the awful playing conditions, it held up and we won the coveted Spittoons for our prize. It would be the only time I would win this tournament, but I would participate in it every year and see a lot of my fellow sales reps and club pro friends.

Everything was good with Mom. Marc was still in college, playing in golf events and doing well. Mom also started a tinnitus (ringing in the ears) support group as my dad suffered from this disorder, which was still relatively unknown around the time of his death. Mom would have an expert on the field come to her house every few months to speak to the six or nine people who were currently showing symptoms of this disease. They always thanked her for her efforts to help them. In a small way, I also felt my mom was being helped mentally with her kind acts by hosting the meetings.

During the middle of my fall run, I was also told by our new Sales Director from Canada that I would have to trim my territory. I believe this was a simple act to get my account base more under control, as fewer accounts would be easier to maintain. At the end of 2001, I still had close to 250 accounts, which was a lot.

I was advised to come up with a new map rendering my new territory less the area I was willing to give up. For me, this was a very easy choice, so I submitted my plan and map to him when it was time to do so. I gave up my three New York City accounts and the few accounts that I had in the Met Section, which were all in the northern Westchester County area. I also gave up several accounts in the southern part of my Connecticut region, including most of the accounts in the New Haven area and accounts on the shoreline. This would trim my accounts down to around 180 or so, and it would also take quite a bit of sales volume from me. I was not concerned about that, as with fewer accounts to tend to I would have the ability to work the territory smarter and pick up more sales as time went by.

For the record, I had the New York City area (Manhattan only) for 16 years. During that time frame, I would have made close to 200 visits (all by train), literally walked 200 miles, and stayed in several of the city's nicest hotels including the famed Waldorf Astoria. I also had many enjoyable meals along the way, including a wonderful evening at the famous Sparks Steakhouse when I was entertaining the staff of The World of Golf. I was fortunate to have had this area for the company all those years and the memories will last a lifetime. The thing I will cherish the most is my close working relationship with all those accounts that I worked with so closely over those years. We all had some wonderful years over this period.

48.
EXCELLENT TESTIMONIALS
FROM FORMER ACCOUNTS

When the year 2002 arrived, and when I went to the PGA Show in late January in Orlando, I worked with my new account listing. I was working my 19th Show, but I now had the fewest accounts ever in my career with the company.

One of the most significant adjustments I had to make in my years working as a PING rep was getting used to the constant rollout of new equipment. Back in the early days of my selling career, we had the Eye2 model, which lasted for ten years from 1982 to 1992 and is still one of the best-selling iron models in history. Then in the next eight years, PING would introduce four more models: ZING, ZING 2, ISI series, and i3. Once we got into the new century, a new model name was introduced every two years, or so it seemed. The industry had been doing this marketing strategy for many years, and it was just a natural procession for PING to join this practice.

I will not bore you with all the details of all the model changes from 2002 to my last days with the firm in July 2009, but the many changes required countless hours of product learning along the way. The only constants that remained were the account visits and the demo days. The ever-increasing popularity of such demo days caused me to give up my golf membership at The Edison Club due to lack of time to play golf, as demo days were most popular at private clubs on the weekends. I even had a tech rep to help me out in my later years with the company.

One of the tasks that each rep was asked to do each year was to find worthy candidates to become "Authorized PING Fitting" accounts, thus making the trip to Arizona to be appropriately trained to become fitters. We all took this seriously, but I always thought the best way was to present the facts to each potential account and let them decide. Most of the accounts that I could get on board wanted to be a little different and wanted to give their members the best fitting experience they could, so finding the accounts was not that hard. In the year 2000, I had 30 such accounts spanning my entire territory of upstate New York, Vermont, western Massachusetts, Connecticut, and the three New York City accounts. I was always trying to get new accounts to join each year, and I always had a shortlist of potential pros that I would pursue, but sometimes it took a little longer than planned.

One account that I had in mind was Derek Sprague, the head pro at the Malone Golf Club in Malone, New York, which is in the dead center of the northern part of the state only ten miles from the Canadian border. I tried unsuccessfully to get Derek on board for four or five years, but I finally got him to commit to the program in 2005.

We always helped our iron fitting accounts to do a nice demo day for their members, usually three or four hours long. Every year, for Derek, I would make a four-hour drive to his facility to conduct these demo events. The golf pro was usually always out there with us, assisting his membership along the way and aiding us in selling products, which was always the goal at such activities.

Derek would have several more successful years with PING while at Malone and became the 39th President of the PGA, serving 2014 to 2016.

Here are some testimonials from a former account, Ryan Hall, who was the head pro at Golf Club in Avon (Hartford), Connecticut:

"Stuart Miller was my PING rep for many years during my tenure at The Golf Club of Avon. Every spring, I had a big demo day representing all the major companies in the industry."

This was common practice for a golf pro back in those days—staging a one-day demo day with a litany of companies on hand.

Ryan would go on to say, "Not only was Stuart the first to arrive to set up, but he was also always the last to leave. His attention to detail and the ability to follow up with me was unparalleled. He was a great fitter, and my members appreciated his guidance."

Ryan, as a top club pro, knew how important it was for him to be "walking the line" as I liked to call it—being out on the range during the entire time of the demo day to work with not only us sales reps but also his members, helping to guide them when buying equipment. We would have successful demo days because of golf pros like Ryan Hall.

Ryan would go on to say, "Furthermore, Stuart was the only golf rep to represent his brand himself. All the other companies (he mentioned them all) had "tech reps" who were part-time employees that weren't exceptionally knowledgeable of their products. Not the case with Stuart. He was a true professional, and he took these strenuous days very seriously. His attention and effort lead to sales and customer satisfaction."

Mr. Hall's final comment was, "That has always left a lasting impression with me. He cared...and I always appreciated that about Stu."

Deep down, I truly feel that most club pros had the same sentiments that Ryan demonstrated. They were all able to achieve so much with our help during such demo days. It certainly made them look excellent in their members' eyes by providing top-notch service.

On average, I would do between 50 to 60 demo days a season. When my days as a PING rep ended, I estimated that I did close to 700 of these. If I averaged four hours at each one, that would come to 2800 hours (117 days in a row, 24 hours a day) of demo days. If that doesn't make you a little tired nothing will.

One other former golf account of mine, Fred Lux, Jr., whom I mentioned earlier in my journey, also recently reached out to add some words on my behalf:

"I met Stuart Miller in 1982 in Poughkeepsie, New York, at Dutchess Golf & Country Club, where I was the head professional since 1980. Stuart was taking over as my PING rep and covering the northeast. Sometimes sales reps' only interest is selling you product and breaking in as a new guy is not always easy. Stuart was a very polite-mannered young man and extremely dedicated to doing a good job and selling PING products."

Fred would add that we hit it off very well from offset and bonded pretty much instantaneously. He tried to give me as much business as he could and build up a good PING account. He would then add, "Stuart and my family became very friendly over the ensuing years and enjoyed Stuart's personality and friendship. I saw Stuart about five or six times throughout the season. We'd have lunch or dinner with my wife Judi, and sometimes Stuart slept over at our home." It was true that my relationship with the Lux family would be one of my closest relationships in the golf business, and this friendship remains to this day.

In his email, Fred also mentioned how I met his oldest daughter, Eve, when she was only seven years old and paid close attention to her golf career over the years, even following her later in her life as she competed in the U.S. Women's Amateur. Eve just turned 45 years old and is the club pro at a private club in the Charleston, South Carolina, area. Fred would finish by saying, "Stuart went well beyond being a golf rep. He became much more, a loyal friend to my family."

One last testimonial comes from a golf pro mentioned quite a bit in the early stages of my new role as a PING rep in the early '80s, Mike Rosenquist. These are his words describing me:

"My times spent with Stuart Miller, the BEST golf salesman I encountered during my career as a PGA life member. I first met Stuart in 1982 when he became my new PING salesman. Having a PING account since 1972, I was sold on PING as a product ahead of the field in quality, playability, and fair price to the golf professional that gave them a chance to make a reasonable profit without a large outlay of money.

"I always found Stuart to be full of enthusiasm and ideas to help promote PING products, which helped me better serve my membership and profit for myself. Stuart was always available for demo days, which gave my customers a great chance to test the new PING clubs. I believe I was one of the first PING accounts to receive a demo cart around 1997, which really helped me fit and promote PING golf clubs."

As a side note, Mike was my best customer in the North Country of upstate New York for the years I called on him, from 1982 to his retirement in 1999, so we had a terrific run of 18 years.

Mike would conclude by saying, "After retiring in 1999, I always spent time with Stuart during his demo days for the next ten years to help him and my past members to make the best decision on new equipment. Stuart has been and still is a personal friend that I enjoy talking to about the golf business, both now and then, and what we believe it will be in the future."

It is always very gratifying to receive plaudits and praise from your accounts, both former and current. It just makes you feel so good to hear positive things; it makes all that work you put into your career worth it. And that, my friend, is what life is all about.

49.

TESTIMONIALS FROM MORE IN THE INDUSTRY

Here are additional testimonials from three individuals saying that I have impacted their lives differently; they are all touching in their distinct way.

First is an exceptional lady named Helen Duffy, who for 20 years worked at PING in the credit department. Helen was the person I would send credit apps for when I would get a brand-new account on board with the company, and she would set the account up properly on the computer. Helen started her career with PING in June 1979, just one year after me, in the golf ball division, which had recently been launched. I never met Helen as we were both on the manufacturing side of things and in different buildings. She would later get a new job in the front office a year later and keep that position until her retirement in early 2000. Helen was in charge of new accounts, and that is when we met for the first time.

Since Helen and I have stayed in close contact for the past 20 years, I asked her if she would like to say a few words for my project. She was on board.

Helen recounted her time at the company: "My position required me to be the contact person for the reps and for the pros that wanted to open an account with PING. I loved the interaction with both. Most of the reps, like Stuart, started out working at the factory in various positions, mostly directly out of college." She added, "I knew most of the reps personally and their families as well; in a lot of cases watched them grow into very fine men and gals. I can't say enough good things regarding the sales force. They were all devoted to the company and the product and represented both magnificently!" Helen would conclude by saying, "They all also continued to keep in touch with many reps by phone calls and Christmas cards and time to time lunches when they were in town, and it continues to this day, 20 years later. Stuart has always made it a point to keep in touch even after he left PING and ventured out on his own, and I have deeply appreciated it."

Like I said in the introduction, a very classy lady indeed.

Next up is Brent Skinner, whom I initially met back in 1985 when we were both members at The Edison Club. Brent would have been a junior player at that time. Here are some excerpts from Brent on how our paths touched:

"I remember how I looked at Stuart's interactions with PGA Professional Rick Wright from when I was about 12 years old and thinking to myself, 'That's what I would like to do for work when I get grown-up.'" Brent explained how his family grew up in the same neighborhood as his childhood friend Tom Wright, Rick's son, in Clifton Park. His parents were members at the Edison Club before Brent was born. When he became old enough to golf, his dad would drop him off at the club on his way to the General Electric plant in Schenectady. Brent explained how he and Tom were very close and played a lot of golf together during their formative years.

Brent went on to say, "Around 1986, Footjoy had sent in director chairs to good accounts as promotional tools and I can't tell you how many hours we spent in those chairs (unless Rick kicked us out of the shop). I would see Stuart come into the shop to meet Rick wearing a shirt and tie and maybe a sports coat. I specifically remember him driving a white Lincoln Continental and parking sometimes in the loading zone if he was making a quick delivery. I admired and looked at the relationship he had with a guy who I had so much respect for."

Brent would conclude by saying, "It was obvious that Rick trusted Stuart and PING, and that allowed Stuart to take his business to the next level. I carried the impression that Stu made on me in those adolescent years through college and eventually to my first job out of college in a golf shop."

I am glad to say that Brent became a sales rep for Mizuno golf in 1999 and was the youngest sales representative for them at age 23, which was the same age I got my sales gig with PING. He proudly declared, "The relationship skills I observed between Rick and Stu vastly helped me to land this job." It is very touching to hear this : When Brent was working as a rep, he related this story to me, which was great to hear back in the day. Brent exited the golf business in 2016 after spending 17 years as a golf rep. He still marvels at how I have been able to sustain my career, now spanning almost four decades. We remain friends to this day.

The last story is about a young man who recalls a story from 34 years ago that genuinely helped chart his career path. To this day, I do not remember the event, but that doesn't matter. I am just glad to have played a role in it.

The setting was also 1986 (same time frame as Brent Skinner), and it was summertime. A young junior golfer named Jeff Beauregard from Keene, New Hampshire was working during summertime recess at Crumpin-Fox Golf Club in Bernardston, Massachusetts, the same club where I would win a car with a hole-in-one six years later. Jeff was only 16 years old and worked in the pro shop for new head pro Ron Beck. Ron asked me a favor. He asked if I would consider giving Jeff a personal use discount for a set of PING irons.

Jeff remembers the story as if it occurred just yesterday: "I remember Stuart coming into the pro shop and putting his order pad on the pro shop counter. He then said to me, 'Young man, what can I do for you today?' Jeff said he would like to get a set of the new PING Eye2 beryllium copper irons: 3-9 irons, pitching wedge sand wedge, black color code, ZZ-65 shafts, standard length, and Dyla-White grips." He also asked for a personal use discount. Jeff says I replied, "Absolutely." Again, I don't recall this exact moment as I met so many people and helped all of them if I could. I remember Ron Beck asking me to do this, so he saw something special in Jeff for sure.

Jeff would become a PGA member (still is today) and worked mostly in the Missouri Section. That was where he befriended a PING rep named Jerry Waitulavich, whom I worked with early in my PING days at the 19th Green Driving Range. Jerry was the final influencer for Jeff, who wanted to become a PING rep. He was fortunate to move to Phoenix and be employed at the company. In 2004, at age 29, he became a PING rep in the Dallas, Texas, area. Jeff is still an active rep for PING, but is now anchored in Austin, serving that area and the state's vast southern region. When I was in the sales force, Jeff and I would always talk about things. I am proud to say that he is one of what I like to call the "Elite 4" of PING reps with whom I stay in close contact with to this very day.

When I reached out to Jeff to hear his story, he again told me that what I did for him all these years ago was "one of the nicest things anyone ever did for me." That pretty much sums it up.

50.
SUMMING UP THE LAST FEW YEARS

If younger folks would do their best to find their passion in life early, they, too, could go on to have the success that I have experienced. It has been an incredible ride for me. I have been pressing these keys on my laptop computer to express my life journey. I have done quite a few things in the golf industry, both on the golf course but mostly in the golf shop and on the golf range. As I have said a few times before, I have been fortunate to find a job that I truly love, and for that reason, I have never really worked a day in my life. How many people can say those words?

As I stated previously, the PING company that I first started to work for in 1978 and for my first 20 years as a rep is not the same company that I was working for in my last ten years or so. There were, for sure, a lot of new demands and requirements for the job. We were being evaluated more often by our regional manager. The once close relationship that I had with members of upper management like John Solheim and Doug Hawken was evaporating. The new sales management foundation created in early 2000 had, for sure, put a buffer zone, and those once available figures were now insulated. Hey, I get it and I can understand, but this was so different from my heritage and upbringing with this great organization. It was discouraging to me and honestly was a personal let down. My internal fortitude and respect for the PING name kept me in the game, especially for my last few years. The most important element that kept me at my peak performance was my relationship with my accounts. I lived for my accounts. Always have and always will.

Here is a story that I have found entertaining:

The scene was The Sagamore Resort in upstate New York in September 2005. The NENY PGA Section was conducting a merchandise show for all its members and several golf reps were there to sell their wares. It was the night before the show, and I was in the lounge of this great resort having drinks with my all-time favorite sales rep friends Steve Sormanti and Jeff Dibona—both representing top tier clothing brands in the industry. A new rep joined us for this occasion, Derek Travers, who was the new hard goods rep for Callaway Golf in the New York region. For some reason, we were talking about a new tech rep who was working with Steve. This person happened to be a younger female and soft on the eyes. I mentioned her name and said half-kiddingly that I might make a play for her (again, I was just having fun with the thought). Derek chimed in and said, "She is way too young for you, so I think I will also ask her out." Now the battle was on. That is when I said to everyone, "Okay, here is what we have here to compare. On this side, we have a rookie (Derek) and a gazil-lionaire (indicating me)."

You really had to be there to get how funny it was, but I have never heard Steve and Jeff laugh as hard as they did. Even Derek, who was fast becoming our new friend, had to chime in, "You win this one." That was one of those moments in time you freeze in a bottle and, when you get together with old friends, it is uncorked, and the laughter resurfaces again.

I also wanted to touch a little on my continuation of being a golf spectator at golf's biggest events. In 2006, I attended the last day of the U.S. Men's Open at Winged Foot with new friend Derek Travers. This was my second Open at Winged Foot (I also attended in 1984) and my third Major there, as I also attended the 1997 PGA. Since Derek was a big-time Callaway supporter, he was rooting for Phil Mickelson, and honestly, so was I. But it just was not meant to be. To this day, that would be the last men's major championship I have attended live, but I hope to catch another one in future years. This particular pro golf event would mark the 40th that I had attended or played in (the pro-am portion of the tournament). That is quite an achievement in its own right.

I also wanted to compare my job status over all these years to success in a professional golf event. I have been a pretty good golfer along the way, even winning a few events through the years and having some high finishes. To me, being a sales representative for

PING for all those years was my major accomplishment in life and in the game of golf. This was, in golf terms, my "major" victory.

There was also a change at the company concerning our employee status. We were independent sales agents during the majority of my time as a PING rep, which meant you were paid a commission and you were responsible for all your expenses—including your health insurance. I believe it was around 2001 that we became employees of the company and were put on their health insurance plan. This leads me to my next story. I would keep reading in our company's monthly newsletters about employees who had reached company milestones such as working ten years, 20 years, or even 30 years.

One day, I reached out to Stacey Pauwels, Karsten's granddaughter and daughter of Alan Solheim, who I have known most of her life, about the status we sales reps had since we were now employees. (Stacey from what I can recall was working closely with all employees concerning many things.) In other words, do we qualify for such milestone achievements, too? She seemed intrigued when I brought it up, as I could immediately sense that I may have had a point.

Sure enough, at our next major sales meeting in Arizona in August, those sales reps who qualified for these awards would be recognized and presented with a gift, the same one that the employees at the factory would be given. I remember the year: it was 2007 when these presentations were being made to the sales force. If you were to backdate to my first year of employment in May of 1978, I would have been eligible for the coveted 20-year award in 1998. That was presented to me that evening. I was honored. Since this was being retro-activated through the years, there were quite a few reps honored that night.

My name was called, and I remember to this day the sense of joy and happiness I felt as I walked up on the stage and was given my gift. It was a very nice ring, like the kind you get when graduating from college. I took a picture with both John Solheim and Doug Hawken. For the record, I also wanted to make it known that I wasn't sure how long my career with PING would go on, so at such large company gatherings, I took many photos with fellow reps. I really did appreciate the camaraderie with all of them and needed some memories.

It did not take long for me to be recognized again on the big stage—at our sales meeting in 2008—as I now had officially reached the 30th year milestone. I believe that there were only two of us who were honored with that prestigious recognition that night. When my name was announced by no other than Stacy, I knew she and all in attendance were very proud of me for all my years of devotion to the PING family. I was presented with a beautiful watch from EBEL with my name etched on the back. I was able to get a photo shot one more time with John and Doug. Sadly, it would be my last photo with them together. And sadly, this would be my last sales meeting.

51.

LOSING MY JOB
AFTER 28 YEARS

As we all remember, the great recession of 2007 to 2009 was a tough time for many Americans.

Some say between six and eight million workers lost their jobs due to the credit crisis, which seemed to overflow into all areas of life. I will never forget the day that I, too, lost my job.

It came about on a Monday in the second week of July 2009 in a parking lot of a Dunkin Doughnuts in Enfield, Connecticut, at about 10:30 am. I had just finished up sponsoring the Pro-Jr. event in Burlington, Vermont, the day before and was heading back home when I got a call on my cell phone from my regional manager at PING. He wanted to know if he could meet up with me as soon as possible, and I told him I had an appointment scheduled the next day in the Hartford, Connecticut, area at 1 p.m. He kindly asked if we could meet just off I-91 in Enfield to discuss a matter. To be honest, I had no idea what this meeting was going to be about, absolutely none.

We met at the designated area, and I was asked to sit in the car with my supervisor as he had set up a conference call with the home office. I found it odd. When the person on the other end was the human resources manager, I suddenly had this empty feeling in my stomach as I just felt there would be something said that I had never heard before in my lifetime. And sure, enough that came true. I was told, "As of this moment, you are no longer an employee of Karsten Mfg. Corp." I was 100% stunned and taken aback.

The recession had been taking its toll on PING, as they had been offering early retirement benefits to many long-standing employees. Many had taken the deal. Others were also let go, as I was.

Being a privately owned family company also had its challenges in these difficult times, and they had to make these painful decisions. In my 28 years as a field representative for PING, the final ten as an employee, this was the first time that sales reps were part of the attrition program. The company had decided to let one rep per region go.

I was the one rep in the Northeast section of the country and my area would be the easiest to fill, so this made the most sense. For the record, I was not terminated by the company due to work performance. At that time, I was among the top sales performers in my region; it was due to financial constraints only. Either way, I was still feeling somewhat distraught.

As the gentleman was finishing his conversation with us, I heard him say that a package would arrive for me the next day from FEDEX. A lot of information would be contained, and I would have to sort through it all.

The call ended, and I said my goodbyes to my former regional manager as our business relationship was now over, too.

As I got back into my Chevy Suburban, I drove to see my first account of the day: Howie Friday, the head pro at Tumble Brook Country Club, a charming 27-hole private club in Bloomfield, a lovely affluent suburb of Hartford. He would be the first pro who I told about my situation. In subsequent weeks, I would tell all my accounts that I was no longer their PING rep. Many of them did not believe the news.

As I walked back to my car after my visit with Howie, I also was thinking for the first time in 28 years of my life (and at that time I was only 50) that I no longer had the job I was so fortunate enough to have. All those years representing one of the most outstanding golf companies in the world...that chapter in my life had just ended...or had it?

The very next day, while at my Clifton Park home, the FEDEX package arrived before noon. There was a lot of information and a few checks and commissions on past orders and future orders not yet shipped. There was also a fascinating non-disclosure agreement, maybe 15 pages long. I didn't read all of it at that time. The letter said that I would get a severance check from the company. PING would send me a dollar value for every year of service I had in the company (31 years). I would get that check only after I sent in the document. It was classy on PING's part to send me this money. They didn't have to do this, but as I have said countless times, the Solheim-led PING company is a very classy organization. First-class all the way.

This money would indeed be beneficial to me, as my world was being turned upside down. There was also some mention in the package about health insurance that I could access through the federal government, COBRA. I remember that it cost me something like $300 a month, a low figure as then-President Obama had worked out with Congress that this cost would be attainable for millions of Americans (like me) recently displaced from the workforce. After July ended and when new figures were released, it was revealed that 270,000 individuals lost their jobs that month and that this was the lowest monthly number of casualties in 18 months. Just imagine the carnage that had taken place in that period.

After being out of the workforce for less than 24 hours, I had two hard things that I needed to do as fast as I could.

I had to tell my mother, Elayne, and my brother, Marc, the lousy news. Both had relied on my financial support. Mom was over, as usual, helping out for the day, getting things sorted out like she always did. I don't remember the words I said to her. I just told her that I am no longer the PING rep, letting her know that my job was eliminated due to the current economic crisis. I do recall her reaction as I saw her trembling for the first time in a long time when I passed on the bad news.

"I just want you to know there is nothing to worry about. We are all going to be just fine," I said. Then, I told her about the severance package the company had agreed to pay me, along with the commission checks that had just come in. She quickly got her emotions back under control, and I knew she was comforted a little bit with the news of that check coming my way.

She was still upset about what happened to me. I told her that I, too, was still upset and that I was going to protest this decision and see if I could get my job back. Next, I had to tell my brother the news.

Marc was back in school, re-dedicating his life to his education since his short stint as a professional golfer did not work out. He had made a significant personal decision that he wanted to be an engineer. That required more schooling. I had helped him out financially for his first go-around with college, but he was going on his own this time with student loans. When I gave the bad news to him, he was very emotional, which surprised me a little. He was defending me and wondering why in the world would PING let someone like me go. Over the years, Marc had met many of my fellow PING rep colleagues, and Marc knew I outworked all of them. He then said something that has resonated with me to this day.

"How could they let you go? You are the best rep by far for them. You are the last PING man to do this for them and do everything for them as long as you have worked for them."

I calmed him down and told him about the severance package. He started to relax. I said that I would not just accept this news and was going to fight to get my job back. The company had just sent me my flight information and ticket for the company's annual sales meeting in mid-August in Arizona, so I planned to go to Arizona and attempt to meet face-to-face with John Solheim to see if I could salvage my job.

It was Thursday, only two days after I was laid off. I was on the phone, calling all my top accounts and telling them what just happened to me. Everyone I spoke to was distraught at the news and really couldn't make any sense of it. Many asked if there was anything they could do, and I just said that it would be totally up to them if they wanted to voice their opinion. By the end of Friday, I had called most of my top-tier accounts. I was exhausted and pleased with myself because I had so many golf pros on my side in protesting this decision. I guess if you have something to fight for, you just naturally do something.

I also forgot to mention that on the very next day after I got the news about my job, I had a golf game that had been set up for a few weeks with Steve Sormanti of Nike and Derek Travers of Callaway at Albany Country Club.

It was a beautiful July morning. I believe it was around the time that we were all hitting our approach shots into the first green that I gave them all the bad news. They all looked at me as if I was crazy. They couldn't even comprehend that ever happening to me since they all had followed my PING career and knew how devoted a worker I had been over the years.

We were all out to play the great game we all love, so I wasn't going to let some lousy news spoil a nice day on the links. They were amazed at how I could continue to play, but they all knew I would be okay one way or the other. They knew who I was and what I was capable of doing. I explained that I would be reaching out to all my top accounts in the next few days, alerting them all to the news. I was going to fight hard to save my job.

I believe it was on Sunday that I visited one of my best friends, Dave Lupo. We went to his sister-in-law's home because she was having a garage sale. Dave was a long-time sales rep in the golf industry and represented numerous top brands throughout the years, including Cobra, Taylor Made, and Ashworth. I was playing golf with Dave five years ago when he was working as an independent rep and was told that his job was being discontinued during our round.

I told Dave what had just happened to me. We were talking about my options. I needed to hear some thoughts from my friends and get advice on what to do next. I was in a transitional period of my life and had some time to reflect. The only thing I knew for sure was that I had no accounts to see or no item to sell. That, for now, was over.

By the end of July, I was getting copies of letters and emails that had been sent to the company from at least two dozen of my accounts explaining their disappointment in my job being eliminated. The letters were very touching. For the first time, I sensed that if I didn't get my job back (and the odds were very poor), I could become an independent golf rep.

It was the early part of August, I had used the ticket the company had bought for me, and was in Arizona. I stayed with my brother Marc at the Tempe home that we all had purchased only two years earlier as a place for him to live while attending ASU and for me and Mom to stay when we visited Arizona. Marc continues to live there to this day. I reached out to John Solheim's office and left a message with the secretary that I was in town and wanted to meet him in person. The second night I was in town, Marc and I decided to see an Arizona Diamondback baseball game. Sometime in the first few innings of the game, I got a call on my cell from John. I told him I was at the game, and he agreed to reach me the next day.

I believe it was late morning when he called me. I was standing in the living room and was just trying to figure out why my job was suddenly taken from me after 28 years. I could sense that John struggled with his words. It is never easy to have these conversations, which is most likely why we did not meet in person.

I remember telling John, "You know John, I always thought I could control my destiny" (mostly meaning my time with the company). In this case, I was not.

John replied, "Stuart, you still can do that," or something along those lines. I really did not know what he meant at that specific time, but I did figure it out a few weeks later. I remember John telling me that we would always be friends and to stay in touch. Right then and there, it was officially over. My **PING** career was now a thing of the past.

52.
DECIDING ON THE PATH FORWARD

Now that I reflect on that day in August of 2009 when I realized that my attempt to keep my sales position with my former company failed, I realize that I pretty much immediately put in motion plans for a new path forward. I brought the program book from the 2009 PGA Merchandise Show to Arizona. It had all the major golf companies' information, which I could use to plot my next moves. My plan involved making a list with categories at the top of at least six to eight categories of golf products from golf bags to accessories to apparel. Then I would put down the companies underneath each category. The goal or intent was to try to find some companies within this framework that did not have anyone representing them. I knew who all the reps were anyway, and I just avoided every company with an existing sales representative.

All those years of paying attention to segments other than hard goods were about to pay off for me. Within the first day of this exercise, I already had four to six companies that fit this description. The next day, I began to make some phone calls to see if I could find some companies to represent as an independent sales rep.

I still had a few days left on my trip before my flight home to New York. I used them wisely, trying to secure some new lines so I could potentially go out and sell for the fall run, which would begin in early September. The first company that I called up was CMC, which was based in nearby Scottsdale, and from the listing in the PGA show directory had Bob Burg in charge of sales. I had met Bob for the first time in the early 1990s when he was associated with ex-PGA Tour player Danny Edwards in helping to launch Royal Grip. He left the company after its sale in 1997. The first time I reconnected with Bob was when I approached him about the CMC line in my upstate New York territory. Bob knew exactly who I was and told me he was disappointed to hear the news of my predicament but quickly said that I was hired to be his new rep in New York. He told me the company had a current rep that covered central and western New York and that I could have the northeastern New York section. This was great as that is where I lived, and I could efficiently service these accounts. CMC was a full-service accessories company that made repair tools, hat clips, golf towels, and a myriad of golf-related products that were all customized. The only companies I knew that were like them were Miller Golf out of Randolph, Massachusetts, and Golf Design out of California. I just knew that this brand would be very popular for me and my accounts, especially for events.

The next company I called was Town Talk, which makes headwear. They are based in Louisville, Kentucky, and have been in the business since 1919. I spoke to the company president, Joel Gary, and mentioned my situation. He told me he would look at the map and do his best to fit me into an area that was not currently being serviced. As it turned out, I was also able to handle the northeastern New York section with Vermont, western Massachusetts, and the northern part of Connecticut.

The next company I reached out to was Straight Down Clothing, a relatively unknown brand that came out of San Luis Obispo, California. Quite honestly, I had never heard of this place before. I spoke to the sales manager in Florida, and he told me the company was quite interested in hiring me, but he just needed me to talk to one other inside sales manager. I recall owning an outerwear item from this company that I'd bought a few years prior, and I thought the item was very nice. I also talked to the national sales manager on the phone.

I shared the information that when I was with PING and we were selling apparel, I would consistently rank in the top ten in sales. She seemed to like that, and I was hired to be their new sales rep for portions of upstate New York, Vermont, western Massachusetts, and Connecticut. In less than one day, I already had three companies to sell for. The creation of Stuart Miller Golf Sales LLC was a success. I couldn't be more excited.

I told my brother, Marc, what was happening with these new companies. He wasn't the least surprised, as he knew I would be a big asset for anyone who hired me. Mom was very excited for me and was a little surprised how fast things could work out in this industry.

As soon as I got home to Clifton Park, I reached out to Peter Tavares, the Director of Golf at nearby Saratoga National Golf Club. Peter was the gentleman who stepped in at this facility when David Nevatt left in 2003 to help create another facility in the Philadelphia area. I wanted to have lunch with him and pick his brain. We ended up having lunch out on the veranda of the clubhouse, as it was a spectacular late summer day in Saratoga Springs. Peter had been one of the many golf pros who'd sent in a letter to my former company expressing his concern on the decision. He was also someone I had gained a lot of trust in over the years, and I needed to hear his thoughts on things.

I told Peter I was deciding to become an independent golf rep and said to him that three companies had already hired me to represent their brands. I explained who they were to him as well. I just remember him telling me that since I already had the contacts in place, switching over should be an easy transition. He also said that since I had been such an excellent partner for the section being a long-time sponsor, that would undoubtedly help me ease into this new role. I also told Peter that I was in contact with a few smaller companies about being their rep. As I had the potential to have around four to six different lines to sell right off the bat, Peter told me I should give it a shot and that I would need to meet up with them during my fall run to show them my product lineup. That lunch helped solidify my decision to embark on a new career.

53.

THE FALL RUN
BEGINS AGAIN

By the second week of September 2009, I was ready to get back on the road. This would be my first ever "fall run" as an independent golf sales representative but would be my 28th overall. I had made several appointments to see my accounts in the "North Country" as I liked to call them (golf courses located at the top of New York State). I would see roughly a dozen accounts that were scattered from Plattsburgh to Massena. I was still driving my Chevy Suburban, which had plenty of room for me to bring along my rolling rack and sample clothing from my new Straight Down line and all my hat samples from Town Talk and items from CMC.

As I was heading up Interstate 87, better known as the Northway, to see my very first account at the North Country Golf Club in Rouses Point just a few miles north of Plattsburgh, I was filled with anxiety as I was not sure what was going to happen on the very first day of my brand-new job. Looking back at this moment now, a lot of things happened to me in those eight weeks after losing my job of 28 years. It is hard to imagine how far I had come and how I had metamorphosed from selling one company to many. Honestly, I couldn't be prouder of myself for this period because it was a defining time in my life and eventually would show my real character as a person and as a sales representative. I was going to find out if I could genuinely be a proficient salesperson.

I can tell you this with no hesitation. I was prepared and ready to go. I had all the catalogs I needed and most of my samples. I figured I was brand-new at this, and none of my accounts would expect perfect presentations. The first pro I met up with gave me an order of 36 shirts from Straight Down, which I did not expect, but I was on the board with this line. I sold other items as well, so I was on my way.

The second stop was Malone Golf Club. I had about an hour's drive to get there. The head pro there was Derek Sprague, and he was a very loyal club pro, so trying to break into his shop with my new companies would not be easy.

The entire process of writing this book has been based on moments that occurred in my life over the past four decades, and I have done the best I could to bring them to light on these pages. I am going to try to illuminate the main events in the past ten years in my new role. I knew there would be many unique moments that would help define this new period in my life, but I had no idea one would happen on just my second sales call.

I was showing Derek and his longtime assistant pro John Dotte several neat items from CMC in a meeting room they had at the club when Derek said this:

"I could never imagine Stuart selling anything else in his life other than PING." As I was looking for the next product to show them, I replied, "How in the heck (I used another word) do you think I feel?" Laughter erupted from the two club pros. Talk about an ice breaker. That was it. I seriously believe the way I handled that very moment brought me a more significant opening order. I ended up with only an order from CMC for some repair tools, towels, and hat clips, but it was a start. Remember, the sales gauge was at zero right now, and I only had one way to go. That was straight up.

I spent my first night on the road in Potsdam, having dinner at the Potsdam Town & Country Club with the former head pro Mike Rosenquist, who was now the superintendent, and a few of the members who knew me. It was quite enjoyable to be hanging around such friendly people at a club that I had so much success with at my former company. I shared the new lines I was selling with all of them, and they all seemed to enjoy hearing what I had to say.

I remember having success with most of the golf pros I met up with on this three-day, two-night trip. I got home on a Friday afternoon and spent the next few days getting all the orders written and sent in. The following week was going to be a light week for me, as I had the president of Town Talk, Joel Gary, coming up to work with me for a few days.

I picked Joel up at the Albany airport on Tuesday, and we drove directly to see James Cronin, the owner of Cronin's Golf Resort. This was a family-owned resort in the town of Warrensburg, about a 45-minute drive north of me. It was a classic, old-school resort with about ten cabins for lodging on property and 18 exciting golf holes nestled near the Hudson River. James always supported me when I had PING and wasted no time helping me with my new career.

Joel helped me a great deal in presenting all the caps to James. I believe I left with an order of over 200 units, which was a very nice order indeed. I told James I would stop by later in the season to show off my other lines to him.

After we left Cronin's, we took a trip to Hiland Park Country Club a little south in Queensbury and presented our products to the Director of Golf Jim Jeffers. Jim and I went way back, as he was an assistant pro at The Edison Club several of the years I was a member there. He ended up winning the PING Stroke Championship I sponsored many years previous twice, with the first victory in 1994.

I was quickly learning the many styles of caps that my Town Talk line had. Jim was very helpful in picking out the several styles he liked. Then, we zeroed in on the actual colors and units to buy. Again, he gave me a whopper of an order of around 160 units. Town Talk had a unique discount program for any account: an order of over 144 units (12 dozen) would get a 10% discount on all items.

After two very successful appointments, we ended up going to have a late lunch. We went over more of the company's guidelines while Joel was with me. Afterwards, we stopped in to see my best former account Rick Wright, who had just accepted the head pro job at a brand-new golf course called Fairways of Halfmoon in Mechanicville.

Rick could not buy as much as the previous two visits since his pro shop was much smaller and he had to take it slow at first. He did order 72 caps and some other items. We were three for three on appointments for the day.

I dropped Joel off at the hotel for a little break. We would meet again for an early dinner. Joel was great, and I learned a great deal about my new hat line. I took him to the airport early the next day for his flight back home to Louisville.

54.
GETTING THE HANG OF THINGS...AGAIN

As the fall was finally approaching, I could sense the passing of the time with the weather slowly beginning to cool down. Fall was my favorite time of the year for many reasons. Football season was starting, both in college and the NFL, and this would be my escape from work on the weekends. The main reason I loved fall was the beginning of the end of another golf season. This also meant that it was time for me to go out on the road again for the next 14 weeks to write up business for next spring.

Everything was dissimilar this time around as I was selling something different for the first time in almost three decades. The only two constant factors were dealing with the same account base and selling. I loved to sell, and I loved my accounts. How in the world could I go wrong?

One of the very first things I did in my new role really paid off, and to this day, I am very proud of what I did and even more proud of the outcome. CMC discontinued some business products that I found to be very interesting and thought I could use them as a great public relations tool. I had met up earlier with a marketing friend who created my business card, and we took the same logo I used for the card and made a ball marker that would be put on all these items.

Let me briefly explain how the logo worked as this process would become second nature to me in the coming weeks. You would take your club logo or even your business logo, like in my case, and it would go on the marker disc that would go on a ball marker or hat clip. When you are out playing golf and you want to mark your ball, you would use this disc from your repair tool. I had my logo on all of them. I believe the price was $50 for the set, and I ordered ten of them. I planned to give them to my best former accounts.

When I saw Rick Wright a few weeks before to show my Town Talk hat line, I also presented Rick with these items. I set it up by saying, "Thanks, Rick, for all your support all those years with PING. I wanted to give you these items as a small gesture of my appreciation and welcome you to one of the new companies I represent, CMC." The account holder would always be very thankful for the items, and it always got me in the door. You had to spend a little bit of money to make money. I always believed in that, and even more so with my new business.

I also remember talking to some of my accounts about seeing them a little later in the fall. I wasn't quite sure how they would react to my new product lineup. One, in particular, said, "Don't worry about us. Just show up and let us know what you are selling. We will figure it out from there." In other words, they were very nice to me. If I read them right, they were saying just show up and we will take care of you. That pretty much is what happened to me that very first fall run.

I remember going up to Vermont in my third and fourth weeks, seeing about ten accounts each week. I wasn't doing a lot of business there, but it was an excellent opportunity to visit my loyal pro shops and see what orders we could write. While working in that area, I also got a call from the sales manager from Straight Down. He wanted to meet with me in Syracuse shortly to see some accounts. This individual was new to the company and living in southern Florida. Part of his new responsibility was building a new sales force on the eastern seaboard.

I remember driving over to Syracuse and getting off the exit. I met him right near the toll area. The plan was to just go in my car for the two days we were working together. Then, he would drive over to Rochester to work in that area on his own. So, the Syracuse area was the furthest west I would drive (at that time) in New York state for this line. Despite this happening over ten years ago, I believe we met up with three or four accounts that first day.

We visited Bellevue, Drumlins, and Cavalry Club that first day and Lake Shore Country Club the next morning. All these clubs were great private clubs; only Drumlins was a high-end daily fee course. They were all perfect facilities for this line, as it was grouped in the premium category right along with industry heavyweights

Peter Millar, Donald Ross, Foot-Joy, and Fairway & Greene. All the pros we met up that day gave me good-sized orders.

As a close observer of all these companies while I was doing my former job, I knew the industry trends better than others. It was kind of a hobby for me to know these sorts of things. I was always a quick learner.

I had to be responsible for selling so many lines. I would soon learn that having a wide variety of products to sell could be used as an asset and the odds were very good that someone was going to require something.

After our first day on the road together, we went to Rico's Restaurant, a wonderful Italian landmark that had been in business for several years. I had the shrimp scampi, and it was excellent. We also discussed the events that'd occurred during the day and some strategies for moving forward. We would see one more account in the morning, and that pro also gave me a spring 2010 order.

The Straight Down company was founded in 1987 and, for years, was known as a West Coast company trying to move east. It was started as a volleyball clothing company, as the words "straight down" are used to describe spiking the volleyball. I have even heard those words during Volleyball matches on TV. It was mainly a line of fleece items that would be used as outerwear or layering pieces. The product was exceptionally constructed and had a beautiful hand finish to it. Men's styles made up most of the line, but there was a good representation of women's styles. There were also some polos and pants, but outerwear was their niche, and that was what I was going to push first.

All my life, I was a clothing man and loved to buy only the finest items, from cashmere to merino wool during my PING clothing selling days. I even once bought a Bobby Jones shirt from a PGA Tour event I attended in California in 2000 that cost me $125 with tax. I was not afraid to buy expensive goods. The way I saw it was that those items I purchased years ago are still in my closet and faring very well to this day. You get what you pay for. I could sense that Straight Down would be a good line for me. I just needed some time to cultivate it in my new territory.

I said goodbye to my new sales manager as he was on his way to cover the Rochester, New York, area, which would also become part of my territory in a very short time. I could sense he was very pleased with my performance and was glad to have me on the Straight Down team. He also mentioned that the founder and owner of the company would like for me to come to their California headquarters in mid-November to help with their annual golf event and check out the company's facility. I told him I would be there. That would be it as far as seeing sales managers on the road for the rest of my fall run. I was on my own, but that was fine with me.

The rest of the country was slowly starting to bounce back from the financial meltdown a few years earlier, but it would still require several more years to fully get back to normal. At that time, the golf industry was still doing well. I was so fortunate to still be an active part of it.

55.

MY FIRST SUMMER: NO MORE DEMO DAYS

The rest of my fall run in 2009 went very quickly. I was only going to those accounts with whom I had an excellent relationship and had done profitable business. One of the first things I did before my fall run was make a list of such accounts in each of my four states. I just did the math on how many I could see in a day, a week, a month. I ended up with about 120 potential accounts to see.

I stuck to my routine, trying to see at least three accounts per day or 12 a week for this mission's 12-week grind. In retrospect, I would have to say I had a solid "first" fall run as an independent sales rep. I was getting that taste of victory again, albeit slowly. Don't forget, I was starting at the bottom. The only place to go was up.

I was calling this my "phoenix" moment, as I genuinely climbed from the ashes with my sales career and took it to new heights. But it, for sure, would not be a comfortable ride as there were many challenges in the coming years.

The main early challenge for me was attempting to sell obscure brands, compared to just one brand that most accounts knew well. Having golf brands that were not that well known in my area was not an easy undertaking. Most reps who came from an in-house position like I did have a difficult time in the transitional period. For me, that was not going to be an option. I knew what I was doing, but more importantly, I had a plan (call it a five-year plan) as I knew this process would take some time.

All I have to say about that is this catchphrase that I have used a lot in my life as a golf rep: "People buy from people." It is as simple as that. In other words, relationships are the key to success in any enterprise, and great relationships are the key to more significant sales and higher income.

Everything was good on the home front. Mother was still working with her lawyer on the case she had against the government for my dad's untimely death and doing her monthly tinnitus meetings. Marc was doing well at ASU; he was successfully working on a master's degree in electrical engineering. He was taking courses that would make him an invaluable employee one day.

However, my personal life was again put on hold as doing this new job required a lot of my time and focus. I was pouring all my energy into it. I am pretty sure I was still upset with being let go from my former company after all those years, but I used that as motivation to show everyone that I could still do it. I am sure that would be the case for anybody who experienced what I went through.

As I mentioned earlier, I was invited to come to Straight Down's event in mid-November. This region was tough to travel to, so for convenience I booked a flight to Phoenix. On my way back, I stopped there to see my brother Marc for a few days. I arrived in San Luis Obispo (or SLO as the locals like to call it) Thursday.

When I arrived at the hotel, there was a small reception for us in the lounge area. I was wearing a dress shirt and sports jacket since I was not sure of the dress code. The first person to greet me was a fellow sales rep, Ricky Bryner, based in Richmond, Virginia. The first thing he did was make fun of my attire, saying, "Stu, you are in SLO, where everything is casual. Let me buy you a beer." I accepted, and a pleasant evening was underway. I liked Ricky right on the spot. I would also see my sales manager, and he would introduce me to several Straight Down reps from California.

The next day I remember helping with the merchandise tent the company had set up at the host club, San Luis Obispo Country Club. It was a pro-am event where a professional would play with a scratch golfer in a best-ball event for two days. It had a purse of over $100,000, so it was a big event. A lot of well-known PGA Tour players were competing, including golf commentator Gary McCord as well as Steve Pate and Tom Lehman. I also ran into my long-time friend and former classmate Dan Forsman, a Tour veteran from nearby Provo, Utah.

I remember having breakfast with Dan and his partner and telling them about my departure from PING. After talking with him for just a short time about my new career, Dan was convinced that I was on my way with my new adventure. I also had a chance to meet up with the owner of my new premier clothing company. He was glad to have me on his team and appreciated me making the long voyage to be at the event. After a few days of watching some golf and meeting many of the employees at the main plant, I was on my way to Phoenix to see Marc for a few days before heading home to New York.

After the holidays, a new year was now upon us, as well as a new decade. I would call this the "Decade of New Beginnings," as that is precisely what I was going through. For the next ten years, there were many companies I would represent and then with no reason or rhyme would not. Being an independent rep was like being in the wild, wild west as sometimes the only known factor was the unknown.

It was late January, and I was about to go to my first ever PGA Merchandise Show as an independent rep. This would be my 26th overall show. I was a bit nervous due to my new career path. I did not know what might happen. Before I stepped into the sprawling Orlando Convention center, I prayed to God, asking him to allow me to do my best job and have a successful show. I was also sporting a new look, as I grew a beard during mid-December and decided to take it with me to the show. It would be the third time in my career that I had a beard, but the first time I took it to the show.

I stayed at one of the hotels on the main road and had one of the buses pick me up in the morning to take me to the center. Once I walked the few hundred feet to get to the main door of entry into the actual show floor, guess who was the very first person I saw as the door swung open? It was John Solheim. I had not kept in touch with him since my departure, but I am sure he knew I would stay in this industry as it was him who said, "You can still control your destiny." I was not sure what that meant but had a feeling I would find out soon.

Just mentioning that I was a PING hard goods rep for 28 years helped me find new jobs in this industry. In the future, it would also allow me exposure to clubs that I might not be in otherwise. In other words, it was all good, and I took running into John as a good omen and nothing more. We said our quick hellos and wished each other good luck for the three-day show.

During the show, I spent most of my time at the Monterey Club apparel booth and often made the five-minute walk to get to Straight Down. I had over 20 appointments in all and was very busy for the first two days.

After a successful show, I realized that my commissions from the show would easily pay for my expenses. I caught an early flight home on Saturday and was back in New York in the early afternoon. I called Mom and told her of my success at the show.

My birthday came in February. I was now 51 years old and felt very good. I was a member of the local gym, going a lot in the winter months, which were my downtime. Ever since turning 40, I had been going to the gym to keep in shape for my job. Driving was always the most challenging part, and staying in shape helped me stay alert and make it through some grinding times.

As part of being a new independent sales rep, I chose to be in what we called the "soft goods" area of the market instead of the "hard goods" part I had made my entire career in at my former company. As a tribute to PING, I would never enter that market segment again; those days ended when my days with PING ended. I would only do soft goods. To celebrate this moment, I went to the liquor store and bought three bottles of fine champagne. Since I was no longer making hard good sales anymore, it also meant no more demo days, and I had to celebrate that. I never dreaded demo days, but I was happy that I no longer had to deal with them. When I got to mid-May, I would open the first bottle and make a toast to the 20 demo days that I did not have to do this past month. I am not much of a drinker, so I only had a glass or two and poured the rest down the kitchen sink.

I thought I would get only one chance to do this ritual, but I ended up doing this two more times in mid-June and again in mid-July. I was delighted with my new role in the golf industry.

56.
NEW LINES TO SELL

The spring of 2010 would be my first ever as an independent salesman. During my winter downtime, I was trying to figure out a game plan on how I would schedule my account visits. It was not a big deal, as everything was a learning curve for me, which was perfectly fine. I was genuinely excited to be doing this new venture. Now that I look back on it, there were several reps whom I have known for years that have gone from working for a big well-known golf company to delving into the independent world and carrying several companies. They all went on to have productive careers, and many are still active, with a few retiring in the last few years.

Now that I was a soft goods rep and didn't have to deal with demo days, which pretty much dominated my spring and early summer schedule, my emphasis was on seeing accounts for apparel sales. I also got started a little later, as I wanted to give all my accounts time to acclimate to the season opening. My focus was going to see those clubs to which I could show my Straight Down clothing line, with hopes of securing fleece orders for fall when the weather turned colder.

My new clothing line had a tremendous product offering of outerwear items, and that was going to be my focus early on. My goal was to sell the pro a sampling of their product, which would make the account want to buy a little more on the next order. I just looked over my account base for each state and selected accounts for the spring/early summer visit.

At that time, trying to sell apparel was always of paramount importance. Still, while I was with the account, I would always talk about all the other lines that I represented to make the pro/buyer fully aware of what I carried. These golf accounts were seeing dozens of sales reps all the time, and you had to instill in their memory what lines you carried. That is why I would put a sticker with my info on every catalog that I would give an account on a visit. When I was long gone, and they picked up the CMC catalog, they would see my name and call me first instead of the company. As I was an old-school rep, I always preferred my accounts to contact me with orders instead of calling the companies.

My sales manager from Straight Down also called me in the late summer and had some new exciting news for me. He told me that the company was so pleased with my performance that they wanted to extend my territory coverage by adding the Rochester and Buffalo markets. He wanted to come and work with me in early October to visit several accounts and present the new line. I was very excited about the news and a little nervous because I was going to places that I had never been before as a golf rep.

The very first we met up with was Oak Hill Country Club in Rochester, the same Oak Hill that I was a spectator at for both the 1989 U.S. Open and the 1995 Ryder Cup. We brought in two rolling racks of our product into the club's bowling alley area just down from the pro shop. I presented both the men's line and the women's line to long-time head pro Craig Harmon and his buyer. I must confess I was very nervous about the presentation, but I knew my sales manager was there to back me up.

This club had been only exclusively doing the ladies line with my new clothing brand. The pro was old school (now that sounds familiar) in that he was loyal to his vendors, and trying to break into the men's market would be a challenge. If you were in, you were in. It was hard to crack in; thus, no men's products there. That would be the case, but at least he let me show him the men's line anyway. At the end of the presentation, we did receive an excellent spring order for the women, which was most appreciated.

I believe we also meet up with the pros at Cobblestone Creek and Monroe Country Club, receiving spring orders from both accounts.

We traveled to a town called Weedsport and decided to stay there. In the morning, we crossed over to Buffalo, where we had a few appointments set up. We met with the pro at Niagara Falls C.C., John Boss. John gave me a terrific order, including around 36 polos. I can't remember who else we saw, but my manager was going to catch a flight to take him home, and I would stay one more night since I had a few more appointments the next day with brand-new accounts. These were, for certain, exciting new times for me.

I had a next step I was taking to prepare me for success in my new life as an independent salesman and especially to fast-track my Straight Down clothing line. Earlier I had gifted ten of my best accounts from my former company with CMC products to get me on board. Now, I was going to create the Stuart Miller Straight Down advisory staff program. The plan was to find outstanding young assistant golf professionals at very nice private clubs that were already placing Straight Down orders with me. I would try to get the assistant pro on board to help me promote the line and sell it. I would offer the new candidate two shirts and one fleece item, all crested with both the club logo and the Straight Down logo. The ultimate goal was to have this young assistant pro become a head pro, and hopefully, I would have an instant new customer with all my lines. I also extended this program to key buyers of clubs, as I also felt I needed to have this extra exposure at "key" clubs to help me promote and grow the brand.

I did this with the women's products buyer at Oak Hill as well as an outstanding young golf assistant pro at Monroe, also in the Rochester, New York, area. I would expand this program over time.

Here is a memo written many years ago by one of my current accounts, Glenn Carlson, who was an assistant pro at the time but is now the head pro at Torrington Country Club in Goshen, Connecticut, on the subject of the relationship between sales reps and assistant professionals:

THE IMPORTANCE OF THE RELATIONSHIP BE-TWEEN SALES REPS AND ASSISTANT PROFESSION-ALS: (written on March 19th, 2001)

Why do I feel relationships are important? For the assistant professional, I feel that getting to know the reps can only help you in your quest to become a head professional. Forming early relationships with reps can head to long term friendships and business contacts that can help you land your first job. It's the sales reps that you know and trust the most that you are going to want to sit down with first and seek guidance or help from before meeting all the others that follow. Sales reps are our link to the inside scoop; they provide valuable information of the section and surrounding areas. They know of job openings.

I also feel this relationship is important for the sales rep. For young assistants, making contacts is important; they create a sense of security or acceptance when reps pay a little attention to them. For older assistants (which Glenn was), I think the stakes are higher for the reps. We are looking for a trusting, respectful relationship, and we are making ties with the industry. We will be replacing the older pros, hence spending our money with you, the reps. I think meeting reps for a professional is like a job interview—that first impression can last a long time. The great reps make great first impressions and try to help the assistants as much as they can. Little things like gloves, balls, and hats go a long way with younger assistants.

Glenn relayed a bad experience with a sales rep, and I will give a quick summary of that. Glenn was working with the head pro, dealing with a clothing rep. The club was already committed to their previous purchase, so they could not place an order at that time. Glenn wanted to see if he could get some product to try out and wear in front of the membership to see what feedback he would get. The sales rep. refused to do so and made some negative comments to Glenn about not knowing the business, which made a poor impression on him. When Glenn did get that coveted head pro job a few years later, this salesperson came calling. Glenn remembered him and said he was not interested (for a long time).

When I became an independent sales rep, Glenn was one of my early supporters, which I appreciated. About that time, Glenn sent me this same memo to let me know why he chose to continue to do business with me after my PING days. I have kept this memo all these years as a constant reminder to myself to respect and pay attention to all the assistant professionals who are in my territory. In this group, there are many Glenn Carlson's (potential future customers).

57.
SOME INTERESTING TIMES

The next two years, 2011 to 2012, were exciting times. I picked up more lines and got more comfortable in my new role, and my sales continued to grow. I could feel myself getting more relaxed in what I was doing, which also improved results. Many things occurred during this time frame—all for the better.

I met a nice woman named Julie and started to date her during in the spring of 2011. I am not 100% sure how we met, but we seemed to get along quite well. She was about ten years younger than me, but that did not seem to be an issue. I remember when we went on our first date, I suddenly came down with a cold and was not feeling well. I did not reach out to her. Finally, after more than ten days, she called me to see what was up. This surprised me and pleased me as it meant she was interested in me.

We ended up going on our second date, and I found out that she'd recently split up with her boyfriend. I kept my distance after that as I certainly did not want to be part of any rebound relationship, as they rarely work out. I kept this as a fun relationship and would only see her every few weeks, because this was the perfect time to take things slow.

During this time, Mom was also learning more about our legal case against the government regarding my father's death, as her lawyer was pressing on with the matter. He said that we were doing well with our pursuit of justice, but we were still a few years away from knowing the outcome. The case was still being heard, and that was the most important issue.

Speaking of Mom, she was getting a little older now (she turned 76 in 2011), and since we were both watching our pennies, I thought it might be an excellent time for her to sell her home in Malta and take some of the profits to help us all out. She was okay with the idea of selling her place, but she had no idea where she was going to live. I did not say anything (knowing exactly where she would be living). I wanted to see what her reaction would be. I remember her saying, "Son, if I sell the house, where am I going to live?"

I then said, "Well, where do you think you want to live?"

Then I added, "You will be living with me, of course, Mom."

When I said that, I could just see the relief pouring out of her. She was so pleased to hear that. We were all getting a little older now. I was 52, and my younger brother Marc was 37. I believe the ultimate goal was to one day get Mom away from the cold, harsh winters in New York to Marc in Arizona. The main goal now was to get the house in order and prepare to sell it.

We had this conversation in 2012, and we ended up selling Mom's home in October of 2013. A vast industrial manufacturing complex was being erected only five minutes from our house. It was called GlobalFoundries, and the father of the family who bought Mom's house was coming to town to work there.

Bouncing back to my time with Julie, we ended up having a super time that summer, but her father tragically died of a heart attack, and she ended up getting back together with her ex-boyfriend. I did have a wonderful time dating Julie, and she rekindled my hope of one day meeting that special person after being a bachelor my entire adult life.

I have always lived by myself. This new situation would take some time to figure out. At the time, it was the best decision for all of us—and we certainly made the best of it.

Mom was officially no longer doing her tinnitus meetings, so she ended up working for me a little bit as a secretary. Hence, her workload was more manageable. One of the positives, of course, with this new living arrangement was the cooking. Mom was an excellent cook, and when I was home, she made all the meals for us.

As far as new product lines to sell, I did pick up a couple of interesting companies that were not mainstream corporations, and it made things interesting. The most important thing that happened in early 2012 was that I decided to buy a Show Van from the FootJoy rep becaue they were being treated to brand new Sprinter Vans, which were the latest craze. It was now time for me to drive around in a van that my customer could sit in and see all the products they may want to buy. It was a 2005 Chevy van, maroon in color (the van on the cover of this book). It had about 80,000 miles on the clock, but it was in great shape, and I got a great deal for it.

I went to a local welding shop and had him create a unique display system in my van using two older rolling racks. I had three rolling bars, allowing all my apparel to be displayed. The van was set up with a hard-acrylic floor installed over the carpet, and I would roll around on a stool. I had the front chair moved, and I would rotate it for the account to sit in. I would sell that way. It turned out to be a very effective way for me to sell going forward.

I reached out to my long-time friend Brent Kendall, the **PING** rep in Virginia, to see if he would be interested in buying my blue Chevy Suburban from me. It was a 2008 model, and I believe I still had two years of payments left on it. We reached an agreement that Brent would make the remaining payments on the vehicle, and it would be his. He flew up in July of 2012 to drive the truck home.

If I were to add up all the product lines I was now carrying, it would be close to 20 (with many tiny ones in this mix). One of my sales mates at my former company also went on to be an independent salesman. He told me, "Remember, you are not married to any of these companies, and you are free to leave them anytime you wish." I remember him saying this years ago, and I would heed this advice several times in the upcoming years. The other crucial piece of advice that I got from an independent sales rep was that "discretion is your best friend," meaning you do not need to tell the companies you are representing any of the other lines that you are carrying. The companies, mostly small, are fortunate to have you out on the front lines talking up their products and selling them. You must remember the entire selling process starts with us, the sales reps. We are the ones that get things started.

58.

MY FIRST EVER MERCHANDISE TENT EXPERIENCE

As I reflect on the year 2013, I would have to say this was my break-out year as an independent sales rep. Many good things were happening.

This PGA Show was my fourth now in my new job, and boy, was it a doozy. During December of the previous year, I had heard through golf circles that the OGIO golf bag company was looking for a new sales rep in the upstate New York territory only. I found a contact person, dialed the number up at their Utah headquarters, and put my name in the mix for consideration. A few days later, a gentleman called me to do an interview over the telephone. I told him of my 28 years' experience in this area and how I had sold many golf bags during this period. I told him about the other lines I was currently carrying and that I did not have a bag line presently and would love to have one. I did not hear anything for about a week. I thought this could be a real winner and momentum shifter for me, so I didn't want to squander the opportunity. I called this person back again and said that I really would like to represent the brand.

"What do you all say?" is what I asked him. Without much hesitation, I was hired right then. I was so pleased because I knew I could sell some golf bags.

There was also a new company that I became involved with called Nexbelt. This was a belt that had a ratchet fastening system instead of a traditional buckle. It was a game-changer, for sure. I remember getting my sample sent to me, and I did not open the FEDEX box for a few weeks. I had attempted to sell some belt lines before with no success, so I wasn't motivated. It was mid-July, and temperatures outside were quite hot, so I was feeling a little sluggish. One week later, I finally opened the box and took the belt out, and the first thing I said was, "This could work," reciting the same words that Tom Hanks said in the movie *Castaway* when part of a lavatory washed ashore on his island, giving him a sail to escape with. I fiddled around with it for a few minutes, and I knew we had something special.

As I headed to the 2013 Merchandise Show, I was going to be representing the following brands: Straight Down, OGIO, Nexbelt, Town Talk, CMC, Sunfish headcovers, and a few other small brands, including Art and Stone, a marble company. I was starting to build a superior nucleus of companies with a lot of variety and name recognition. This could help me continue to move forward in establishing my brand during this period.

I didn't know what I would wear to the show, as I would have to share booth space with both Straight Down and OGIO. Both companies were expecting us reps to be busy with as many appointments as possible. Although I was brand-new with OGIO, I was able to get six confirmed appointments, and I had around 12 with Straight Down. That was a number that could work. To solve the apparel dilemma, I just wore a dress shirt, sports jacket, and tie for the show's three days. I was neutral as far as logos in each booth, which worked out perfectly.

The show was a great success for me, and I was delighted. I also met up with my longtime friend and PING rep Lee McCormick, who invited me to have lunch with him. It was great to see him for the first time in a few years, and we got caught up on a lot during our time together. Lee is one of the "Elite 4" reps with whom I stay in touch, along with Jeff Beauregard, Brent Kendall, and Tim Reardon.

I got back to New York and was there for only a few days, because I decided to travel to Arizona to stay with Marc for a week and attend the Waste Management Phoenix Open on the PGA Tour. I went on the first day of the tournament and hung out for the day with a few friends, including Derek Travers. Derek had a similar issue with Callaway just a few years after my dilemma, as his job in upstate New York was going to be eliminated. Still, he was offered the Arizona territory, which he took.

It was great to hang out with him for the day. We had a great time. How could you not have a great time when you are in a place in early February wearing shorts and a polo with the temperatures hovering in the mid-70s and an abundant supply of sunshine? I believe we were among over 100,000 spectators who watched the best players perform.

I also returned to the PING campus for the first time since my departure in July 2009. I had it all arranged for me to come and see quite a few people so I could get through security protocols. I also had lunch with a few of the marketing folks while there.

I remember when I was in the employee parking lot getting ready to leave, I saw a young John K. Solheim, John's son and potential chairman-in-waiting, arriving. He was about 20 yards away, parking his car when I heard, "Is that Stuart Miller?" It is just so lovely when you are remembered.

I shouted back, "Is that you, John K.?" We shook hands, and that is when I said, "What kind of car is that?"

John was so proud of his Tesla. I had not heard of them much, as they were a California company and hadn't gotten much exposure yet on the East Coast. We chatted for a few minutes, I got him up to date on my independent rep news, and that was that.

I was soon back in New York again, dealing with the cold winters and occasional snowstorms. I got some winter things done in preparation for the new season, but I also had one more trip to make to break up the winter break.

My long-time friend Mike Rosenquist from Potsdam, New York, invited me to come and visit him at his new winter home in the Biloxi, Mississippi, area. It was the third week in March, and the weather there was starting to warm up. Mike was a member of one of the clubs in the area, and we played golf every other day for the eight days I was visiting. We also went one day to see the Senior Tour players play.

This was my 44th official professional golf event as a spectator and my 49th overall Tour event attended. We walked the course and saw a lot of action that day, including watching Fred Couples play his last few holes. It is always a fun day when you are watching the game's best go at it.

While I was at home getting ready for the start of another golf season in the Northeast, I also got some great news: My marble company, Art and Stone, was authorized to be in the large merchandise tent at that summer's PGA Championship at Oak Hill Country Club. The owner of the company, who would usually attend, told me I would get my full 10% commission on the entire invoice of the product sold during the event, but I had to be at the event site for the week handling all the prep work, and I had to pay my travel expenses.

I booked a room at the hotel that I had been staying at in Rochester as soon as I could for the week to get a better rate. The event was not going to be until August 5-11, so I still had things to do in my area.

Another interesting thing happened to me during the late stages of the winter break, just before the final snow covering melted and green pastures appeared. I got a call from my new boss at OGIO, the national sales manager, asking me about my territory. I told him that since it was still only the end of March and snow was still present, I had not yet gotten on the road to see accounts because they were not even open yet. Only one week passed, and I again got a phone call from this gentleman asking me if there were developments with sales in my territory. That is when I had "the talk" with him.

I asked my new supervisor very politely and professionally not to call me again regarding sales in my brand-new territory for the foreseeable future. I told him that he hired me to create new sales and opportunities for his brand in my area, so he needed to allow me to do that. I said that it will take some time, and you will have to be patient and let me make it happen. He never called me again. He allowed me to do my thing, which is what I did. I was opening new accounts and selling products to those established accounts. Things were happening. It was all good, as they say. I emphasized OGIO, Nexbelt, and CMC, but I also gave equal presentation time to my other big line—Straight Down.

Also in 2013, I decided to forge a sponsor relationship with most of my sections. I started in early May by sponsoring a Pro-Asst. tournament in the Central New York region. I sponsored a Northeast New York Classic Series event in July and two other events that took place in the fall.

Mother was also busy at her home, getting everything ready for a potential buyer. We officially put the house on the market in June.

Before I knew it, the PGA Championship week was upon me. I left for Rochester on a Tuesday to get into the tent area on Wednesday and get my booth area all prepared.

I had been in these super-sized merchandise tents before when attending past major tournaments like the U.S. Open and Ryder Cup but had never worked as a vendor before. All the vendors on site met with the PGA people on Wednesday to go over the rules, regulations, and requirements we had to uphold for the right and privilege of selling our wares in the tent.

I had a reasonably small display area at the far end of the main tent, which was fine. It was also close to one of the tent's final staging areas, where customers could check out. I was in a place best described as the accessories area, as I was surrounded by vendors selling golf towels, golf repair tools, Tervis tumblers, and logoed golf balls. I was responsible for ensuring that my Art and Stone area was fully stocked with coasters (with a retail price of $10) and coaster sets in a custom box (retailing for $40), and magnets ($5). That year's brand-new product was a Christmas ornament, which also sold for $5. I was given space on the slat wall area for my magnets.

Each vendor also had a reserved spot outside of the tent in a staging area, which would house all our inventory. Each day, you would go back there to grab more items to fill up your space as necessary. All the vendors were doing this—especially the hat vendors and the apparel vendors since they were the most popular sellers. The tent was a selling machine. I had never seen anything like it. Fans were continually flocking into the tent to grab as many souvenirs as they could.

I did find that from time to time I could escape and wander onto the course to see some action or grab a bite to eat. It was, for sure, a long day since we would arrive at a particular parking lot, get shuttled to the course, and be in the tent from 8 a.m. to 5 p.m. every day.

My boss at Art and Stone told me that by the end of the second day, 75% of the inventory should be gone, and by the end of Saturday, it should all be sold. We could scan barcodes every few hours to see how our sales were going. My product was selling, but not as fast as predicted. I did notice the ornaments were not getting any action.

After the first day, I went to a Michael's craft shop at one of the local malls while grabbing some dinner and bought a display that was meant for hanging jewelry. I made it so I could hang some ornaments on the display. I put about six such ornaments on display, and when potential customers were looking at the more popular coasters, I would point out the ornaments. It helped me sell them faster.

I also remember running into a few celebrities in the tent. On Saturday, Colin Montgomerie was looking at some items on the slat wall when I was filling up the magnet board. I started to talk with him. He had just become eligible to play on the Senior PGA Tour, and I complimented him on his fine play since he had made the top ten in his first three starts. He thanked me for noticing his fine play and asked me what products I was representing. I showed him my booth area, and he walked away with one of the coaster sets that had the PGA logo on all the coasters. That made my day, for sure.

I was hoping to have all my products sold out by Saturday so I could go home on Sunday, but that was not the case. I spent Sunday there, occasionally seeing some golf but mostly watching it on TV. Jason Duffner would go on to win his first major, just edging out veteran Jim Furyk.

The good news was that I had very little product left after Sunday, and there was going to be a special sale for all the staff of the event, who could come on Monday and buy the rest of the product at cost. The person in charge of the vendors told me I could leave Sunday afternoon and did not need to be there on Monday as he would make sure my product was safe and would sell out. I drove home later Sunday and was home around 8 p.m. I was exhausted.

The listing of Mom's home was generating plenty of interest, and a few weeks after the PGA, we got a firm offer on the home from people who wanted to move in as fast as possible. We officially closed on the house in early October, and Mom moved in with me at that time. I was super busy with the fall run, but I made sure to only be gone two nights a week during the first month so we could figure things out with a new living arrangement, which we did. It was great to have Mom at my home. It was a significant change for sure, but it was the right thing to do at that time.

This was my fifth fall run as an independent rep and 31st overall. Having my van for the first time made for a great selling experience, and I am confident my spring orders were the best ever. It was now time to reflect on another successful season and enjoy the holiday season that was upon us. It would be our first Christmas together at my home.

59.
BUILDING A BRAND FROM SCRATCH

I was getting ready to start the 2014 golf season, which would be my fifth season as an independent salesperson. Common sense would be for me to establish my brand (company) Stuart Miller Golf Sales first. But I want to build the "core companies" of my sales portfolio while trying to distinguish myself against my competitors. What plan could I concoct that would lead me to success?

The very first step for this project was to secure the right companies to represent. There is a lot of volatility, and many factors play into these decisions. After I started selling as an independent rep in the fall of 2009, I knew that golf pros would be buying my products due mostly to my credibility and the relationships that we had built up over the years. The only unknown factor was how the product would be perceived by the members. I was only concerned at that time about getting the product in the door. The one thing that I could control in this business setting was how many items sold on that very first order. The last thing I needed was someone to order way too much and have it not sell. I purposely monitored how much was coming in on that first order. I wanted it to be successful and sell out so that it would be counted as a win in the account's eyes, and thus, a re-order would be plausible. At the same time, I was not putting any extra pressure on the buyer, and they always appreciated this.

In the early years, I also picked up an accessory line called Gregory Paul and an outdoor rainwear company called Sunderland of Scotland. The accessory line was exclusively duffel bags that were great for events. I would usually sell at least 100 at a time, and retailing at $80 each, my commission on them was always very nice. The Sunderland brand was quite interesting, as I found a niche with my customer base. This would be considered their rainwear company. Rainwear was dominated by Foot Joy and Zero Restriction, a unit of Fairway & Greene. I was able to coax many of my accounts into this line based on price, selection, and quality. The product was very nice. I worked for a pair of gentlemen from Birmingham, Alabama, who had licensed the corporate name from the United Kingdom. A typical wholesale order would be around 36 units or $1,500. When I started to make these sales regularly, they began to add up.

Here is the problem with companies like this. You just don't know how long they can sustain themselves and be in business. My third rule in building my brand from scratch was to know when to drop a line that wasn't making the grade. The problem with my duffle bag company was a lack of inventory, which led to a potential problem of not delivering for an event. That would be the ultimate disaster. For that reason alone, I stopped carrying that line, and ultimately, they exited the golf business. The Sunderland brand lasted only three years with me, as the owners decided not to renew their license agreement. That was okay because my Straight Down line was starting to take off, which was my next focus in building my brand.

My sales went up every year for the first four seasons that I was representing Straight Down in the premium apparel space. Now that I was in the year 2014 and I had more territory with them, all indications were that sales would continue upward. During this entire time frame, my goal never wavered: I was only interested in getting the outerwear/ fleece items to the clubs on a limited basis. I wanted to start with small orders, and as the product was received well by the members, I knew we could grow the business there. That was my focus, and I indeed succeeded in reaching that.

I mentioned earlier that I also created a program to get Straight Down products to assistant golf pros at select clubs that were doing business with me. This would allow for more exposure from individuals who interact with their members and hopefully lead to more brand awareness. The ultimate goal was to have these golf pros eventually land their head professional job one day. The likelihood of them opening an account with me to put the Straight Down brand in their shop would be increased. This has only happened to me a few times in the seven years I have run the program, but you can't put a price on the free advertising you are getting with them wearing it at the club on a routine basis. I try to give every staff member two polos and one fleece every season.

I had the former buyer at Oak Hill C.C. on the staff, and when the new buyer came on board, I offered her the same deal. Speaking of Oak Hill—in the fall of 2013, we had all heard that long-time head pro Craig Harmon would be retiring from the job he held for over 35 years. I was meeting in my van with one of the more experienced assistant pros. I told him that if Craig were sitting where he was, I would appreciate his consideration for finally bringing in the men's collection of outerwear fleece from Straight Down into his shop. I recommended going with the Fairway and Foothill models, which were made in the U.S.A. and were considered stalwarts in our lineup. I said doing 24 of each style with four colors in each one would be a great start. Wouldn't you know it, I did receive a PO from the club in a few weeks for that same quantity. The buyer did tell me to hang onto the order and that the new incoming pro would have to make that final decision on whether to bring it in or not.

Fast-tracking to the 2014 PGA Merchandise Show where I had an appointment with Oak Hill. Before the meeting to go over the women's line, I first had the pleasure of meeting the newly appointed head pro Jason Ballard, who had spent the last five years of his career at Augusta National. I remember the conversation as if it happened yesterday.

"Hi, I'm Jason Ballard, the new pro at Oak Hill."

"So glad to finally meet you, Jason. I'm Stuart Miller, and I'll be your Straight Down rep."

"Tell me, Stuart, why is your stuff so expensive?" Those were the first words out of my new contact person at my best Straight Down account. How do you answer that one?

I remember looking Jason straight in the eyes and saying, "Well, Jason, we do things different at Straight Down. By adding more steps in our process, it costs money but makes our product special."

I remember him putting his right hand on my left shoulder and looking me in the eye. He said, "Consider the men's order approved." I was so relieved at that point. The company was finally going to get men's products into the Oak Hill pro shop for the first time. I would spend the next hour with the buyer picking out her ladies' order for the fall season with Jason occasionally looking on. He was continually talking with fellow PGA pros, who were still congratulating him on his new position. Jason would have success immediately at his new post, winning the 2020 PGA Merchandiser of the Year Award for Private Category. Shortly after our meeting ended, I had to find the company's owner and my sales manager and give them the great news.

My belt line, Nexbelt, also required me to try to partner up with the proper places by placing some free products with staff members. The previous year, I'd given the entire pro shop staff at Oak Hill a complimentary alligator strap belt so they could try it out. It turned out to be successful, and I am selling my Nexbelt line to them to this day.

Not all my lines will resonate with all my accounts. You do the best that you can. The one thing that I have learned in the first five years of this new job is that you must earn your place in the pro shop. Your place refers to floor space. Every product I represent is sold by at least six to 12 other competent sales reps. You pick your battles when you can when fighting for this space. A lot of it has to do with where you live. Years ago, when I worked for PING, I coined the saying, "Territorial Dominance," which simply meant if you can't dominate pro shop sales in the immediate area where you live, you are doing something wrong.

With my new set up, I was trying like crazy to sell my core products to everyone within a two-hour drive of my home. My core products include CMC (repair tools and towels), Town Talk (headwear), Straight Down (depending on the pro shop's membership), and Nexbelt belts. I must admit I have done an excellent job of securing a lot of this business. Loyalty plays a massive role in my industry. Having all these relationships with these golf pros at all these golf clubs is key to longtime success. I do my best to sustain these relationships and, if possible, improve on them.

When I started my new venture, I would set up a file on my laptop computer for all the different companies I represented. Let's take CMC, for example. I would then enter each account individually, and any orders or other documents would be stored under their account. I would keep track of how many accounts I had. This was an excellent way to track how successful I was with each company in increasing its brand exposure in my territory. You never know when you will add an account, so it is hard to plan or gauge this. I often would put down a club's name and list it as "potential" with a date of when I might have given a free item in hopes of landing a new client. Most companies will work with you on the cost of these goods. In many cases, companies will have promo offers where they will pay for the items. Working together is key to sustaining both sales and growth for all the companies I represent.

It is very important follow up with your accounts. I have been told by many of them that I am the best rep in doing this.

On a personal note, concerning my mother's pursuit for justice in the wrongful death of our father, things finally paid off with her winning the case. The settlement was a very significant amount, as all the pension money from his death in 1986 was paid, and she received it all in one check. It came during the middle of summer. The next month, she got his pension check and has been receiving it every month since. You could say it was a financial reprieve for the entire family as Mom was very generous in giving portions of the settlement to all of us to help out with our situations. I was so happy for Mom after all those years of fighting for justice. She is writing her book on this subject and hopes to have it published someday in the near future.

Later that summer, I drove with Mom to the Niagara Falls area, where we had lunch with her lawyer Peter and his wife. This trip to western New York was the first time Mom and I had made such a trip in our state, and we did it all in one day. Mom was exhausted for sure, but I drove the entire 600 miles, and I too was tired. Our family has been so fortunate, and someone for sure was watching over this entire process to help with the outcome. It was a glorious end to a hard-fought crusade.

60.
RELIABILITY IS KEY TO SUCCESS

Following up with your accounts on all matters is always the right thing to do as you illustrate firsthand to your pros that you care about their business. It usually guarantees that the order will ship out correctly, which is always a good thing. Over the years, I have learned that doing this consistently with every order, no matter who the account is, reinforces this habit. The right golf pro will see this and will remember the reasons that they do business with you. They want to work with reliable people; they want to shine in front of their membership.

One of my longtime friends and fellow sales representative Jeff Dibona told me in the very first years of doing independent rep work that "golf pros that like you and respect you will start to call you for tournament favors and tee gifts." Boy, was he right on the money. I did not do many tournaments in my first three to four years. However, I have been increasing in this category every season since year five. At this very moment, I would have to say that 40% of my overall business is tournament driven.

I have a theory on why my event business continues to increase. First and foremost is trust and relationships. Once you get your foot in the door with a pro and you deliver on the event gift and it is popular with the members, you have passed the first test. Since the pro knows you and your company are reliable sources, there is a great chance you will get a second go. This record can play over and over. Taking care of an account's tournament needs never gets old or goes out of style.

Also, there is the boomerang effect. Golf pros like to talk to other golf pros, and if you are considered very reliable, you will get those calls from other accounts. A new cycle will begin. I am not naïve enough to believe I am the only rep who gets phone calls for events. There are several, but from what I've witnessed, the list is small as not all sales reps have earned that trust. I have earned that trust and respect from my accounts, but so have all the companies that I represent as they play a significant role in an event's success.

At this moment, I would like to include a testimonial from my account base since I have become an independent salesperson. This comes from Dustin Jones, who operates his golf academy and has a store to sell his merchandise in the Utica, New York area:

"Stu Miller, the sales rep. Describe Stu: interesting, funny, intelligent, and a little off the wall!! I met Stu in 2009 as an assistant professional at the Yahnundasis Golf Club. When I first met him, I wasn't sure if I liked him or if he irritated me! It didn't take long to understand his deal. Stu was the last of the old-school sales reps, and he understood his product and, even more important, his customer. I became the head professional at the Yahnundasis Golf Club in 2012, and Stu was one of the first sales representatives to call me and ask me how he could help. I genuinely believe he cared about me as a customer and a golf professional. He wanted to make my bank account grow along with his. This is a trait that doesn't exist much anymore. Over the years, I always try to give Stu a shot at every order I can…because he did that for me."

To this day, Dustin does as much as he can for me, and that is all I can ask for. We have become great friends, and you can't put a price on that.

At the Yahnundasis Golf Club, former head pro Mark Jorgensen and Dustin introduced me to a blanket company called Touch of Class out of the Boston, Massachusetts, area. I had a meeting with them, and they gave this blanket to me and said you should give them a call and rep for them. So I did.

I called the phone number on the hangtag and spoke to the sales manager. It was an elderly gentleman who was from the Boston area, and since I have family from Salem, we got along instantly. He was quite happy that I reached out to him, and he immediately made me a sales rep for my area. To this day, I continue to represent this fine knitted blanket company.

I have to mention one last company to you all that I have represented now for seven years—the Sunfish Headcover Company, which is based in the Nashville, Tennessee, area. The company was created by two childhood friends from the South and formed around 2010. I have been with them most of the way. They make outstanding products but are small. It is hard sometimes for them to compete with some of the big names in this space. They do the best they can, and they have been great for tournament gift items that are in a higher price range.

As I marched on in 2015, I entered my sixth year as an independent rep and 34th overall as a golf rep, my 37th total year in the golf industry. I was soon to be 56 years old. I was prepared to do battle for a new year. My best-selling brands in volume were still Straight Down and OGIO. I was having success with CMC, Nexbelt, Sunfish, and Town Talk. I dropped two niche companies during this time frame: Art and Stone (coaster company) and a pottery company that made coffee mugs. Over the previous few years, I had opened up close to 60 accounts for each of these companies.

Like I said earlier, you don't have the final say in when your time is done with companies. I never dwelled on times like this, but instead thanked them for the opportunity and wished them all good fortune in the future. This would give me more time to focus on my core companies, which I embraced with full force.

61.
THE ART OF
SPONSORING EVENTS

Another major ingredient needed for success: sponsorship of PGA Section events. At my former job, PING and I would combine our resources. We were a major and consistent sponsor for all my sections, including the Northeast New York and Connecticut Sections and the Vermont chapter of the New England Section. These sponsorships ended during my last few years with the company.

As I was establishing myself as an independent representative, I knew that to fast track my career, getting involved with different PGA Sections that covered a large swath of area would be the way to go. I started a "relaunch" of being a sponsor again for the same sections I had done in the past. I was now doing it on my own and representing my brand. It was going to be an exciting time for me.

It would start in 2010, with my return to sponsoring the Vermont Match Play Championship held in the last week in September at ultra-prestigious Ekwanok Country Club in the village of Manchester. The club dates back to 1899 and is a Walter Travis design. I have been fortunate on a few occasions to play this terrific and demanding golf course.

The executive director of the Vermont PGA, Dave Christy, reached out to me in the spring of 2010 and wanted to know if I would be interested in reclaiming bragging rights as the title sponsor of this event. Dave was the head pro at the Country Club of Barre for over 15 years, retiring in 2000 for his new role. He had been around for all the years that PING and I sponsored the event.

The event comprised the 16 leading point winners during the season's tournament schedule. They would all convene at Ekwanok for the championship. I would show up first thing on the first day to greet all the players and hand them a tee gift for coming to the event. Each year, I would find a nice item from one of my vendors and always have it decorated with the event name. I would then arrive the next day to watch the last few holes of the championship match and then take a picture of the eventual winner. I would then order a nice marble plaque from my vendor at the time, Art and Stone, and send it to the winning player.

I also donated some cash to increase the purse for the competitors. This sponsorship ended in 2017, but it was a good ride while it lasted.

In 2011, I relaunched my sponsorship efforts with both the Northeast New York and Connecticut PGA Sections and continue to do so to this present day. Please see the two photos of myself on site at events for the Connecticut Section and the NENY Section.

Since my territory was expanded in 2013 by Straight Down, I also picked up two more Sections: The Western New York Section (comprising Buffalo and Rochester) and the Central New York Section (from Syracuse to Binghamton). I also started sponsoring the Pro-Assistant Championship in both sections. This is always a well-attended event and enjoyed by all. I continue to sponsor both events to this day.

When you are spending money in Section sponsorships, try to maximize the moment. With every event I am associated with, I partner up with one of my vendors to find the perfect tee gift for that event and always have them decorated to make the event even more memorable. I am always present at the event to greet every participant and hand out the gift. I work closely with all the tournament directors of each section, and they have told me that it means a lot to all the players when a sponsor is present at an event. For the most part, these are active accounts of mine, and all the assistant pros are potential clients down the road.

On average, I spend about $1,500 per event. With the four events I am doing today, this is about $6,000. This is all from my pocket. The companies I work for always give me their best price on the actual tee gifts. The way I look at it, you must spend money to make money. I am a major sponsor for four PGA Sections, which has allowed me to gain access to the pros in these respective sections. It has also allowed me to sell more. The entire concept of being a sponsor in the Sections I am involved with is an essential part of my business plan. I know that my account base in each section I represent is grateful for my sponsorship efforts. In 2016 I was also honored to be voted as the Sales Rep of the Year winner for my home section/ the NENY PGA Section. First time a winner of this coveted award as an independent rep and second time overall in my career.

2016 Special Awards
Sales Representative of The Year
Stuart Miller
Stuart Miller Sales
STUART MILLER
GOLF SALES
PGA

62.

MAJOR SETBACK: LOSS OF A PILLAR COMPANY

As I mentioned earlier, I picked up the OGIO golf bag company at the start of the 2012 season—the third year of my new career. I also mentioned that I had to adjust my wardrobe for the PGA Show to blend in at all the booths I was working. There is another event from this show that stands out to me:

I was attending the 2017 PGA Show. It was early afternoon on day one of this two and a half day marathon. I was positioned in the OGIO booth, waiting for my next appointment to arrive. Standing a few feet from me was a gentleman who was OGIO's Vice President of Product Development. He had been with the company for well over ten years and was a driving force in creating new products for them and helping our reps to understand the products we were selling. He was very good at his role, and I was glad to be associated with him.

I remember this individual saying to me, "Stuart, I just wanted to tell you how fortunate we are to have you on our team. I cannot tell you how many of your accounts have come up to me during the show to express their pleasure in working with you. So, thank you for that."

I was stunned at hearing those remarks. I knew I was doing an excellent job for the company, and I always knew I did as well for my accounts as I could, but to hear these words from a high-ranking officer was a pure delight. I thanked him profusely for those kind words. I also added, "You know, if I was a jerk during my time as a sales rep for PING, I would not be standing in front of you today. I always knew my job with them was not forever, so by being consistent with my account base helped me to evolve into this new role."

I had seen some reps who worked for massive companies and had very nice positions, but when they were let go from these firms, they could not make it on their own in the same industry. I never wanted to be one of those people.

As it turned out, this would be my last PGA Show with OGIO. During the last quarter of 2017, the Callaway Corporation purchased the OGIO company and all its assets. This also meant that my job with them was officially terminated. This was the first and thank goodness only time this happened to me during my new career as an independent sales rep. I gave them six years. When I left, I had increased their overall sales in my territory tenfold. I was disappointed this happened, but I saw the silver lining of the situation. I would never have to carry ten more sample golf bags in my van to show accounts. My time selling golf bags was over.

The official date of the transfer of sales reps occurred on April 1st of 2018. I got my full commission on every order I had written for the Spring '18 shipment. This was done very nicely and professionally.

In this business, when one door closes, another one opens. I became a sales representative for New Balance golf shoes and Sundog eyewear in 2017. I represented nine companies at the beginning of 2018: CMC Design, Monterey Club, Nexbelt, New Balance, Straight Down, Sundog, Sunfish, Town Talk, and Touch of Class blankets. I was very content with this amount. At one time, I had over 20 companies that I was peddling, many of them very small. I was very comfortable with the number of lines I represented and felt I could improve everyone's sales in the coming years.

During the beginning of this same season, I got an invaluable tip on selling from one of my competitors (more of a friendly foe), Steve Sormanti. Steve had also had his recent share of misfortune, as he was let go from the Nike golf brand in 2016 after being with them for over ten years. He is now repping the Callaway apparel line through their license agreement with Supreme International for New England and is one of the company's leading salespersons. I have mentioned Steve quite a few times already, and I have to refer to him again for giving me this excellent tip. I call it the "Sormanti Chat."

Steve is one of my closest friends in the business, and we talk at least once a week during the season, mostly about business and accounts. If he sees a place that I should go to, he will share that with me and vice versa. I talked to him about my Straight Down line and how it did not fit into many courses I called on due to its higher price. That is when Steve told me that I needed to start to ask accounts about how much pro shop credit they dole out during a year. He suggested that members might want to spend a little more money on a particular item in their pro shop using such credit. It was like a light bulb went off for me.

Please understand that the entire time I had been building up my Straight Down account base in my territory, I was plenty busy with the accounts I'd opened up. But any good sales rep wants more. The "Sormanti Chat" has now become a handy tool for me in attempting to establish not only new Straight Down accounts but new accounts for all the brands that I rep. I have convinced more than a half-dozen accounts to become Straight Down customers, and my list is continuing to grow. I must thank my good friend Steve for his fine tip.

63.

GETTING MORE TESTIMONALS IN MY NEW ROLE

At that time, I was now entering the 2019 campaign with nine companies to represent. I was more confident and poised to have one of my best years ever as an independent golf rep.

I would like to add a few more testimonials that I have received from current accounts and even from one of the companies that I rep for. Let's start with Roger King, who is currently the Head Golf Professional at the Sugarbush Resort Golf Club in Warren, Vermont: "I first met Stuart in 2001 when I accepted the PGA Head Golf Professional position at The Country Club of Barre in Barre, Vermont. I never owned my own pro shop and had never done business with the PING golf company. I was excited to carry such a well-respected company in my pro shop as well as playing their great equipment. My memories of Stuart revolve around his helpfulness in my early years as well as his exemplary customer service. From day one, Stuart made sure that I had the most up to date information, knowledge, and equipment in my pro shop. He would make sure to check in or stop by often throughout our seven-month golf season. Not only did Stuart take care of my pro shop needs, but he was also one of the few sales representatives who understood the importance of taking care of the professional staff. I think that is a great business practice. He would make sure to periodically give my staff or myself a nice gift, usually logoed with our names on the item. It is a very personal touch. Not only was it a nice gesture, but it also showed that Stuart looked at our relationship as more than just a number. To this day, I still use many of the items he gifted to me."

Let me just add that when I worked for PING and covered the state of Vermont, I tried to find a few key clubs and work with the head pro to make that a shopping destination for members and golfers in the area. Roger was one of these accounts. I knew he would be an advocate for all my product offerings, and each year his business flourished with me. I am also grateful to Roger that when my PING days ended, our relationship remained intact and he immediately supported the majority of the brands that I carried when I began my new career.

When Roger left his post at C.C. of Barre to go to Sugarbush for the start of the 2017 season, he also brought in several of my product lines. Roger was one of the finest players of the club pros in the section and made some comments on my role as a sponsor: "Stuart's support of me is appreciated, but Stuart has been generous with his sponsorship of many chapters and sections of the PGA of America. In particular, Stuart was the title sponsor of the prestigious VTPGA Match Play championship for more years that I can remember. Not only would he provide tee gifts to all players and added money to the prize pool, he made sure to donate a beautiful plaque to the winner each year. I was lucky enough to win the event in 2015 and still have the plaque hanging on my office wall."

In his final statement, Roger added, "For over 20 years, Stuart has been helping me grow business in my pro shops. He has been nothing but helpful and professional. Any company, including PING, are lucky to have him representing their lines. I, for one, am lucky to have Stuart as a business acquaintance, but also as a friend." For the record, I feel the same toward Roger.

One of the other things that I have prided myself on doing is routinely calling on smaller accounts throughout my territory despite the sales of the account. Case in point is Erik Tiele, the head pro at Waubeeka Golf Links in Williamstown, Massachusetts. I have been calling on Erik for close to 30 years now at all the locations he has been at during that time.

Erik recently commented to me, "Seeing small accounts was something you were always very good at. In my opinion, it is what separates you from the pack of all the other sales reps."

Bottom line is that Erik is good people, and I will see him as often as possible. The amount of business we do is not a high priority. If my products happen to fit in well at his current place of business, that is a bonus. I have several accounts like Erik's that do not do a lot of business in terms of overall sales but are run by nice golf pros who are definitely worth stopping by and seeing.

I also wanted to mention some comments made by one of the vendors I represent. Bob Burg is the president and owner of CMC Design in Scottsdale, Arizona. I previously mentioned that they were the first company to hire me as an independent sales representative. I have known Bob for over 20 years, and he is one of the finest individuals I have had the pleasure of knowing in this industry. Every time I come to Arizona, I make it a priority to stop by their corporate office in Scottsdale to see him and the rest of the team. They are truly one of the great small companies in this industry. When Bob heard I was working on my book, he asked if he could make some comments and was glad to share them with all you:

"Superlatives to describe Stu Miller: hardworking, honest, knows his products through and through, pride in his appearance, respectful, considerate, and detail driven. Any business owner knows how difficult it is to find a nation of "good," let alone "really good" sales reps. Particularly, multi-line commission reps. To make a great living, be a successful golf rep you have to be authentic, love the game, outwork, out-think, and out-serve. Stu is and does all that and more. I never appreciate a teammate coming to me with a problem and no thought or suggestion of a solution. Stu is invested, for the good and the bad. If a problem needs solved, he thinks solution."

Like I said before, I am so honored to be representing a brand that is run by Bob Burg. See photo of Bob and me shot in Arizona in March 2020.

One other testimonial I would like to share with everyone is from Stan McLennan ("Stan the Man") the head golf professional at nine-hole private course Suffield Country Club in north-central Connecticut. Here are his comments: "I have known Stu for over 30 years. He has always been there for me when it came to those special orders and always made sure I was never overstocked. He also was very on the stick with margin builders when overstocked of company inventory. (I kept him informed so that he could make deals with higher profit margins.) Stu is a true salesman, and his time now as an independent rep was a smooth transition from PING. He always studies his products and promotes the best-selling pieces of the line."

Stan was a great account for me with PING, and today is one of my best accounts as an independent rep. I remain close to this day with his wife Joyce and son Brian, who I watched grow up and is now a student at Clarkson College in Potsdam, New York.

I believe I have saved the best testimonial for last. These words come from James P. Jeffers, who has been my friend approaching 35 years now. We first met back in 1986 when Jim was an assistant pro at The Edison Club. He is currently the Director of Golf at the Hiland Park Golf Club in Queensbury, New York, where he has worked for ten years. Now, in his own words: "As a Golf Professional, it's always nice to look back on the people that had the greatest influence in the course of their career. My list is very short but formed from purpose and intent, and the people on it are impactful, memorable, honorable, and worthy of all the respect I can afford them. Stuart is perched very high on that list and for good reason. Through all my years working as an Assistant Golf Professional, Stuart had a unique way of showing me the true essence of professionalism. In most cases it was not in the spoken word, but more his actions and the reactions he elicited from others that became one of my greatest tools from learning interpersonal skills. Stuart was and will always be a true to the bone, aggressive yet flexible, forthright and competent sales and marketing genius. Above all else, Stuart has perfected the lost art of listening."

For the record, Jim is a three-time winner of the Section Championship of the Northeast New York PGA. All these events were sponsored by me and PING. Since I have become an independent sales representative, Jim has supported as many of my lines as he can and continues to do so to this day.

Jim would continue by saying, "He takes the time to listen, always making you feel like the most important person in the room. When I became a Head Golf Professional, I watched as Stuart expanded not only his business prospects but also his charitable endeavors through tournament development and sponsorships. His efforts speak volumes to his deep commitment to promoting professional excellence and transformative personal growth. I am excited for Stuart during this time of discovery as he shares his life's lessons in this book. Perhaps we could all take a page from the book and learn to listen...just once, listen. You may be surprised by how much you learn."

64.
WRAPPING THINGS UP

The entire time I have devoted to this book has been during the COVID-19 outbreak. I started writing on Friday, April 3rd, and today is Friday, July 24th, 2020.

When I returned home from a two-week vacation in my home state of Arizona visiting my brother and mother on Monday, March 10th, the entire world changed. That is when this virus became very real, with more people getting infected and, in some cases, dying. It was all so new to all of us at that time, and the only logical thing was to ask all Americans in certain locations to stay home and be in quarantine for the next eight weeks. At least that is what happened to me as I was living in upstate New York, and the epicenter for this virus was in the metro New York City region. The economy started to shut down due to this mandatory order.

All I know is I returned from a spectacular trip and was so much looking forward to getting my new year in golf sales started, but everything changed. I was watching the Players Championship on Thursday, and during this telecast, the word was spreading that the March Madness NCAA Basketball tournament had been canceled due to the virus. Then the golf event was canceled after Thursday's first round, and all future events were put on hold. Then the NBA and NHL also stopped playing. Every league in sports hit the pause button, including spring training in Major League Baseball. I may have seen one of the last games played that spring while I was in Arizona when I attended a game between the Arizona Diamondbacks and the Cleveland Indians the day before I flew home. I am only mentioning all this as my life, too, was now on hold. My normal spring traveling would've been happening, but that, too, was altered.

When I heard the news that the governor of New York had mandated that we New Yorkers all stay in our homes for the next eight weeks starting on March 16th to stop the spread of this virus, I had to figure out what to do with my time since I was going to be isolated in my home all by myself.

My mother, Elayne, started to write about her journey since the loss of our father five years ago in order to keep busy and to get it published one day. Hopefully, the book will give hope to other families in her same predicament. She also wanted me to one day write about my life as a traveling golf rep during my almost 40-year career. As I said earlier, I was a writer early in my life, and she always thought I had it in me to continue writing one day again.

I said to myself, "If there was ever a perfect time to do this, it would be now." I commenced writing on Friday, April 3rd around four in the afternoon. I have been composing story after story ever since, reaching deep into my memory bank to uncover the important stories and events that played a major role in my life as a salesperson in the golf industry. Entering this chapter, I have written 63 of them and close to 300 pages in total. I did not know how much I would write about, but I believe I covered a great deal.

For those of you who are still reading, I hope that you have sensed the amount of pride and satisfaction I have in all my years of being associated with the Solheim family and PING, from my work as a part-time PING employee in my college days to being a sales rep for them for 28 years. During my time with them, I achieved so many great things in the game of golf and life. They allowed me to succeed in life, and for that, I can never thank them enough.

I have always been an optimist, and when the bad news came with my sales position being eliminated, I quickly rebounded and found myself a new home as an independent golf rep. Going from working for just one major company to now representing a cadre of smaller companies has been such a blessing in its own right. It has allowed me to meet so many new people and work for some extraordinary smaller golf firms. It has been a lot of fun, for sure.

Since this is the final chapter in my book, I wanted to share some stats that I have recently calculated that you might find interesting. I do work in a business based on numbers and figures, so why not share some with you?

I have been on the road as a traveling sales rep in the golf industry for 28 years with PING and ten as an independent. During this time, I have driven an estimated 1.5 million miles, have been to 36 PGA Merchandise Shows, stayed in hotels over 2,000 times, eaten in well over 2,500 restaurants, did close to 800 demo days during my time with PING, made close to 18,000 sales calls, sponsored close to 100 PGA sectioned events, attended around 60 professional Tour events including multiple majors and two Ryder Cups, participated in five pro-ams as a player, met and called on over 2,500 PGA golf professionals, and so much more. Please see photos taken when attending the 2020 PGA Merchandise Show in Orlando: first image is with Tim Quirk, Director of Golf Leatherstocking Resort in Cooperstown, NY, with the Ryder Cup and photo of myself in front of the Straight Down booth, also at the 2020 PGA Show.

That is what happens when you start to add things up. I never brought up financial figures in this writing, as that is all private information and does not need to be divulged. Many of you reading this book have first-hand knowledge of this, and that works for me. I said several times that I earned a very nice living working for PING. This was godsend for me when I transitioned well into my new role.

As I was never married (except for my job) or had a family (except all my golf accounts), I could save well for my adventures in life. I am still young at 61 years old, but I am getting older in rep years since this is year 39. The years just have a way of creeping up on you with all the travel we do during the year.

What does the future hold for Stuart Miller?

I guess you can say I have an inner spark to continue to succeed in anything that I do. I have narrowed the roster of companies that I represent to nine and will keep that number for the rest of the 2020 season. I might dial it back a little for next year. I continue to strive to find ways to be a better salesperson in this industry. That goal continues to motivate me to practice my craft and represent all my brands, bringing them more success. All future growth is somewhat on hold due to the pandemic, but this will pass, and normal life will go on (hopefully sooner than we know).

The other day I went out and played my first round of golf in close to two years. I played 18 holes in 90-degree heat and high humidity, and I made it through the round pain-free. I have been battling back issues that have stopped me from playing. I was still okay to do my job. I was sure sore the next two days, but I already have plans to play next week at least two more times. Being on the golf course again was the best therapy for me during these uncertain times, and it just brought back so many memories of what playing the game of golf has meant to me all these years. Being pain-free gave me hope to revive my golf career again and try to play more in the future. I feel that is very much needed at this time in my career.

I happened to join a group of three senior golfers during the round, which I played at Cronin's Golf Resort, my #1 account. I went out solo and joined them on the par-three sixth hole. All I can tell you is that as we had a cold beer after the round; they all complimented me on my swing and how I handled myself on the golf course. I shot in the mid-80s, but hey, I will take it for my first round in two years. They could see my game, and my swing was there, which helped with my confidence.

Putting the virus situation to the side, I hope to keep doing this golf selling job for several more years. I always said I would keep doing it as long as it is enjoyable. My good friend Steve Sormanti (67 now) is officially retiring from his golf sales career on August 1st, and we both came into this business at about the same time. However, I feel good and will continue. I have things I want to improve on. Who knows, maybe one day I will move back to Arizona and work for a golf company out there. Or maybe this golf writing thing will catch on and become a new career for me. I am just taking it one day at a time and trying to stay safe and healthy.

I just wanted to close by saying how therapeutic writing this book has been for me. It helped keep my sanity during these uncharted times. I am so fortunate to have my mind still firing on all cylinders, which has allowed me to dig deep and pull all this information from the past and bring it back to life. It has been a joy to write this, and I hope that you all find it enjoyable as well. If your name is mentioned in it, thank you again for finding your way into my life and being a part of this wonderful journey in the game of golf.

Made in the USA
Middletown, DE
28 October 2023

41528208R00159